"Sri Lanka's experience as a small open economy is fascinating. Policy itself has had many twists and turns, which provide an excellent basis for analysis of the impact of policy alternatives. Sarath Rajapatirana has excellent qualifications to undertake such an analysis, as an academic economist, as an economist at the World Bank, and as a policy adviser in Sri Lanka. This is an invaluable study, focusing upon globalisation and its interaction with domestic development policies. It will be of interest to all those analysing the political economy of growth in developing countries."

Anne Krueger
Senior Fellow at the School of Advanced International Studies, Johns Hopkins University and the Herald L. and Caroline Ritch Emeritus Professor of Sciences and Humanities in the Economics Department of Standford University

"Sri Lanka achieved independence in 1948 with high hopes that it would prove the best bet among all post-colonial nations in Asia. However, during the ensuing seven decades, Sri Lanka's economic performance has fallen way behind the fast-growing East Asian economies, rapidly converging to the levels of its South Asian neighbours. This well-crafted book provides a penetrating analysis of Sri Lanka's economic policy and performance, with emphasis on policy slippages that hindered reaping gains from the promising initial conditions. It enriches our understanding of opportunities for and policy challenges of achieving economic advancement in this era of economic globalisation. The analysis is well informed by the relevant scholarly literature and the author's extensive experience as a development practitioner. The exposition is repressing and insightful."

Prema-Chandra Athukorala
FASSA, Emeritus Professor of Economics, Australian National University

"Challenges posed and opportunities offered by globalisation to a country must ultimately be assessed in the context of that country's economic history. In this brilliantly written and highly readable book by Sarath Rajapatirana, who has witnessed globalisation up-close when he worked at the World Bank and also has an intimate knowledge of Sri Lanka's economy, offers precisely such an account. The book is a must-read for scholars, policymakers, media persons, teachers, and students interested in understanding the evolution of the Sri Lankan economy in the age of globalisation."

Arvind Panagariya
Professor of Economics at SIPA, Columbia University

"This coherent and wide-ranging book combines political history and economic analysis to illuminate the character of Sri Lanka's development since 1960. The author's focus is on the country's encounter with the forces of globalisation. While he is a staunch proponent of 'globalisation-friendly' government policies, his advocacy gains traction by being balanced and nuanced in its approach. Rajapatirana has worked for nearly a decade as an economic adviser to successive Presidents of Sri Lanka. This hands-on experience shapes the book and makes it highly relevant not only for students but also for economic policymakers in small developing countries more generally."

Vijay Joshi
Emeritus Fellow of Merton College, Oxford University

POLICY CHALLENGES
OF
GLOBALISATION
IN
Sri Lanka

POLICY CHALLENGES
OF
GLOBALISATION
IN
Sri Lanka

Sarath Rajapatirana

World Scientific

NEW JERSEY · LONDON · SINGAPORE · BEIJING · SHANGHAI · HONG KONG · TAIPEI · CHENNAI

Published by

World Scientific Publishing Co. Pte. Ltd.
5 Toh Tuck Link, Singapore 596224
USA office: 27 Warren Street, Suite 401-402, Hackensack, NJ 07601
UK office: 57 Shelton Street, Covent Garden, London WC2H 9HE

Library of Congress Cataloging-in-Publication Data
Names: Rajapatirana, Sarath, author.
Title: Policy challenges of globalisation in Sri Lanka / by author Sarath Rajapatirana.
Description: New Jersey : World Scientific, [2025] | Includes bibliographical references and index.
Identifiers: LCCN 2024039488 | ISBN 9789819801138 (hardcover) |
　ISBN 9789819801145 (ebook) | ISBN 9789819801152 (ebook other)
Subjects: LCSH: Globalization--Sri Lanka. | Sri Lanka--Foreign economic relations.
Classification: LCC HF1365 .R36 2025 | DDC 337.5493--dc23/eng/20240920
LC record available at https://lccn.loc.gov/2024039488

British Library Cataloguing-in-Publication Data
A catalogue record for this book is available from the British Library.

Copyright © 2025 by World Scientific Publishing Co. Pte. Ltd.

All rights reserved. This book, or parts thereof, may not be reproduced in any form or by any means, electronic or mechanical, including photocopying, recording or any information storage and retrieval system now known or to be invented, without written permission from the publisher.

For photocopying of material in this volume, please pay a copying fee through the Copyright Clearance Center, Inc., 222 Rosewood Drive, Danvers, MA 01923, USA. In this case permission to photocopy is not required from the publisher.

For any available supplementary material, please visit
https://www.worldscientific.com/worldscibooks/10.1142/14050#t=suppl

Desk Editors: Kannan Krishnan/Kura Sunaina

Typeset by Stallion Press
Email: enquiries@stallionpress.com

*I dedicate this book to our children Anusha,
Chandima and Sanjaya and our grandchildren
Priyanka, Deran and Nikhil.*

Preface

It is reasonable to ask why there is a need for another book on globalisation when there are books on the subject by the leading economists of the day. The answer is that these books have analysed globalisation from a world perspective and there is a need to examine the issues related to globalisation from a single country's view, from the ground level. A country study that is done at a ground level clarifies the challenges of policy formulation. This book analyses the issues related to globalisation through economics informed by history, politics and the ideologies of different governments of the country over time. Sri Lanka has an interesting history. Given its strategic location at the centre of South Asia, it was subject to colonial rule for over 400 years under the Portuguese, the Dutch and the British. This book examines the 60 years from 1960 to 2020 closely. During this period, Sri Lanka underwent many changes in its economy, ideological positions and connections to the world economy through trade, foreign investments and migration, both inward and outward. The book analyses the economics, politics and the ideological context of policy making in Sri Lanka with respect to globalisation and the effects of those policies on the country.

The world has changed due to the global financial crisis and COVID-19, and many developing countries including Sri Lanka have undergone changes. Their economies were recovering slowly. Since 2020, Sri Lanka has been facing the worst economic crisis in its history, which allows us to examine the policy challenges throughout the period to sort out the reasons for its poor performance. Sri Lanka, which had a favourable start in both GDP growth and income distribution, faltered and became a poor performer in contrast to neighbouring countries and those in similar initial conditions in the 1960s. An examination of Sri Lanka's history reveals the change and continuity of economic performance. This is a good start to analyse the reasons for the crisis that took place in 2020. This book contributes to the understanding of why the country has come to the present predicament.

This book notes the positions on globalisation taken by the leading economists of the day, Jagdish Bhagwati, Dani Rodrik, Joe Stiglitz and Martin Wolf. Dani Rodrick and Joe Stiglitz hold more pessimistic views on globalisation, while Bhagwati and Wolf hold more optimistic views. The former hold that globalisation has not helped increase the economic growth of developing countries and has led to worsening income distribution in these countries. This book evaluates these positions. The journal *The Economist* disparages globalisation as "slowbalisation."

In contrast to earlier books, this book examines positions on globalisation from a single-country perspective and establishes the veracity of the different claims.

About the Author

Sarath Rajapatirana is currently Economic Advisor to President Ranil Wickremasinghe, the President of Sri Lanka on economic reforms since 2022. He holds a B.A. Economic Honours degree from the University of Ceylon Peradeniya. He was awarded a Fullbright scholarship to read for a Masters degree (Development Economics) at the University of Massachusetts and a Masters degree in Economics (International Trade) from the University of Minnesota. He read for a Ph.D at the University of Minnesota has an ABD. and a Ph.D. from the University of Colombo.

He was a staff member and later a consultant of the World Bank for over 30 years. His main contributions at the World Bank were as Director and main author of the World Development Report on Trade and Industrialisation in 1987, Director and co-author of the research on Macroeconomic policies of Developing countries which led to the book "Boom Crisis and Adjustment: Macroeconomic experience for Developing Countries" coauthored with Professors Ian Little, Max Corden and Richard Cooper. He has led World Bank missions to three continents Asia, Sub-Saharan Africa and South America. Upon retiring from the World Bank Sarath Rajapathirana joined the American Enterprise Institute as a Visiting scholar where he led seminar, written papers and books with Professor Prema-Chandra Athukorala, Dr. Ravi Yatawara and Dr. Luis Guash. He has authored and coauthored six books and published 63 articles. Google Scholar has found more than 1500 citations of Sarath Rajapatirana's work.

Acknowledgements

I am grateful to Chehara Amaratunga, Araliya Weerakoon and Anandi Premarathne for their excellent help in preparing this book for publication.

Contents

Preface		ix
About the Author		xi
Acknowledgements		xiii
List of Figures		xvii
List of Tables		xix
List of Abbreviations		xxi
Chapter 1	Introduction: An Economic Analysis Informed by History, Ideology and Politics	1
Chapter 2	Movements Towards and Away from Globalisation	15
Chapter 3	Through Eminent Eyes: A 50-Year Retrospective as a Background to Globalisation	49
Chapter 4	Ideology and Economic Policymaking: A Framework Applied to Sri Lanka	85
Chapter 5	The Impact of International Financial Institutions on Globalisation: World Bank's Analysis in the 1970s and 1980s	111
Chapter 6	The Role of International Financial Institutions in Globalisation: The International Monetary Fund (IMF) and Its Role in Sri Lanka	147

Chapter 7	Industrial Policy Versus Policy Towards Industry Debate: The Sri Lanka Case	153
Chapter 8	Avoiding Inflation in Sri Lanka in Order to Benefit from Globalisation	181
Chapter 9	Export Growth and Appropriate Macroeconomic Policy: A Necessary Nexus	209
Chapter 10	Globalisation, Poverty and Income Distribution in Sri Lanka	245
Chapter 11	The Future of Globalisation in Sri Lanka	249
Chapter 12	Conclusions	257

Bibliography 263

Index 279

List of Figures

Figure 1.1	Trade, as a Percentage of GDP in Sri Lanka and the World (1960–2019)	4
Figure 8.1A	Indices of Tradable Price (PT), Non-tradable Price (PN) and Real Exchange Rate (RER), 1990–2007	206
Figure 8.2A	Colombo Consumer Price Index Base (2010=100) and Year on Year Inflation in Sri Lanka (1960–2008)	206
Figure 8.3A	Revenue/Grants, Expenditure and Overall Fiscal Balance (as a percentage of GDP) in Sri Lanka (1960–2008)	207
Figure 9.1	Sri Lanka Trade Trends, 1960–2012: Exports, Imports and Trade (as a percentage of GDP)	210
Figure 9.2	Merchandise Exports as a Share of GDP (1960–2011)	210
Figure 9.3	Sri Lanka's Share of World Exports, 1960–2012 (Per cent)	210
Figure 9.4	Monthly Movements of the Real Effective Exchange Rate (REER), 1995 (M01)–2011 (09)	213

Figure 9.5   Trade Balance as a Percentage of GDP in Sri Lanka
               (1960–2012)   213

Figure 9.1A   GDP Growth (Annual Percentage) (1960–2012)   243

Figure 9.2A   Sri Lanka Trade as a Percentage of GDP
               (1960–2012)   243

List of Tables

Table 1.1	A Measure of Integration: Trade to GDP of Sri Lanka Compared to the Trade to GDP Ratio of the World (1960–2019)	5
Table 1.2	Standard Deviation of values relating to Trade, Net Migration and FDI in Sri Lanka (1960–2019)	6
Table 1.3	Real Interest Rates, Trade to GDP, Gross Capital Formation and Net Migration for Six Periods in Sri Lanka (1960–2019)	7
Table 1.4	Imports and Exports as a Percentage of GDP for Six Periods in Sri Lanka (1960–2019)	7
Table 2.1	Sri Lanka's GDP Growth and Sectoral Distribution (1960–2019)	16
Table 2.2	Sri Lanka's Globalisation Indicators (1960–2019)	18
Table 2.3	Political Regimes, Policy Orientation and Globalisation	23
Table 5.1	Share of Sri Lanka's Tree Crop Exports in World Exports	122
Table 5.1A	Historical Data; Rates of Change (Constant Prices)	136
Table 5.2A	Structure of the Economy	136

Table 5.3A	Macroeconomic Balance (as a percentage of GDP)	137
Table 5.4A	Financial Indicators (as a percentage of GDP)	137
Table 6.1	Sri Lanka: History of Lending Commitments with the IMF as of September 30, 2018 (in thousands of SDRs)	150
Table 8.1A	Basic Indicators of the General Price Level, 1987–2008	204
Table 8.2A	Indices of Tradable Price (PT), Non-tradable Price (PN) and Real Exchange Rate (RER), 1990–2007 (2002=100)	205
Table 9.1	Nominal and Effective Rate of Protection: Nine Agricultural Commodities for 2009/2010	233
Table 9.1A	Implied Overvaluation of the Rupee During 2005–2012 (Nominal Rates)	243
Table 9.2A	Macroeconomic Outcomes and Macro Prices (Annual Averages and Rates)	244
Table 10.1	GDP Growth Rates and Income Distribution Under Different Regimes (1956–2012)	247

List of Abbreviations

ADB	Asian Development Bank
EFF	Extended Fund Facility
EU	European Union
FDI	Foreign Direct Investment
FTA	Free Trade Agreement
GOSL	Government of Sri Lanka
GSP	General System of Preferences
GCEC	Greater Colombo Economic Commission
IMF	International Monetary Fund
IPS	Institute of Policy Studies
SBA	Stand-By Arrangement
TFP	Total Factor Productivity
WTO	World Trade Organisation
SLFP	Sri Lanka Freedom Party
UNP	United National Party
LTTE	Liberation Tigers of Tamil Eelam
GDP	Gross Domestic Product
CBSL	Central Bank of Sri Lanka
IDA	International Development Association
SOE	State-Owned Enterprises
OECD	Organisation for Economic Cooperation and Development
MLA	Monetary Law Act
WTO	World Trade Organization.
TRIPs	Trade Related Property Rights
CEPA	Comprehensive Economic Partnership Agreement

ASOE	Australian Model of a Small Open Economy
REER	Real Effective Exchange Rate
FEEC	Foreign Exchange Entitlement Certificate Scheme
LSSP	*Lanka Sama Samaja Party* (Lanka Socialist Party)
QR	Quantitative Restrictions
CRA	Convertible Rupee Accounts
CFA	Cease Fire Agreement
UPFA	United People's Freedom Alliance
VAT	Value-Added Tax
ERP	Effective Rates of Protection
ITC	International Trade Centre
TB	Treasury Bills
NRP	Nominal Rate of Protection
CCPI	Colombo Consumer Price Index
OPEC	Organization of the Petroleum Exporting Countries
FMRA	Fiscal Management (Responsibility) Act
PPP	Purchasing Power Parity
JVP	*Janatha Vimukthi Peramuna* (People's Liberation Front)
CEM	Country Economic Memorandum
MEP	*Mahajana Eksath Peramuna* (People's United Front)
CP	Communist Party
WFC	World Financial Crisis

Chapter 1

Introduction: An Economic Analysis Informed by History, Ideology and Politics

As stated in the preface it is reasonable to ask why there is a need for another book on globalisation when there are many already by leading economists of the day, such as Jagdish Bhagwati, Joseph Stiglitz, Dani Rodrik and Martin Wolf. While they have different views, they are dealing with the same subject matter. These books were published on globalisation in the early 2000s. In *Globalisation and Its Discontents* (2002) and *Making Globalisation Work* (2007),[1] Stiglitz took on the issues of globalisation before most other economists did. Stiglitz's concern that globalisation could lead to increase in poverty and worsening distribution of income was yet to be confirmed. Jagdish Bhagwati, in his In Defence of Globalisation (2004), found that when other economists started probing the arguments of those who saw no benefits in globalisation, ended up finding problems with globalisation rather than addressing some downside risks. Better policies can mitigate these risks. Dani Rodrik in *The Globalisation Paradox: Democracy and the Future of the World Economy* wrote about "hyper globalisation" when there were hardly any barriers between a particular country and other countries, much like the situation within a country. He

---

[1] Stiglitz moderated his view in his second book on globalisation by noting that countries can make globalisation work. However, more recently Stiglitz has claimed that globalization would lead to greater poverty and worsening of income distribution in poor countries. This claim has to be verified by more research. In this study we did not encounter such situation.

considered the European Union to be a hyper-globalised entity, where there are also no policy conflicts with respect to the movement of factors of production and money with similar interest rates and exchange rates. Rodrik was also a sceptical about globalisation, underscoring the view that the disadvantages of globalisation exceeded its assumed benefits. Martin Wolf in *Why Globalisation Works* (2004) found that the benefits of globalisation exceeded its costs. The world has changed since then with the World Financial Crisis (WFC) in 2008–2012.

1.1 What is Globalisation?

Globalisation is a process that brings the world together by linking goods, services and factor markets. Stiglitz defined it as the closer integration of the countries of the world through the increased flow of goods and services, capital and even labour. He claimed that problems of globalisation have a bearing mostly on developing countries, where 80 per cent of the world's population lives.

Globalisation takes place due to the enormous reductions in the costs of transport, and communication and changes in policy regimes from inward-looking economic regimes (associated with high protection) in goods and factor markets to outward-looking economic regimes (associated with low protection). Both technology and policy drive globalisation. Changes in technology reduce the cost of international transactions through shipping, and communication makes the management of international production processes easier and more cost-effective through such processes as just-in-time delivery of inputs. Changes in policies that have liberalised trade and opened capital markets have allowed the savings of developed country to be invested in developing countries, which leads to reduced costs of capital. In addition, there are learning effects that arise from access to new technology that allows countries to move to the technological frontier sooner than in the past. Technology transmission has sped up. The WFC that began in 2008 dampened the enthusiasm for globalisation for some of its advocates, and the slow recovery that began in 2010 led to renewed pessimism about it. Following the Global Financial Crisis (GFC), Greece, Italy, Spain and Cyprus have experienced reduced growth, high unemployment and adverse effects on income distribution. Some countries have shown a faster recovery than others because they have efficient markets.

As it is with most processes, globalisation is measurable, if somewhat imperfectly. Different measures exist for the different aspects of globalisation, such as trade, capital and labour. Generally, a few measures can be used to measure globalisation, ranging from increasing trade with the rest of the world to opening a capital account and permitting the efflux and influx of labour. In Chapter 2, the Sri Lankan case of globalisation is reviewed to provide a prototype of the policy challenges of a small open economy.

1.1.1 *Goods and Services, Labour and Capital Integration*

The integration of goods and services, capital and labour markets, or what is now termed as globalisation, is in one sense inevitable, given the advances in technology and the reduction of man-made barriers to policy reforms. Economic theory has anticipated these movements. With respect to trade, two well-known models of international trade — the Heckscher–Ohlin and the Stolper–Samuelson models — are relevant. The first predicts that countries will export goods intensive in the use of their abundant factors in exchange for goods intensive in the use of their scarce factors. The Stolper–Samuelson model predicts that (with some restrictive assumptions applied to the Heckscher–Ohlin model) when the country is open to trade, there would be a rise in the prices of the abundant factors and the fall in the prices of the scarce factors. Thus, labour-abundant poor economies will experience a rise in wages and a relative decline in the rental of capital. With even more restrictive assumptions, building on the Heckscher–Ohlin model, it is predicted that factor incomes will tend to equalise in line with the Factor Price Equalisation model developed by Samuelson. The conditions that underlie these models are so restrictive that, for all practical purposes, they cannot be used with any degree of precision to predict income growth, income levels that can be achieved or their distribution. However, it is also observed that while complete equalisation of factor prices would not happen, there has been a convergence of incomes observed in the last 30 years. This has been observed by the higher growth rate of incomes of some of the poor countries, such as the East Asian countries, compared to the growth rates of the advanced industrial countries. Attempts to model the relationship between globalisation (mainly via trade) and poverty have been made recently with reference to South Asia. And, the results suggest a positive relationship between liberalising trade and export of labour and poverty reduction in some broad yet qualified terms.

The link between capital markets in poor countries, such as those in South Asia, and those in developed countries is not well established as yet,

4 Policy Challenges of Globalisation in Sri Lanka

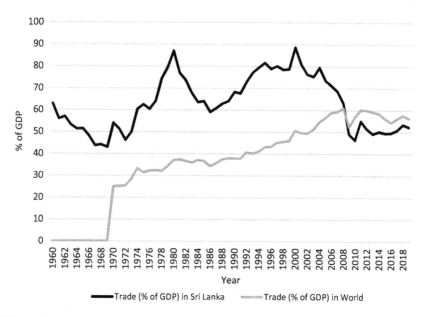

Figure 1.1. Trade, as a Percentage of GDP in Sri Lanka and the World (1960–2019)
Source: The World Bank, World Development Indicators.

given that the former does not have developed capital markets. For that very reason, the turmoil in the financial markets, with the WFC in the advanced countries, has left the poor countries relatively unaffected save for the reduction in foreign demand for goods of these countries.

In the context of the above-described theoretical possibilities, there is an important story behind the following statistics. The world's goods, services, capital and labour markets have integrated in the last five decades under a self-driven and to a large extent self-generating process. The process is far from complete. The ratio of Trade to Gross Domestic Product (GDP, the value of goods and services produced in a country usually during a year) for the world is around 56 per cent on average (Figure 1.1 and Table 1.1). It has the potential to grow to 70–80 per cent in the future, taking into account the increasing "tradability"[2] of the world

---

[2] Tradability is the property of a good or service that can be sold in another location distant from where it was produced. A good that is not tradable (is called non-tradable). Non-tradable goods, can only be consumed in the economy in which they are produced; they are not exported or imported.

Table 1.1. A Measure of Integration: Trade to GDP of Sri Lanka Compared to the Trade to GDP Ratio of the World (1960–2019)

Time Period	Trade (% of GDP) in Sri Lanka	Trade (% of GDP) in World
1960–1969	51.11	—
1970–1979	60.24	29.96
1980–1989	67.98	36.63
1990–1999	76.31	42.11
2000–2009	72.67	54.39
2010–2019	50.85	57.55

Source: The World Bank, World Development Indicators.

economy as further technological changes reduce transport costs and man-made trade barriers in agriculture, services and the remaining pockets of protection. Even today, there is little prospect for a new round of multilateral trade negotiation; the proposed Doha Development Round (DDR) could not be implemented mainly because there was no agreement among the principal countries with respect to the agenda. And, what was agreed upon in the Bali Ministerial Conference was much narrower compared to the original ambition of the DDR with regard to agricultural subsidies, trade facilitation and greater support for the least developed countries. The WFC that led to a world recession did not give much impetus or scope to reduce trade barriers further. Overall, there is greater scope for the trade to GDP ratio to be raised in such circumstances. There are still pockets of protection among industrial countries, particularly with respect to garments, textiles and agriculture, as well as an escalation in the tariff structures in some developed countries. Average protection levels in developing countries are about double those of developed countries.

Equally, with better information, improved supervision of financial institutions and greater convergence of rules of conduct for financial transactions after the WFC, there are greater opportunities for further capital market integration. In fact, in the first wave of globalisation during the 1890s to 1920, world capital markets were more closely integrated than they are now, thanks in part to fixed but stable exchange rate regimes and the access provided to financial resources for commercial banks by their head offices. In the late 1990s, the financial crises in Mexico (1997), East Asian economies (Thailand, Indonesia, Korea and Malaysia in 1998) and Russia (1999) dampened the initial enthusiasm for the integration of financial markets that arose with the ending of the debt crisis of the 1980s. While the threat of a systemic collapse never occurred in the financial crises of the 1990s, any plans to open capital accounts in developing countries were shelved. The WFC occurred in 2008, leading to a collapse of large financial houses in New York, such as Lehman Brothers, and created less enthusiasm for the integration of capital markets. European financial markets were saved by government intervention after some countries went to the brink, such as Greece, Spain, Italy and Cyprus. A slow recovery began in 2011.

Capital flows to developing countries resumed (refer to Tables 1.2 and 1.3), following a hiatus in the mid-1990s associated with the Mexican debt crisis which was called the "Tequila crisis," and thereafter some recovery from the shock associated with the WFC during 2008–2012. Despite the shock, the more open economies have resumed growth. In nearly all countries, currency crises have abated, including those in the Eurozone. Perhaps it was unrealistic to expect stability to return as the fiscal problems, high debt and appreciated real exchange rates persist though at a lower scale than in the immediate aftermath of the WFC.

The integration of goods and services is greater than what measures such as the trade ratio suggest due to the "slicing of the production process." Production processes are "disintegrated" as no country produces all the components of a good. Many leading experts agree that the integration

Table 1.2. Standard Deviation of Values Relating to Trade, Net Migration and FDI in Sri Lanka (1960–2019)

Time Period	Trade (% of GDP) in Sri Lanka	Trade (% of GDP) in the World	Net Migration (Per 1000 Population)	FDI (net) Inflows (% of GDP)
1960–1969	6.47	—	0.20	—
1970–1979	10.59	3.62	0.80	0.44
1980–1989	8.71	1.09	1.44	0.34
1990–1999	4.99	3.02	1.11	0.73
2000–2009	10.79	4.34	1.42	0.35
2010–2019	2.43	1.88	1.53	0.33

Source: The World Bank, World Development Indicators and United Nations, World Population Prospects: The 2022 Revision.

Table 1.3. Real Interest Rates, Trade to GDP, Gross Capital Formation and Net Migration for Six Periods in Sri Lanka (1960–2019)

Time Period	Real Interest Rate (%)	Trade (% of GDP)	Gross Capital Formation (% of GDP)	Net Migration (Per 1000 population)
1960–1969	3.06	51.11	15.55	−0.88
1970–1979	6.18	60.24	17.49	−2.78
1980–1989	13.55	67.98	26.23	−3.46
1990–1999	15.87	76.31	24.87	−3.73
2000–2009	4.09	72.67	25.54	−1.23
2010–2019	3.94	50.85	31.57	−3.84

Source: The World Bank, World Development Indicators and the United Nations World Population Prospects: The 2022 Revision.

Table 1.4. Imports and Exports as a Percentage of GDP for Six Periods in Sri Lanka (1960–2019)

Time Period	Imports of Goods and Services (% of GDP)	Exports of Goods and Services (% of GDP)
1960–1969	26.77	24.34
1970–1979	32.04	28.20
1980–1989	40.64	27.34
1990–1999	42.60	33.71
2000–2009	40.77	31.90
2010–2019	29.65	21.19

Source: The World Bank, World Development Indicators.

of production across frontiers due to the slicing process is bringing about more competition and therefore greater static and dynamic gains from trade (Krugman, 1995; Feenstra, 1998; Frankel, 2000). When traditional aggregates are used, such as the levels of exports and imports, they do not capture the underlying intra-industry trade that is taking place. In Sri Lanka, the same phenomenon has taken place (see Table 1.4). Thus, the same level of exports and imports in a country today compared to 1980 would have more intermediate goods, due to greater imports and exports of intermediate goods. Such trade in intermediate goods is not captured in the final goods as in the usual measures of trade.

Today, services are growing twice as fast as goods. This is because services are akin to luxury goods, have low elasticities of substitution and experience rising prices. The rapid growth in services is providing more opportunities in the global market. New trade-in services go beyond tourism, port services and international transport. They include the rapid growth of financial services as well as informational and technological services. There is a huge potential for the latter. Bangalore is perhaps more integrated with Silicon Valley in California than with the rest of India with respect to the purchase and sale of information technology services. But, at present, nearly all developing countries are net exporters of services.

The integration of capital markets takes place as a result of domestic capital market reforms in developing countries and the resumption of capital flows following the debt crisis in the early 1980s. In the 1990s, foreign direct investment (FDI) flows increased six times compared to the 1980s, partly due to the growth in trade in intermediate products, but slowed down due to the WFC. FDI is an efficient conduit for technology transfer and market access. However, FDI is concentrated in a few countries. New research shows that FDI is a *sine qua non* of trade for newcomers. It not only helps alleviate the constraints of national savings but more importantly also helps bring in new technology and provides access to well-established markets for products developed by the principal investors in industrial countries.

Labour markets have remained flexible as a whole in developed countries in contrast to many developing countries, including Sri Lanka. Legislation passed in 1971 (Termination of Employment of Workmen Act No. 45 of 1971 of Sri Lanka) has made labour markets much less flexible, discouraged FDI and led to high unemployment. Negative economic shocks have led to greater unemployment in that part of the developing world. This is one reason for the resistance to globalisation, even in some developed countries. Efforts are presently being made to bring about reforms in labour markets in some developing countries to increase their flexibility and enable them to withstand external shocks as well as absorb new technology more easily.

Following the oil crisis in the mid-1970s and early 1980s, there was an increased demand for labour in the Middle East. Bangladesh, India, Pakistan and Sri Lanka responded by reducing the barriers to labour movements that had existed in the past. As a result, there was a rapid increase in labour efflux that led to large remittances from the Middle East.

At one stage, these remittances accounted for nearly 50 per cent of Sri Lanka's foreign exchange earnings.

However, the invasion of Kuwait by Iraqi in August 1991 and the collapse of oil prices prior to that reduced the rate of growth of remittances. In respect of more advanced countries, labour movements slowed considerably because of tightened immigration policies and the use of highly selective regulations, such as the issuing of H1-B visas in the US. With the WFC, there was again a dip in labour demand from developed countries. Special efforts were made to attract skilled labour with high academic and information technology (IT) skills. President Trump tightened immigration policies in the USA with border controls.

The withdrawal of Iraqi troops (2009–2011) and the coming of peace in the region led to an even greater increase in demand for labour by the Middle East and an increase in labour movement from Sri Lanka to the region. Even the new war in 2003, the ousting of Saddam Husain and the continued conflict in Iraq did not lead to the abatement of demand for labour from Sri Lanka to the Middle-East, and remittances continued to be more than 50 per cent of foreign exchange revenues.

It is clear that there have been a variety of reactions to globalisation. With time from then and now, we need to analyse multiple factors to globalisation. The historical, ideological and political aspects of globalisation and the resultant challenges for Sri Lanka form the principal subject matter of this book. This study is conducted at the ground level to get more details and explore more avenues with regard to the interaction of Sri Lanka with the globalised world.

Thus, during the 1960–2019 period, the economy of Sri Lanka went through a number of vicissitudes, increasing and decreasing its participation in the global economy at different times. Reflecting on these movements, the economy progressed and regressed with time. Given the longer periods and variety of views, we have a much wider canvas than in the early 2000s when globalisation became a topic of interest to eminent economists. This book proposes to sort out the main issues at play and bring the different analyses to a set of conclusions that would be valuable to developing countries like Sri Lanka with a small open economy. For that purpose, we note the changed views on globalisation from the initial acceptance by mainstream economists to doubts raised by eminent economists, like Paul Krugman who remarked that globalisation is associated with worsening income distribution.

It is noteworthy that four types of conclusions were recorded in the analyses of globalisation by eminent economists. These are as follows: First, there are net disadvantages to globalisation according to Stiglitz and Rodrik, who claimed that it increased unemployment and poverty and worsened income distribution. Second, a majority of citizens were worse off after globalisation compared to the situation before increased globalisation. Third, not all countries were worse off as claimed by those who stated that freer trade and foreign capital inflows were disruptive. It should be noted that China, India and Vietnam have experienced unabated growth even with the disruption in global production networks. Finally, there has not been a clear identification of effects arising from technological change (fall in wages due to greater recourse to capital substitution in place of labour) and reduction in incomes due to COVID-19 lockdowns. A good final reckoning of the COVID-19 pandemic is necessary before making strong condemnations of globalisation.

By looking at a single country, Sri Lanka, we can better evaluate the implications of globalisation and assess the true emerging picture of globalisation to undertake necessary reforms to increase the benefits of globalisation.

Like other countries, there has been concern in Sri Lanka about globalisation, which has been expressed in newspaper articles since 1990. Until 2005, no Sri Lankan government had formally expressed any concern, but it seemed well aware of the likely impact of globalisation. However, with the new left-of-centre government that came into power in 2005 under the leadership of President Mahinda Rajapaksa, there was concern expressed about globalisation. It was announced that under *Mahinda Chintana* (or the views of Mahinda), the guiding tenets of the government, the government aimed to make Sri Lanka "the Miracle of Asia," with more dirigiste and interventionist policies, as an important alternative to what was considered the previous government's "neo-liberal" economic policies.

In society as a whole, there was more ambiguity regarding globalisation. There seems to be a better understanding of the issues involved among some circles than in popular discussions spawned by the media. The popular discussions are certainly more negative and in some sense defeatist. How can a small country compete with more advanced and larger countries? This is the refrain in the newspapers. It is noteworthy that the Sinhalese newspapers read by a majority are more pessimistic about globalisation than the English newspapers that have a better-informed readership. Besides, news in English newspapers is not filtered like the news in Sinhalese newspapers, which have a more nationalistic editorial staff.

1.1.2 *Methodology*

The methodology used in the book is to provide a narrative on globalisation and the factors that determine its outcomes. For that purpose, seven specific periods are identified that are closely associated with changes in governments brought about by by-elections with one exception.[3] The seven episodes provide an account of the movements towards and away from globalisation.

This methodology of using a narrative provides a way to look at forces at work in a small open economy without using a single closely specified economic model. One reason why a purely economic model was not pursued is that it would have had a very narrow focus, leaving out important historical, political and ideological factors at play. This is because of the difficulties in specifying and estimating such a model with macroeconomic, microeconomic and institutional elements having their influence. Instead, the narrative found in each chapter is informed by economic theory to a large extent and is placed in the context of the particular time period and its political milieu.

1.1.3 *A Brief History*

Sri Lanka's strategic location and its colonial history under the British assured that the country was integrated to some extent into the world in three important aspects: international trade, foreign direct investment and labour movement. Today, Sri Lanka would be described then as somewhat of a globalised economy, as during the British period. While there had been trading in the pre-colonial period (before the Portuguese and the Dutch arrived), there was limited trade among the neighbours and beyond, due to the demand from Europe for spices, gems and even elephants which were objects of trade.

Even before the British period, there was trade, especially during the Dutch period, in the coastal areas of Ceylon (the name given

---

[3] Refer to Chapter 2: Movements towards and away from Globalisation; subheading: History, Ideology and Economic Policies in Sri Lanka.

by Westerners). The Dutch were inveterate traders, unlike the Portuguese who were more interested in taking over ports and spreading the Roman Catholic religion. The British, given their dominance of the seas since the 17th century, were also interested in trade, especially through the British East India Company.

Later, in the 19th century, the British formally conquered the whole country in 1815 and their interest in economic matters created strong links with other British possessions in the Southern and Eastern parts of Asia.

There were large capital inflows from the British which were British investments, in today's parlance established plantation crops in the country are exported. While the early interest in coffee shifted to tea due to the coffee plants being infested with "Blister Blight," tea took hold with large investments in the Central Province and the Southern Province. British tea and rubber companies hired labour from India and led to some of the earliest labour movements in the Asian region. Tea and rubber were exported, while coconut was cultivated by local farmers and sold in the domestic market. Tea and rubber required substantial labour input for their cultivation and were the main plantation crops, cultivated and maintained by British-owned firms. These estates were examples of well-tended and managed properties.

Using modern parlance, Ceylon under the British had open trade, capital inflows to establish Tea and Rubber plantations, and labour inflows of indentured labour for the estates. In 1975, the government of Sirimavo Bandaranaike nationalised tea estates, parts of which were owned by the British and Sri Lankans.

Thus, the historical background shows that there were aspects of globalisation present in the country as early as the 1840s. Trade, FDI and the labour movements, which are the three principal aspects of globalisation as defined by Joseph Stiglitz and others, prevailed in Ceylon. It was only in the 1960s under Prime Minister Sirimavo Bandaranaike that there was a movement away from globalisation, given the influence of the socialists (Trotskyites and Communists) in her coalition government.

It can be said that the movement away from globalisation was in the post-colonial period of 1956 to the 1970s when left-of-centre politicians who were ideologically driven took over the plantation sector. Following this period, there were three important aspects with respect to globalisation: the nationalisation of plantations, a reduction in FDI and a restriction of labour outflows wherein workers were not allowed to move to other countries in the region for employment.

1.1.4 The Structure of the Book

This book is structured as follows: Chapter 1 is the introduction, which does some ground-clearing. Chapter 2 provides details of the different periods and movements towards and away from globalisation. Chapter 3 provides a historical background to the development that was to come later, based on the ideas of some of the leading economists of the world who were invited to visit Sri Lanka (Ceylon). Chapter 4 discusses the changing ideology, which plays a significant part in determining the policies in Sri Lanka. In Chapters 5 and 6, the role played by international financial institutions like the World Bank and the IMF, respectively, in small countries like Sri Lanka is evaluated. Chapter 7 discusses how many developing countries identify industrialisation with development, with Sri Lanka being no exception. As a result, they had government-sponsored industries paying little regard to follow comparative advantage in establishing government industries. Chapter 8 looks at the detrimental effects of inflation on a small open economy like Sri Lanka. Chapter 9 discusses exports, which are a critical factor for narrow-resource-based countries like Sri Lanka. Chapter 10 provides a mainstream analysis of the link between globalisation, poverty and income inequality. Chapter 11 looks at the future of globalisation as informed by the issues in Sri Lanka that prevailed after the COVID-19 pandemic. Chapter 12 brings together the analyses from all the previous chapters. It provides the conclusion and we note that economics alone cannot explain the impact of globalisation on small developing economies. Consequently, this book brings together economics, history, politics and ideology.

Chapter 2, which follows the major drivers of globalisation, asks the reader the following: Has globalisation slowed down as argued by the *Economist* magazine, which called it Slowbalisation, has it gone too far as Dani Rodrik claims or has it gone far enough as questioned by Martin Wolf?

The Sri Lankan case is most interesting, given that the movements towards and away from globalisation have been influenced by 10 changes in government over this period. The direction and extent of globalisation are tracked through policies with respect to foreign trade, FDI and movement of labour across the frontier.

Meanwhile, the COVID-19 pandemic intervened, creating an adverse effect on GDP growth, poverty reduction and income distribution. Fiscal expenditure increased due to the purchase of vaccinations and the enforcement of safety regulations. There are also cost implications due to lockdowns that led to a significant decline in output.

Chapter 2

Movements Towards and Away from Globalisation

2.1 A Brief History

Liberalisation is a movement towards globalisation. It allows relative prices to determine the allocation of resources. The liberalisation of the economy in 1977 allowed Sri Lanka to benefit from globalisation compared to other South Asian countries. Sri Lanka has not been subject to currency or capital account shocks such as those other East Asian countries suffered from in the late 1990s. Equally, it has not done as well as the East Asian economies. In fact, one stated ambition of Sri Lanka as articulated by politicians and officials (at least before the East Asian Crisis) was that Sri Lanka should become like an East Asian economy. Sri Lanka's movements towards globalisation created opportunities for trade, capital and labour movements. But it didn't continue over time and, around 2005 with a change in government to a more left of centre and somewhat nationalistic government. Over the next 5 years, the trade regime became more protectionist, in part due to the ideology of the party that came into power in 2005, which was more left-oriented and nationalist, and in part due to the need to raise trade tariffs and taxes to finance the war against the Liberation Tamil Tigers of Eelam (LTTE) separatists.

Two factors have to be recognised when considering the impact of globalisation on Sri Lanka, both of which are internal due to which the country's ability to benefit from globalisation was limited. These factors are first, the civil war against the LTTE that went on for nearly 30 years, ending in May 2009 with the elimination of its leadership in battle.

Table 2.1. Sri Lanka's GDP Growth and Sectoral Distribution (1960–2019)

Time Period	GDP Growth (Annual %)	SD[a] of GDP Growth Rate	Agriculture (%)	Industry (%)	Services (%)
1960–1969	4.66	1.97	36.17	17.24	46.61
1970–1979	4.23	2.37	28.97	26.08	44.95
1980–1989	4.15	1.47	27.24	27.02	45.74
1990–1999	5.26	1.05	23.65	26.36	50.00
2000–2009	5.00	2.59	14.71	28.72	56.54
2010–2019	5.40	2.88	7.91	27.80	56.38

Note: [a]SD = Standard Deviation.
Source: The World Bank, World Development Indicators.

Second, the changed ideology led to a lack of consistency in the overall economic framework of the country (Table 2.1).

The civil war had a pervasive influence on the economy of Sri Lanka. First, the war inhibited the inflow of resources for economic activities, both foreign direct investment (FDI) and foreign assistance. Second, the north and east of the country were not available for productive activities. This inhibited faster Gross Domestic Product (GDP) growth, higher export growth and more efficient import substitution. Third, the raising of taxes on foreign trade and other forms of taxes to finance the war distorted relative prices. Fourth, expenditures related the war led to large fiscal deficits that in turn were financed by inflationary sources, leading to double-digit inflation for almost the entire duration of the 30-year war. This also led to the appreciation of the exchange rate. Fifth, tourism declined significantly. Sixth, manpower that could have been used to produce goods and services was used to destroy a part of the manpower and physical productive capacity on both parties associated with the conflict. It is estimated that the internal conflict, violence and war had both direct and indirect effects on economic growth by reducing physical and human capital accumulation by 2.52 per cent a year from 1960 to 2009.[1] Santhirasegaram and Amirthalingam provided a breakdown of the cost of the war between direct and indirect costs. Finally, following the end of the war in May 2009, many Western countries (the European Union, Canada, the UK and the USA, among others) became less supportive of Sri Lanka's

---

[1] These estimates take into account the civil war from 1983–2009 as well as the civil unrest during 1971–1972 and 1998–1990 due to the *Janatha Vimukthi Peramuna* (JVP) uprisings. Santhirasegaram and Amirthalingam (2010).

development efforts since they questioned the manner in which the last stages of the war were conducted.[2]

As mentioned earlier, the war also inhibited FDI in the country, which denied important benefits of globalisation that would have enhanced the resources of the country, provided support for export growth and improved the management of the corporate sector. Meanwhile, since the country reached middle-income status, international financial institutions (IFIs), mainly the World Bank and the Asian Development Bank, reduced their lending to the country and tightened their terms of lending with respect to interest rates, maturity and grace periods.

With respect to ideology, the impact of globalisation was limited in the following ways.[3] First, changes in governments with widely different ideologies made it difficult to have a consistent policy framework that could be maintained over the long term. Table 2.3 indicates the changes in governments with the corresponding different ideologies. Second, the dominant party that led the coalition after 2005, the *Sri Lanka Freedom Party* (SLFP), leaned more to the left, even more so than earlier. It was hostile to open trade and the use of the price system in general and was not appreciative of the opportunities offered by globalisation.

2.1.1 *The Antecedents*

Like many other small countries, Sri Lanka has participated in the globalisation process by, at times, opening up its economy and, at other times, also putting up barriers against greater participation in the global economy. These vicissitudes are not unexpected in a country that has changed governments through the ballot more than fifteen times since independence in 1948.

---

[2] As of April 2014, Canada not only stopped providing foreign assistance to Sri Lanka but also withdrew its support for the Commonwealth Fund because Sri Lanka held the Chairmanship of the Commonwealth Heads of States Conference. Also, in March 2014, the United Nations Commission on Human Rights (UNCHR) passed a resolution to appoint an independent Commission of Inquiry into the conduct of both sides during the civil war since 2002. These developments illustrate the lack of support for the country's development efforts from the Western countries led by the United States, United Kingdom and the European Union.

[3] See Chapter 4, "Ideology and Economic Policy Making: A Framework Applied to Sri Lanka."

Sri Lanka's left-of-centre parties have predictably opposed globalisation in all its manifestations in trade, FDI and labour movement. However, the opposition to liberalisation has been muted due to the strong stance Sri Lanka took with the 1977 economic liberalisation, which connected the domestic market with the world market in trade, and partially in finance and labour movement. Due to the demonstration of the success of globalisation in neighbouring East Asia and the improved economic performance in Sri Lanka itself, the left-of-centre parties lost favour on their opposition to liberal economic policies, which constitute the gateway to globalisation. As indicated, by 2005, however, there was a movement away from the world market with the government of President Mahinda Rajapaksa due to a clear ideological shift. Most of the indicators showed a reduction in their links with the world market for trade, finance and labour (Table 2.2).

Table 2.2. Sri Lanka's Globalisation Indicators (1960–2019)

Indicator	1960	1970	1980	1990	2000	2010	2019
1 Trade Ratio (% GDP)	62.87	54.05	87.02	68.24	88.64	46.36	52.40
2 Trade Deficit (% GDP)	(−2.96)	(−3.15)	(−22.58)	(−7.88)	(−10.61)	(−7.26)	(−5.14)
3 Overall Budget Deficit (% GDP)	(−6.1)	(−6.4)	(−19.2)	(−7.8)	(−9.5)	(−8)	(−9.0)
4 Current A/C Deficit in BOP[a] (% GDP)	(−3.3)	(−2.6)	(−16.4)	(−4.7)	(−6.4)	(−2.2)	(−2.1)
5 FDI (Net) Inflows (% GDP)	—	(−0.01)	1.07	0.54	1.06	0.84	0.9
6 Remittances (% GDP)	—	—	3.77	4.99	7.07	7.27	8.03
7 Current Transfers (Net) in BOP[a] (US$ Millions)	4.6	11.8	274.6	423.4	997.8	3,660.3	5766.0

Note: [a]BOP = Balance of Payment.
Source: The World Bank, World Development Indicators, and Central Bank of Sri Lanka, *Annual Report*, 2022.

Table 2.2 shows a set of indicators of globalisation for Sri Lanka for the period 1960–2019, after independence from the British in 1948, with Sri Lanka having an open economy and specialising in three plantation crops of tea, rubber and coconuts.[4] During the 1948–1960 period, this open and globalised economy functioned fairly well, and Sri Lanka's participation in world trade and capital transactions (as indicated by flows of foreign direct investments (FDIs) and current account deficits) signified this openness. Based on this openness, the country did well in terms of GDP growth and general welfare. But, by 1960, the openness of the economy was challenged.

This chapter further examines the link between Total Factor Productivity (TFP) growth and GDP growth during the 1960–2019 period. Following the establishment of the determinants of TFP growth in Sri Lanka, in this chapter, one can determine a strong relationship between TFP growth and GDP growth. The main determinants in Sri Lanka for TFP growth are FDI, human capital, trade openness and eliminating corruption. Sri Lanka's growth is strongly associated with TFP growth, a result found in most studies of this nature. The present chapter finds that globalisation-friendly (GF) policies have a clear and positive impact on GDP growth while globalisation-unfriendly (GU) policies have the opposite effect. Going forward, it is crucial to return to GF policies, especially with the challenge of large debt repayments created by a debt overhang. Sri Lanka's growth history, policies and events have led to our present situation. These allow us to understand the reasons for the relatively low average rate of growth compared to East Asian countries over the 1960–2019 period; these circumstances also explain why growth cannot be sustained without a rise in total factor productivity along with consistent policies and events.

2.1.2 *History, Ideology and Economic Policies in Sri Lanka*

Seven distinct periods can be identified in which Sri Lanka was either seeking greater integration with the globalising world or moving away from it.[5]

---

[4]Rajapatirana (1988).

[5]These periods are identified based on the policies adopted by the dominant government of each period. A broad four-way classification of the policies is followed: liberal vs. interventionist and globalisation-friendly vs. globalisation-unfriendly policies. Most of the time, liberal policies turn out to be globalisation-friendly and interventionist policies are

These include (i) pre-independence liberal and globalisation-friendly policies (1920–1947), (ii) continued liberal and globalisation-friendly policies (1948–1955), (iii) interventionist and globalisation-unfriendly policies (1956–1964), (iv) partly liberal and globalisation-friendly policies (1965–1969), (v) interventionist and globalisation-unfriendly policies (1970–1977), (vi) liberal and globalisation-friendly policies (1978–2004), and (vii) partly interventionist and globalisation-unfriendly policies (2005–2019). These policy periods were distinct in their characteristics with respect to policies on trade, FDI, financial capital flows and labour movements, and signified Sri Lanka's intention to either participate in or hold back from the globalising world economy. The distinctions across periods are broadly classified according to the dominant policy regimes of each period. Sometimes, the dominant policy regime can extend over one political party. Thus, the presidency of the SLFP led by President Chandrika Kumaratunga dovetailed into the regime led by the United National Party (UNP) during the 1977–2004 period. This was the exception rather than the rule. It was a case of leftist governments continuing and extending the liberal and globalisation-friendly regimes during the presidencies of presidents Jayawardena, Premadasa and Wijetunga.

(i) *Pre-independence Liberal and Globalisation-Friendly Policies (1920–1947)*

This period saw the transfer of greater political freedom by the British colonial authorities to the local population. There were many reforms in this period from the 1832 Colebrooke Commission reforms to the legislative reforms of 1924 and the Donoughmore reforms of 1931, which among other changes introduced universal franchise.[6] A Ceylonese middle class emerged with aspirations to have political power and to further its economic interests. 1920–1947 was the pre-World War II colonial period.[7]

---

globalisation-unfriendly. Liberal policies are those that allow prices to play a role in resource allocation and interventionist policies are those that interfere widely with resource allocation. There is one exception. During 1995–2001, the government led by President Chandrika Kumaratunga was partly interventionist but globalisation-friendly. Her government followed the policies of the preceding UNP-dominated government.

[6] Sri Lanka was first Asian country to have universal franchise the same year that women got the right to vote in the United States of America.

[7] De Silva, K. M. (2005). *A History of Sri Lanka*. Sri Lanka: Penguin Books India.

In this period, there were some attributes of a liberal trade regime with free trade within the British Empire with a mild barrier in terms of the imperial preference system. There was thus a discriminatory tariff for trade with the rest of the world. Also, the world economy was recovering from the Great Depression of 1929–1932. Recovery was slow in the early years of the depression. Trade and links to globalisation were dominated by British interests.

What prevailed was a colonial ideology. British rule of the whole island became a reality after 1815, leading up to independence in 1948. Save for the Uva Rebellion (1817–1818), there was virtually no significant opposition to British rule right up to independence in 1948, except for some protests during the Second World War when a small Marxist minority and some nationalists opposed the "imperialist's war." At no point was the political regime challenged even though there were anti-colonial sentiments fostered and developed by the Marxist parties and the nationalists since the 1930s.

There were important institutional reforms undertaken during this period that led to a modern state of independence with a sound legal framework including commercial laws and practices, and a system of justice that secured property rights. Many of the laws and institutions required for a modern economy were developed during this period by the colonial administrators and later by the national members of the legislative council.

A uniform regulatory system within the British colonies helped to raise output. The Currency Board System helped to keep the macroeconomy situation stable. There was no International Monetary Fund (IMF), but there were strong rules of behaviour for operating in the Currency Board System which was in operation from 1880 to 1950 when the Central Bank was established. The government of the day (following the Donoghmore Commission-based reforms of 1932, remained in place until the Soulbury Constitution (1947) introduced self-rule. The colonial government (with a council of ministers elected through universal franchise) was motivated to establish pilot industrial ventures to produce essential goods using domestic raw materials. Thus, in addition to existing privately owned industries, such as soap, safety matches, textiles and handlooms, the government set up industries for plywood, steel rolling, glass, acetic acid, paper, ceramics, drugs, tanneries and shoes in the short term. It was a temporary departure from globalisation that gathered further impetus after the Second World War.[8] There was no attempt to change the existing liberal trade regime to protect these industries after the war; they were more like public investments to create industries in the short term to meet the disruption in supplies due to the war.

There were large investments in the export sector during the pre-independence period in tree crops, especially tea and rubber. These were in the private sector, in what is now called FDI, which were mostly from British investors, both individuals and private companies. This was not a formal challenge to the liberal trade regime that existed during the time, but something brought about by the exigencies of the situation. A similar case was to arise in the 1990s when the civil war against LTTE led to the loss of some attributes of the liberal and globalised economic regime that came into being in 1977.

Like capital, coming into the country, there were also inflows of labour to work in the plantations since the 1880s. There was no movement of labour away from the country. There was one exception, which was due to laws imposed by the colonial government that mandated that wages of plantation labour could not be reduced. Plantation managers and owners retrenched labour over the years. In fact, part of the adjustment to the Great Depression (1929–1933) in Sri Lanka was to shed labour rather than adjust through the prevailing gold standard system, which would have meant a cut in real wages instead of retrenching labour.

Five aspects related to globalisation were clarified in the pre-war period. First, a liberal trade regime open to globalisation without overall policy and institutional support could not diversify production or raise productivity significantly to assure higher rates of economic growth. Second, the existence of a currency board assured macroeconomic stability.[9] Third, the government of the day did not try to change trade policy but used other

---

[8] Sri Lanka as a member of the British Colonial Empire had access to a large area for trade, investment and labour movement. In fact, there was significant movement of labour to Sri Lanka when British plantation companies brought in indentured labourers from India to work on tea plantations. Thus, goods, capital and labour were mobile within the empire during the period up to the 1930s. The market size of the British Empire was large, perhaps amounting to more than a third of the global economy starting in the late 1870s. See De Silva (2005).

[9] This was due to what Gamani Corea called "a colonial method of fiscal finance" in his D.Phil. thesis at Oxford, Corea (1953).

measures to meet the changes in global economic conditions. Fourth, with no supporting policies, no adequately trained human capital, no appropriate infrastructure or institutions, there would not have been substantial economic development. The colonial regime supported the development of export agriculture, tea, rubber and coconuts. While it was more of a revenue-seeking regime, it provided a supportive economic environment for British commercial interests. Finally, there were no significant ideological differences between the British administrators and local officials to advance national interests. It was a colonial administration with national officials holding limited power and influence.

Table 2.3 summarises the changes in political regimes, policy orientation, attitude towards globalisation and economic growth. The UNP is unambiguously right of centre in its policy orientation; it had more

Table 2.3. Political Regimes, Policy Orientation and Globalisation

Time Period	Political Regime	Economic Policy	Economic Growth (%)
1950–1955	UNP — Right of Centre	Liberal market economy (GF)	4.26
1956–1964	MEP — Left of Centre	Closed economy (GU)	2.85
1965–1969	UNP — Right of Centre	Partially open market economy (GF)	5.50
1970–1976	SLFP — Left of Centre	Closed economy (GU)	3.59
1977–1993	UNP — Right of Centre	Open market economy (GF)	4.76
1994–2000	PA — Left of Centre	Partially open economy (GF/GU)	5.19
2001–2002	UNP — Right of Centre	Open market economy (GF)	1.21
2003–2004	PA — Left of Centre	Partially open market economy (GF)	5.69
2005–2014	UPFA — Left of Centre	Partially open but interventionist (GU)	6.59
2015–2019	SLFP coalition	Partially (GU) and Partially (GF)	3.56
2019–2021	The period 2019–2021 was a complicated period because of the increased uncertainty of the political environment.		

Notes: Average Annual GDP Growth.
UNP — United National Party; MEP — *Mahajana Eksath Peramuna*; SLFP — Sri Lanka Freedom Party; UPFA — United People's Freedom Alliance; PA — People's Alliance (SLEP led); GU — Globalisation-Unfriendly; GF — Globalisation-Friendly.
Source: The World Bank, World Development Indicators.

multi-ethnic electoral support save for the Marxists. The People's Front comprising the SLFP is a left-of-centre party with nationalist Sinhala-Buddhist majority support. But, its approach to globalisation and market orientation changed after their partnership with the coalition with the Marxist and at times Sinhala chauvinist elements such as the *Jathika Hela Peramuna* (JHP) (National Pro-Sinhala front) and the *Jathika Vimukthi Peramuna* (JVP) (National Progressive Front). It was difficult to classify the government that came into power in the 1994–2000 period under the leadership of Mrs. Chandrika Kumaratunga who was elected as a left-of-centre SLFP candidate but who favoured a more open economy with respect to foreign trade, foreign capital flows and the labour movement. Consequently, her government did not change the globalisation-friendly bent of the UNP which was in power for the previous 17 years. The growth rates indicated earlier do not suggest the success or failure of the different parties. Rather, they show partial correlations between policy orientation and growth outcome. Finally, the end of the war against the LTTE in 2009 brought about peace and a prospect for higher GDP growth. However, although peace was restored it could not lead to higher economic growth because there were no accompanying economic reforms.

As noted in Table 2.3, while there is no clear relationship between globalisation-friendly policies and GDP growth, when there is sometimes high growth with globalisation-unfriendly policies, the period preceding has had globalisation-friendly policies due to spillover effects.

(ii) *Post-Independence Continued Liberal and Globalisation-Friendly Policies (1948–1955).*

At independence, Sri Lanka was a prosperous country, ahead of other Asian countries except for Japan and Malaysia. It had other advantages — its location, open economy, a high level of education, the absence of extreme poverty or inequality, a well-functioning infrastructure, sound administration and well-developed institutions such as a good judicial system, and commercial and civil laws. Of course, everything is relative; these good attributes were present compared to other Asian countries. As later research showed, British colonial rule was an advantage for later development especially with respect to institutions compared to other colonial experiences under the French, Portuguese and Belgians.[10]

---

[10] See Barro, Lucas, Acemoglu and Robinson, among others.

The Sri Lankan post-independence economy remained very much like the pre-independence economy during this period. While the political regime changed, there was hardly any change in the economy. The UNP that won the 1947 election formed a government in 1948 in independent Sri Lanka. In today's parlance, the government's economic policies were open and "globalisation-friendly." One important change though was that trade and economic relations moved beyond the group of countries that constituted the British Empire to the rest of the world. In terms of economic theory, the country faced a worldwide demand curve for its exports and a world supply curve. In terms of capital, the opportunity set had widened even though there was hardly any change in the sources of finance for the country. The government signed a Rice-Rubber Agreement with the People's Republic of China (PRC) in 1953, and Sri Lanka was the first South Asian country to recognise the PRC. It also showed the pragmatic nature of the UNP-led government which in some sense differed in foreign policy orientation from that of the US–UK-led group that did not recognise the Communist Revolution in China in 1949.

During the Korean War (1950–1951), there was increased demand for rubber; Sri Lanka accumulated large foreign exchange reserves and used a part of it to increase imports and build up reserves, which helped to meet the increased demand for imports later without resorting to any trade controls. Macroeconomic management at the time was traditional and cautionary, and the Central Bank advocated the reduction of food subsidies that had been introduced during the Second World War. In 1953, *Samasamaja* and communist parties led a *"hartal"* or strike that led to the resignation of Prime Minister Dudley Senanayake, who had become the second prime minister of independent Sri Lanka following the death of D. S. Senanayake.

Sri Lanka's domestic policies remained very much as in the past framework of maintaining macroeconomic stability, subsidising crucial services such as health, education and the consumption of the main staple-rice. One can safely say that the country maintained a liberal market economy compared to what happened after 1960. It is noteworthy that the government at the time did not consider reforms or approaches to integrate with the world economy. It was not due to an ideological position, but the case for moving towards greater globalisation was not considered by the policymakers in Sri Lanka or other developing countries. Research on the benefits and costs of globalisation was to come later.

The response to the Korean boom was conventional. The Central Bank, which was established in 1950, cautioned against inflation given the increase in reserves from the rubber boom and raised the bank rate by some 200 basis points. And, it also raised the reserve requirement ratio of commercial banks from 10 per cent to 15 per cent. Meanwhile, fiscal policies remained committed to a balanced budget.

There was very limited FDI during this period.[11] Few reasons can be offered as to why it was so. First, after gaining independence, the country had yet to prove that it was going to have good macroeconomic and incentive policies. There was uncertainty with respect to the national government. Second, following the Korean boom, primary commodity prices were not expected to increase again in the near term and no new investment was to take place in the traditional export sector. Third, the country's comparative advantage in light manufacturing and food, drink and production of components and similar sophisticated technology in a vertically integrated production arrangement was yet to be established. There was no such discovery taking place in the newly independent country.

With respect to the labour movement, there was hardly any significant inward migration or outward movement to take up work. One of the first acts of the new parliament of independent Ceylon was to disenfranchise plantations labourers with Citizenship Act No. 18 of 1948 who were brought to the country by British plantation companies from the 1890s onwards. Around one million persons of Indian origin or 11 per cent of the country's population were affected. Their political clout was reduced as was their mobility to move from their traditional workplaces to other parts of the country and travel to India for short visits, short of emigration. Later, the Sirimavo Bandaranaike–Shastri Pact (1964) signed between the Prime Ministers of Sri Lanka and India formalised arrangements for sending back Indian labourers with some cash inducements.

Compared to the earlier two periods, this period saw the sharp delineation of two or three competing ideologies associated with the centre right UNP, the left centre SLFP, the further left *Samasamaja* (Trotskyite) Party, and the communists. Over the years, party lines became hardened between the right-of-centre and left-of-centre parties. A third factor was that the SLFP, which was created by S. W. R. D. Bandaranaike, brought in a more nationalist, Sinhala-Buddhist majority coalition that could challenge the

---

[11] Athukorala, P. and Rajapatirana, S. (2000). *Liberalisation and Industrial Transformation: Sri Lanka in International Perspective*. New Delhi and London: Oxford University Press.

UNP's hold over power in 1956. This clear delineation of political parties and ideologies were symbolised in policies towards globalisation over the whole period of 1948–2012. There was thus continuity and change.

(iii) *Interventionist and Globalisation-Unfriendly Policies (1956–1964)*
The economic policy regimes that existed in the colonial period began to change after the left-of-centre *Mahajana Eksath Peramuna* (MEP) or People's United Front government led by S. W. R. D. Bandaranaike came into power in 1956. The precise year is 1960 when, following strong terms of trade shock, the government instituted trade controls through exchange controls and import quotas.[12] This response was partly motivated by the nationalistic ideology of the MEP (the SLFP-led coalition) and the opportunity was created by the negative terms of the trade shock.

The political ideologies of the leftist parties also supported the introduction of trade interventions. These left-of-centre parties (*Samasamajist* (Trotskyites) and communists) had expressed their desire to change the colonial economic structure which was dependent on plantations and agriculture. In the 1950s, a school of economists working in Latin America had developed a paradigm of import substitution-led industrialisation based on the work of Raul Prebisch, Hans Singer, Dudley Seers and others. These structuralists influenced other developing countries based on the alleged long-term deterioration of terms of trade, trade between unequal partners and what was considered an exploitative FDI. In Sri Lanka too, one saw the movement of the officials to a more structuralist view of the world. It is seen in the Central Bank Annual reports of the mid-1950s.

This period saw Sri Lanka moving away from globalisation and to a globalisation-unfriendly stance. It was a period when intervention moved beyond trade into increased public ownership and state trading with widespread nationalisation. It started slowly at first but moved faster towards lesser participation in the globalisation process. Meanwhile, the MEP government entered into a spate of bilateral payment agreements with the former Soviet Bloc countries and some Middle Eastern countries such as Iraq and Jordan. The main thrust of these payment agreements was to exchange goods and pay off the remaining balances in US dollars. These agreements

---

[12] Prime Minister S. W. R. D. Bandaranaike was assassinated in September 1959, but the economic, political and social policies that he favoured were implemented by his wife Prime Minister Sirimavo Bandaranaike and the party leadership.

were not linked to the global economy but a form of managed trade with countries that had isolated themselves from the global economy and globalisation process. These agreements were not globalisation-friendly but were multilateral trade initiatives of the various trade rounds.

The period 1956–1965 is distinguished by the introduction of trade controls, mostly on the import side, exchange controls and increasing public sector size through the nationalisation of a leading commercial bank (Bank of Ceylon), the establishment of a new commercial bank (People's Bank), transport and some industries. There was relative macroeconomic stability, with low inflation and manageable current account deficits in the balance of payments. However, the end of this period saw the introduction and progressive tightening of exchange controls and increased trade protection. The implications of these two factors were the following. First, Sri Lanka lost a part of its character as an open economy with the imposition of import and exchange controls. Earlier, excess demand for tradable goods would spill into the current account in the balance of payments so that the current account would worsen and lead to a fall in reserves and help to contain excess aggregate demand and the adjustment process. But, this could not happen with the introduction of exchange controls. Second, with the increase in import protection, the bias against exports increased. And, the growth of exports slowed due to external conditions arising from the fall in world demand. The ratio of exports to GDP began to fall after 1960, while the trade ratio (the sum of exports and imports) fell to its lowest level during 1960–1970. One outcome of it was that world prices were no longer as important as before in determining the trade outcome. Another consequence of turning away from globalisation and adopting globalisation-unfriendly and inward-oriented policies was a growth slowdown.[13] Meanwhile, terms of trade decline also contributed to the growth slowdown.

A group of seven leading economists who visited Sri Lanka during 1957–1958 to advise the country on the Tenth Development Plan (1957–1958 to 1966–1967) did not make a particular case for greater participation in the global economy as analysed in Chapter 3, *"Through Eminent Eyes: A Fifty-Year Retrospective as a background to globalisation"* of this book.[14]

---

[13] Athukorala, P. (2012b). Sri Lanka's trade policy: Reverting to dirigisme? *The World Economy*, 35(12), 1662–1686.

[14] The eminent economists were Kenneth Galbraith, John R. Hicks, Ursula Hicks, Nicholas Kaldor, Oskar Lange, Gunnar Myrdal and Joan Robinson. Papers by Visiting Economist 1959, Ministry of Planning.

Their recommendations are in contrast to the present view on globalisation where mainstream eminent economists make a general case for globalisation. The earlier thinking of eminent economists reflected the leading paradigm of the day of import substitution leading to industrialisation behind trade barriers and using economic plans to raise economic growth while maintaining macroeconomic stability and increasing employment.

During this period, many countries in South Asia, including India, Pakistan, Malaysia and Indonesia, began to raise import barriers and initiated non-liberal and protectionist trade regimes, moving away from taking advantage of globalisation. One part of the reason for this action was that free trade was associated with colonialism and another part was the new ideas about economic development that emphasised externalities, market failures and the concept of unfair trade between unequal partners. Ideologically too, these countries opted not to increase their participation in the globalisation process. In the mid-1960s, East Asian countries opted to participate in and reaped huge benefits from globalisation, growing at unprecedented rates compared to earlier and compared to other developing countries.[15]

(iv) *Partly Liberal and Globalisation-Friendly Period (1965–1969)*
The use of price controls and exchange controls of the MEP government led to misallocation of resources which in turn led to low GDP growth. The UNP government that came into power in 1965 made a partial attempt to restore the role of prices by adopting a Foreign Exchange Entitlement Certificate Scheme (FEEC) in 1966 and partial liberalisation of foreign trade. The FEEC scheme was a multiple exchange rate regime. All external transactions were divided into an A category and a B category. Transactions under the A category, which included essential imports (rice, flour, sugar and fertiliser) as well as traditional exports (tea, rubber and coconut), were to be conducted at the official exchange rate. Category B transactions, which included non-traditional exports and non-essential imports, were conducted at an exchange rate with a premium (depreciated rate), and the rate was originally determined by the prices for FEECs. Thus, traditional exports (tea, rubber and coconuts) were converted at a fixed (appreciated) rate of exchange, while the non-traditional exports got a higher rate originally determined in the market for these certificates and

---

[15] Maddison (2001).

carried a premium. Initially, the premium rose as high as 65 per cent when the exchange rate for non-traditional exports rose to this level. Later, it was fixed at 45 per cent. These certificates could be used to import goods from a permissible list (included in category A).

The UNP government at the time made an effort to cut down agricultural imports through a package of measures to increase import substitution in agriculture, particularly rice. While some function of prices was restored with the FEEC scheme, its protagonists did not mind that the system taxed traditional exports, the country's main foreign exchange earner and subsidised unproven non-traditional exports through the exchange rate. Two main macroeconomic effects arose from the FEEC scheme. It helped to raise the price of tradables by a small percentage (due to a small percentage increase in non-traditional exports from a very low base) due to an increase in the production of importables with import substitution policies, particularly for agriculture.[16] However, the bias against exports continued, given the high import protection that became necessary to contain excess demand without spilling into the trade balance. Import substitution in agriculture, at the time encouraged by the UNP, led to greater inefficiency in terms of domestic resource costs (DRCs).[17]

It is also noteworthy that an Aid Group was formed in 1965 under the aegis of the World Bank to increase the role of the IFIs in the country, which led to greater resource transfer from these IFIs.[18] In addition, many bilateral donors began to extend assistance to Sri Lanka after a hiatus during the 1956–1965 period. Developed country governments were more comfortable with the UNP returning to power. The case for globalisation was yet to be made in the country since the success of East Asian economies had not yet begun to be noticed. That came later when the so-called Four Tigers (Hong Kong, South Korea, Taiwan and Singapore)

---

[16] Tradables are exports and export substitutes and imports and import substitutes. Non-tradables are those that do not cross borders, either due to the nature of the good or in response to government controls.

[17] Domestic resource cost (DRC): The value of domestic resources (evaluated at "shadow" or opportunity cost prices) employed in earning or saving a dollar of foreign exchange (in the value-added sense) when producing. domestic goods. See Krueger (1978).

[18] Perhaps even more importantly, they provided analytical support through their economic and sector work. See the contributions of the World Bank in Chapter 5, "The role of IFIs on Globalisation: World Bank Views on Sri Lanka in the 1970s and 1980s."

showed spectacular growth and poverty reduction by participating in the globalisation process, opening their markets, and maintaining macroeconomic stability and competitive exchange rates. Also, at this time, the seminal research on trade policies by Little *et al.* (1970), Donges (1976) and the National Bureau of Economic Research (NBER, United States) project (Bhagwati and Krueger, 1978) was not yet published, but a manuscript of this work was available along with the earlier support of the IFIs once the decision to liberalise the economy was made by the UNP government and provided easy access to finance.

While there was an increase in external assistance during this period, there was hardly any increase in FDI. Following the nationalisation of petrol distribution companies owned by Shell and Caltex in Sri Lanka in 1961, FDI flows to the country declined. This action earned the ire of the United States of America that led to the Hickenlooper Amendment,[19] resulting in the suspension of economic aid to Sri Lanka for a period of time.

The UNP government attempted to induce FDI to come back since the earlier nationalisation of petrol distribution of oil companies owned by the Americans as conducted by the SLFP-led government. The new government pursued the connection between export promotion and FDI. Consequently, it introduced a white paper on FDI which emphasised the "ability to export a greater part of the output as the most important criterion for FDI approval." Various tax concessions for export-oriented ventures were given. In addition, the government of the day relaxed limits on the remittance of dividends, interest income and profits against which a moratorium had been introduced in 1963.

Another aspect of globalisation is the movement of contract labour abroad, which had not yet begun at the time. Such a movement became important in the mid-1980s and provided both additional resources and helped to improve the economic welfare of the rural sector.

(v) *Interventionist and Globalisation-Unfriendly Policies (1970–1977)*
The 1970–1977 period is a remarkable one for the economic history of Sri Lanka due to its strong departure from connecting with globalisation processes in the world, with ramifications for trade, capital flows and the labour movement. The period saw the full flowering of the trade control regime that came into existence in the early 1960s, following a short respite from controls during 1965–1970. Trade controls became most

---

[19] University of Pennsylvania Law Review (Vol. 112:1116).

stringent during the 1970–1977 period. There was a restrictive law passed to take over private firms as well as restrictions imposed on firing employees.[20] Some compared Sri Lanka's controls to the type of controls that were found in the former Soviet Union with one hundred per cent quantitative restrictions on imports. It introduced a huge bias against exports and a wide variance in the rates of protection among activities. At the same time, more domestic price and quantity controls were put in place with the worsening of foreign demand due to the first oil shock.

The left-of-centre coalition included the Trotskyite Lanka *Sama Samaja Party* (LSSP) and the Communist Party which were highly committed to increasing control of the economy. There was a definite and strong ideological shift towards greater control of the economy. The Marxist parties campaigned on the premise that Sri Lanka would be transformed into a socialist economy.[21] Following the victory of the leftist parties, the leading SLFP coalition partner went along with their ideas. Later, the SLFP's enthusiasm for greater control of the economy and takeover of the private property seemed even more pronounced than that of the Marxist parties.[22] As indicated, the SLFP–Marxist coalition took over private property and nationalised the largest bank in Sri Lanka at the time — the Bank of Ceylon. The coalition further nationalised the plantations in 1975 and passed the Business Undertaking Acquisition Act of April 1971 and the Termination of Employment of Workers Act 35 of 1971. The first act dampened private entrepreneurship, while the second entrenched labour union power at the expense of the unemployed. During this period, the first oil shock struck, raising the price of oil sharply and creating difficulties in managing the economy.

To sum up, the whole period of 1970–1977 led to a salutary outcome for trade and capital and labour movements.[23] First, the move from price-based policies to quantity-based policies made an adjustment to external shocks more difficult (complicated by the first oil shock of 1973–1975) and changed the character of the economic regime in drastic ways.

---

[20] See Business Undertakings (Acquisition) Act No. 35 of 1971. This Act may be cited as the Termination of Employment of Workmen (Special Provisions) Act No. 45 of 1971.
[21] Athukorala, P. and Jayasuriya, S. (1994). *Macroeconomic Policies, Crises and Growth in Sri Lanka 1969–90*, (pp. 161–172). Washington, D.C.: World Bank Comparative Macroeconomic Studies.
[22] *Ibid.*
[23] The MEP coalition broke up in 1975 when the LSSP and the CP left the coalition.

Domestic prices were controlled as were interest rates, while the nominal exchange rate remained fixed. The fall in world demand for Sri Lanka's exports and the steady rise in import prices particularly for oil and grains imposed a heavy burden on the economy. Meanwhile, macroeconomic policy remained non-expansive. The Trotskyite finance minister, Dr. N. M. Perera, was inordinately fiscally conservative and his policies at this point were pro-cyclical, reducing aggregate demand rather than maintaining aggregate demand by expansionary policies to offset the decline in aggregate demand due to the oil price increase. This is because the bias against exports increased as import restrictions increased. The supply side of tradable sectors was constrained by nationalisations, and the threat of business takeovers made the reallocation of labour in line with changing incentives difficult. Since there were stringent exchange controls, the exchange rate did not ration resource use, nor did the balance of payments lead to huge losses in reserves since all foreign transactions were controlled. Athukorala and Jayasuriya (1994) showed that the economy was unnecessarily squeezed with tight fiscal policies when the economy was already experiencing a negative external shock from the first worldwide increase in oil prices. However, the squeezing of domestic demand did not lead to a diversion of resources to the tradable sector, particularly exports, given the stringent import control regime in place and expectations that the economy would be controlled even further if the coalition were to remain in power. In the event, the MEP-led coalition was weakened when the Marxist parties left it in 1975. But, the economic policies followed by the government continued to be globalisation-unfriendly.

During this period, the elements identified as a liberal economy were nearly completely abandoned, and the economy ceased to be "globalisation-friendly." Dependence on non-tariff measures (NTMs) as the main instrument of trade policy led to the loss of transparency and predictability of protection. The period 1970–1977 saw high effective rates of protection (ERPs) that distorted the allocation of resources not in line with comparative advantage. High ERPs caused high variance in protection. An overvalued exchange rate with a premium of around 50 per cent in curb markets prevented better adjustment to balance-of-payment deficits.[24]

With the huge expansion of the public sector, more than 70 per cent of manufactured output came to be produced in the public sector with preferred access to finance from state-owned banks and foreign exchange

---

[24] Athukorala and Rajapatirana (2000).

for imported intermediate goods. The reduction in the size of the private sector was brought about by the lower exchange rate for traditional exports and increased taxes. An institutional framework dedicated to continually supporting a free economy was absent. The Ministry of Industries had greater say and access to policymakers than the Central Bank, a normally more globalisation-friendly economic policymaking body. Its advisory role was bypassed. The Minister of Finance criticised the Central Bank in his first budget speech. Worse, a demonetisation of the Rupee was undertaken by the Ministry of Finance without the prior knowledge of the Central Bank. No institutions existed to support globalisation. It was abandoned given the command economy model of the Soviet Union and India that was followed by the left-of-centre government in power (see Table 2.3). While agriculture remained dominant in the private sector, it was subject to stringent prices and transport controls.

There were three important reasons for turning towards globalisation-unfriendly policies during this period: (1) the coalition with the Marxist parties that believed in complete control of the economy, taking a leaf from the Soviet Union and its satellites; (2) as a response to the JVP-led youth uprising in 1971 where the Marxist parties made the argument that the uprising was due to economic conditions with youth unemployment rising while overall unemployment rates reached 24 per cent[25]; and (3) the oil shock of 1973, which began to weigh heavily on external finances. Even with strong import restrictions, reserves fell to less than 2 months' worth of imports by 1974. Rather than using general economic policies, including fiscal and monetary policies, and the exchange rate adequately to allocate resources and aggregate demand and supply, the predisposition of the Marxist–MEP coalition was to use direct controls. The Marxist parties left the coalition in 1975. But, the policies they introduced remained in place.

The role of FDI was limited during this period. The coalition with the Marxist parties was not friendly to FDI, given their ideological position. They were not keen to receive FDI from capitalist countries which they claimed were exploitative in terms of Marxist theory. But, they were better disposed towards raising exports and had introduced a package

---

[25] But, one important reason why unemployment rose was due to the squeezing of aggregate demand by the Minister of Finance, combined with the negative oil shock. Fiscal policy was counter-cyclical.

of incentives for investment for export production, at least on paper as indicated by the Five-Year Plan of 1972–1976. But, on the supply side of FDI, western countries noted the government's unfriendly attitude towards the private sector, the battery of import and exchange controls that were put into place in the early 1960s and the overvalued exchange rate. The government had also introduced stringent performance criteria for FDI. All of these factors created a huge bias against exports, while import substitution in a small country with a limited market did not encourage FDI. One example of the attitude towards FDI can be gathered from the fact that the 17 applications during 1970–1976 made by foreign companies to invest in the production of textiles were refused by the government, claiming that domestic companies were capable of undertaking these investments using the latest technologies. In the event, this proved to be a bad judgement call based on nationalistic and anti-globalisation ideology. Sri Lanka's economic history would have changed for the better if these investments were permitted and if the cabinet paper to establish a free trade zone in the Trincomalee area was not rejected by the cabinet with prominent Marxist ministers.[26]

Labour movements were restricted during this regime. Stringent rules and procedures were introduced to limit the movement of labour, both skilled and unskilled. Exit permits were required to leave the country, reminiscent of what prevailed in the Soviet bloc countries. Foreign exchange for travel was limited to less than $50 for a whole trip. Since tickets could not be bought without foreign exchange permits, travel outside the country was limited. Labour from outside was not attracted to the country given the high unemployment rate and the fact that the government would not issue work permits. There was also no demand for outside labour since it was usually associated with bringing in skilled workers and managers to man FDI-based activities. In addition, all travellers, even those with permits, were required to surrender their ration book even when they were to travel abroad for a couple of days, including those performing official duties and attending conferences abroad. No wonder many highly skilled people with graduate degrees tried their best to leave the country during this time. It was the precursor to what was to come with the ethnic strife that took place starting in the early 1980s until the end of hostilities in 2009.

---

[26]Athukorala, P. and Jayasuriya, S. (1994). *Op cit.*

Thus, all three aspects of globalisation, trade, FDI and labour movements, were severely restricted during this period. GDP growth fell, as did employment; prices were kept from rising due to price controls and there were heavy penalties for the transgression of foreign exchange laws. Some compared the regime to the ones that existed in the Soviet Union at the time. Long queues, food shortages and poor-quality domestically produced goods with no foreign competition were the order of the day.

The MEP was badly defeated in the 1977 election, securing only eight seats in parliament. And, a globalisation-friendly right-of-centre United National Party came into power with a five-sixth majority, winning 140 seats out of 168 seats in the parliamentary elections.

(vi) *Liberal and Globalisation-Friendly Policies (1978–2004)*
Several factors converged to lead to the liberalisation of the economy in 1977, which was second only to Chile (1974) in its timing, speed and intensity[27]: (a) the economy plummeted badly due to the interventionist policies of the period (1970–1977); (b) the huge political mandate of the UNP and the economic hardships due to the interventionist economic regime; (c) the strong ideological commitment of the political party to freer markets; (d) strong leadership of the new Prime Minister, J. R. Jayawardena; (e) the actual economic experience of East Asian countries that had largely adopted liberal economic regimes; (f) coming into stream convincing research on trade regimes (Little *et al.*, 1970), the NBER project sponsored Bhagwati and Krueger (1978) on a new analysis on international trade and the manuscript was available around late 1978[28] to the UNP; along with the of support of the IFIs immediately after the liberalisation to provide access to finance.[29]

---

[27] Michaely *et al.* (1991).
[28] Gamini Dissanayake, a stalwart UNP parliamentarian, used the findings of the Bhagwati and Krueger study for the National Bureau of Economic Research in his speech on the 1976 SLFP budget. See Bhagwati (1978) and Krueger (1978) (this work was still in draft at that time) who criticised the policies of the MEP-led coalition.
[29] Some have claimed that the World Bank and the IMF were behind the liberalisation (e.g. Lakshman (1997a)). However, this is incorrect. The idea came from the UNP leadership and few economists who had a pro-market bent, while a large majority of Sri Lankan economists particularly from academia were more sympathetic to the controlled economy. Chapter 5, "The role of Financial Institutions on globalisation: World Bank's views on Sri Lanka in the 1970s and 1980s," reports that the World Bank was not focused on supporting incentive reforms at the time, but was instead suggesting import controls and

In contrast to the 1960–1977 period, the 1978–2004 period was one of more openness in the macroeconomic framework and a movement towards a liberalised economy. The openness of the economy arose from the replacement of quantitative restrictions (QRs) with tariffs and the adoption of a unified and devalued (by 45.1 per cent) market-based exchange rate (in contrast to the earlier FEEC scheme and the later Convertible Rupee Account (CRA) scheme). The reduction of import tariff rates led to a reduction in the bias against exports combined with a more competitive market-based exchange rate regime. The replacement of quantitative restrictions with tariffs increased the flexibility of the economy, and in combination with the flexible exchange rate, the economy could withstand external shocks better than before, with prices adjusting instead of quantities. This fact alone gave greater confidence to the new government to move towards greater participation in the globalisation process. It was a liberalisation in the classic sense of allowing prices to allocate resources rather than administrative controls. Hence, this period is classified as having liberal and globalisation-friendly policies.

In addition to the trade liberalisation and the exchange rate reforms, interest rates were allowed to be market-determined, which also helped increase the ability to withstand external shocks. In effect, real wages were also allowed to adjust, within limits, with the movements of the real exchange rate (after all, real wages in the non-tradable sector are a part of the numerator of the real exchange rate), defined as the ratio of the price of non-tradable goods to tradable goods. The real exchange rate depreciated by about 45 per cent. Meanwhile, real wages also rose, initially by 25 per cent, but fell to the pre-liberalisation level in 5 years. As expected, tradable prices rose, while non-tradable prices also adjusted over time. The initial boost to the production of tradable goods softened when inflation caught up with the huge public expenditures. It seems that the government's policy of liberalising the economy was throttled by the massive public expenditure boom. With prices allowed to find their equilibrium levels, the economy became more inflation-prone than before. Admittedly, though, instead of the repressed inflation of the earlier period, the new period saw open inflation. This meant that there had to be greater vigilance to guard against open inflation than before (Chapter 8, "Avoiding

---

specific export promotion policies. It was beyond the IMF's terms of reference to advocate incentive reforms and it concentrated its advice on its area of competence of macroeconomic policy and the balance of payments. It maintained this position even in 2013.

inflation in Sri Lanka to take full advantage of Globalisation" provides some background to the inflation at that time, even though the chapter deals with a later period).

Exports would have fared better than in the earlier regimes with the reduction of the bias against them. However, this was not to be, given the competing public expenditure programmes that the government launched in early 1981. In hindsight, we can see that the liberalisation of 1977–1978 was mostly undone by a massive public expenditure programme that included the Accelerated Mahaweli Development Project, the ambitious urban housing programme to build some 100,000 houses and the construction of one million rural dwellings.[30] No doubt, the headroom initially created for the private sector with the new policies came to be limited by the very ambitious public investment and expenditure programmes never seen before in the Sri Lankan economy. This rivals the ambitious public expenditure programme of the post-conflict period of 2009–2012.

There were two waves of liberalisation and globalisation-friendly policies. The first, already discussed earlier, under President Jayawardena, made the initial big bang effort and achieved a larger measure of success in linking the country to the world's globalisation trends through trade liberalisation, financial market reforms and dismantling of the restraints put on labour movements in the earlier periods. But, the two laws passed in the earlier period — Business Undertakings (Acquisition) Act No. 35 of 1971 and the Termination of Employment of Workmen (Special Provisions) Act No. 45 of 1971 — remained in place. Probably, the UNP leader did not want to offend trade unionists from the opposition camp. However, there was much larger headroom created by the new government to give greater freedom to business enterprises and to extend the existing businesses knowing that the new government was friendly to private enterprise. The new government campaigned to change the business environment and provided greater opportunities to non-unionised labour. In addition, some of the commercial lands acquired by the previous government were given back to the owners. This first wave of globalisation-friendly policies dissipated by mid-1995. This arose from a number of factors. First, the leadership of the UNP changed when J. R. Jayawardena resigned and R. Premadasa became president. He was not as committed to liberal economic policies and not as globalisation-friendly

---

[30] Deepak and Rajapatirana (1989).

as his predecessor. Second, the coalition that existed to bring about strong and liberal economic reforms broke down as the results of the policies produced were less spectacular due to high inflation and widened current account deficits. Third, a Dutch disease phenomenon arose with large aid flows that appreciated the exchange rate. Without further reforms, the economy could not perform as well as before. Finally, the war against the LTTE gathered momentum, due to a spate of bombings in the capital and major cities in the central and western provinces.

The 1977–1989 regime of globalisation-friendly policies could not be sustained for several reasons: First, the resolve of the UNP government to maintain a liberal trade regime was weakened as an ideological position, and the reforming coalition lost power within the party. Second, the economy was overheated with large public expenditures on the Mahaweli project, the housing project and similar infrastructure ventures, which led to high inflation in the early 1980s. Third, the exchange rate became highly appreciated due to large capital inflows associated with foreign aid, which was called "Dutch disease." That is to say, capital inflows to one sector of the economy raised domestic prices and appreciated the real exchange rate that acted as a tax on traditional exports and gave a subsidy to imports. Meanwhile, domestic inflation rose (see Chapter 8) and the economy became less competitive compared to the country's trading partners. When the inflows ended, the economy became less competitive.

This situation encouraged President Premadasa to launch a second wave of liberalising reforms in 1990. This reform package included further reductions in tariffs and their variance, a privatisation programme, removing exchange controls on current account transactions, a more flexible exchange rate policy regime and changes to foreign investment. President Premadasa was more interested and attuned to developing the rural sector than forging increased links with the rest of the world. He was assassinated in 1993 and a new president emerged who was neither committed to undertaking further reforms nor had the gravitas to pursue them. His weak leadership contributed to the defeat of the UNP in 1994 after 17 years in power.

After the assassination of President Premadasa by the LTTE in 1993, President D. B. Wijetunga took office as an interim president until 1994. In the election of that year, the UNP lost to the SLFP-led coalition — the People's Alliance (PA) led by President Chandrika Kumaratunga. Her economic policies were not very different from those of the UNP with respect to the liberal and globalisation-friendly policies that existed under the UNP since 1978. One reason for the left-of-centre PA to follow the liberal and globalisation-friendly policies was that they provided strong gains to an electorate that was already experiencing these benefits. It is claimed that the benefit of those policies led to "leading the left to the right."[31] Another reason is that under President Kumaratunga, conservative institutions like the Central Bank and the Ministry of Finance had greater say than institutions such as the Ministry of Planning and Implementation and the Ministry of Industries, which were more influential under the earlier SLFP-led coalition. Finally, by this time, the international experience was beginning to show clearly, especially in East Asia (S. Korea, Taiwan, Hong Kong and Singapore), that liberal and globalisation-friendly policies were raising GDP growth rates significantly.

Under President Kumaratunga, the PA extended the liberal trade policies, privatisation policies and improved the regulatory regime. By the mid-1990s, Sri Lanka was moving away from the earlier policies of intervention in the economy and away from trade protection. It was also during this time that the cumulative effects of earlier policies reached their maturity. The share of manufacturing in GDP rose from 10 per cent in the mid-1970s to over 20 per cent. Also, the export structure changed significantly from land-intensive plantation-based exports to labour-intensive manufacturing, ending the dependence solely on tree crops for manufacturing and rescuing the country from the vicissitudes of declining terms of trade. The economy became more closely connected to the world economy.

What did developments during the 1978–2004 period imply for participation in the process of globalisation? First, the trade and exchange regime liberalisations helped give an initial boost to exports and imports, and the ratio of trade (exports plus imports) to GDP rose to 87 per cent by 1980 (See Table 2.2). However, the impact of trade and exchange rate reforms was later muted by an appreciation of the exchange rate due to the large public investments that raised the price of non-tradable goods significantly. Since public expenditures are relatively more intensive in the use of non-tradable goods (compared to private expenditures), a given amount of expenditure by the public sector produces a higher rate of appreciation for the same amount of expenditure by the private sector. Second, it led to the now well-known and better-understood phenomenon

---

[31] Athukorala (2012b).

of the Dutch disease.[32] The large inflows of capital associated with the public expenditure programmes appreciated the exchange rate to such an extent that the private sector, especially the export sector, could not cope with the competition for factors of production that the public sector virtually commandeered through the foreign assistance funds that it received.[33] Third, because imports were restricted almost for a period of 17 years (1960–1977), with a short respite in 1968–1970, there was huge pent-up demand for imports (made relatively cheaper due to the appreciation of the rupee), the highest for the seven periods analysed in this chapter. Fourth, the current account deficit rose to high levels (to 5.6 per cent of GDP) not only because of private sector imports but also because of the large capital inflows arising from foreign assistance programmes at concessional interest rates, and long grace and maturity periods. Fifth, GDP growth rose to 4.8 per cent for the period, the highest rate seen up to that year. Finally, the threshold level for inflation was breached during this period. Inflation reached the highest rate in the post-conflict period up to this time, at 10.8 per cent. It would be instructive to see how this precedent compares with the later post-conflict period.

With respect to FDI, the new government, led by Prime Minister J. R. Jayawardena in 1977 who later became the president, was committed to promoting export-led industrialisation of which promoting foreign investment was a crucial aspect. To facilitate greater FDI flows, the government set up the Greater Colombo Economic Commission (GCEC) with wide-ranging powers.[34] The GCEC approved FDI in Export Processing Zones (EPZ) with infrastructure standards sought by exporting firms. The incentive package offered by the GCEC included complete foreign ownership, tax holidays for up to 10 years, complete tax exemptions for foreign personnel working in the GCEC zones and duty exemptions for imported inputs for export-oriented firms financed by FDI flows. In addition to the economic zones, the government improved the overall policy environment for FDI country-wide. This was achieved by doing away with most of the quantitative restrictions, lowering tariffs and reducing the variation in tariffs. Free trade status was provided for imported inputs. A scheme of manufacture-in-bond was provided for re-export as a part of finished goods, and cash grants were made to import material for re-exporting

---

[32] Corden and Neary (1982).
[33] Deepak (1985).
[34] The GCEC became the Board of Investments in 1992.

goods. Other facilities were also provided such as 100 per cent foreign ownership of firms producing exports, investment protection and double taxation.

The political climate for FDI was favourable as expected with the UNP Government. The large electoral victory, the stated ideology of the new government and the weakened power of the Marxist and left-of-centre MEP also helped to give assurances to the foreign investors that the country had a globalisation-friendly environment. The new Gaullist model of executive and legislative arrangement arising from the 1978 constitution signalled political stability.[35] The initial attractiveness of the country for FDI under the new government began to vane due to macro-economic instability (rising inflation, large current account deficits) and an appreciated exchange rate due to the large inflows to finance public investments, which created a Dutch disease phenomenon.[36] Moreover, the globalisation-friendly ideological commitment of the UNP began to weaken mostly due to a disagreement between the original reformers and the newly emerging power elite within the party who favoured greater control of the economy than leaving it to market forces. But, the strongest factor against increased FDI came after 1983 with the civil war against the LTTE. Many multinationals wanting to invest in the country decided not to invest due to the political problem of a country besieged by civil war.[37]

Beginning in 1978, labour markets were freer compared to the earlier period. Restrictions on the outward movement of labour were removed. In addition, the freeing of the exchange control regime allowed people to seek employment abroad. And, many did. Thus began a period where net factor income related to labour services became prominent over the years. Another important factor for the large movement of labour and indeed emigration was the ethnic tension that culminated in the 1983 anti-Tamil riots; emigration increased across the board as the civil war escalated. With the increase in incomes in the Middle East from two oil price hikes in 1973 and 1979, there was increased demand for unskilled labour to which South Asian countries responded. In the case of Sri Lanka, the supply response was only possible after the defeat of the left-of-centre SLFP

---

[35] Athukorala (1997).
[36] Athukorala and Jayasuriya (1994).
[37] Harris Corporation and Motorola showed interest in investing in the country, but turned away due to the civil war.

and its coalition partners. In the 1990s and after the year 2000, the labour movement increased and by 2014, earning from remittances became the second most important foreign exchange earner after garments.

(vii) *Interventionist and Globalisation-Unfriendly Period (2004–2019)*
From November 2004, Sri Lanka explicitly reversed its commitment to globalisation-friendly policies. This marked the beginning of the Mahinda Rajapaksa regime with a victory that year when the UNP leader Ranil Wickremesinghe was defeated narrowly. President Rajapaksa was not ideologically predisposed towards participation in the globalisation process. This can be inferred when one reads the *Mahinda Chintana*.

Since 1995, there has not been an important trade reform. What was done in June 2010 was partially by the Rajapaksa government and was reversible and subject to uncertainty. It was not a complete liberalisation and did not support globalisation. Following these "reforms," effective protection rates may have increased as nominal tariffs on intermediate inputs were reduced by a larger proportion than those on the final goods. High tariffs, some as high as 40–50 per cent that had helped to finance the war effort, were replaced by across-the-board 15 per cent tariffs, but many of the other high rates persist. Thus, total tariffs, including both standard tariffs and para tariffs (the tariff equivalent of many charges and taxes that are imposed on imports), raised the level of protection. The trade regime became more protective compared to the 1989–2014 period.

Pursell and Ahsan (2011) noted that the trade policy became restrictive during the 2001–2004 period following the LTTE attack on Katunayake, when a 40 per cent import surcharge was imposed. Many import cesses and para tariffs were introduced to help finance the war. Protectionist trends expanded and became stronger during 2007–2009. There was an ideological commitment to protection supported by many Sri Lankan economists, especially those from academia known for their left leanings. They conveniently ignored the trade liberalisation of East Asia and later by China (starting in 1979 under Deng Xiao Peng) and India (1990) responding to a macroeconomic crisis. The Indian trade liberalisation was led by Dr. Manmohan Singh, but the economy retained tariffs on consumer goods imports. That was challenged by the US in the WTO and India agreed not to seek protection for balance-of-payments purposes, particularly through quantitative restrictions. According to

Pursell and Ahsan (2011), Sri Lanka and Bangladesh are the most protectionist countries in South Asia. As noted, modest relaxation of trade controls took place in June 2010 in Sri Lanka when surcharges were reduced to 15 per cent across the board. Earlier, there were the Value-Added Tax (VAT), Social Responsibility Levy, Nation Building Tax and Excise duties. Then, there was a special commodity levy on 22 essential imports. Consequently, agriculture remains the most protected sector with high tariffs and input subsidies.[38] Valdes (2013) found that the ERPs calculated were 111 per cent for paddy, 907 per cent for fresh milk and 111.71 per cent for paddy calculated for 2010/ 2011 for importables. For exportables, Effective Rates of Protections (ERPs) accorded to value added exports) were negative 31.4 per cent for coconuts and 4.42 per cent for processed tea. Not only were the ERPs high but they also had wide variance, which led to resource misallocation problems.

By 2012, para tariffs and various surcharges had remained in place and the tariff regime is unpredictable. Many *ad-hoc* changes were introduced, particularly in the import of food, fuel and motor vehicles to name a few. For instance, car tariffs were reduced in 2010, but were increased later. Car assembly where value-added at international prices exceed value added at domestic prices is one piece of evidence that the trade regime does not help to increase competitiveness and productivity.

Many para tariffs led to similar protective and revenue effects that created a bias against exports. In 2010, para tariffs were reduced from 39.9 per cent of all tariff lines (a total of 6,520 tariff lines) to 27 per cent. However, the total protection rate increased compared to the pre-2001 period.

Many types of tariff-like devices came to be used and the trade regime became complex and unpredictable with many changes taking place, especially in agricultural imports. Again, the case of motor car imports is revealing. After reducing tariffs from 300 per cent in June 2010, many rates were re-instituted.

A study by the International Trade Center (ITC) in 2010 found that NTMs had created formidable barriers to exports and imports much to the detriment of efficiency. An NTM survey conducted by the ITC found that Sri Lanka was the country most affected by these measures. First, nearly

---

[38] Valdes (2013).

70 per cent of the exporters complained about the NTMs. There are many procedural obstacles and clearances needed from the plantations, the forestry ministry and other authorities. Bribery is rampant. Exporters complain that domestic barriers are severe compared to foreign barriers with respect to issues of certification and meeting rules of origin, among other requirements. The largest proportion of reported NTMs referred to are technical regulations which comprise conformity assessments. In the case of imports, a cluster of charges, taxes and other para tariff measures were also mentioned as formidable impediments to trade.

Second, obstacles are caused by inspections at customs. Complaints referred to very long delays, especially if several government agencies were involved, and sometimes damage to cargo due to manual examinations rather than using x-tray machines. An initiative that requires all relevant agencies to be represented at the same time for a "single inspection," combined with general training of officials, may alleviate frictions at customs and ports.

Finally, there are problems with respect to rules of origin, i.e. no technical import requirements by importing countries. To benefit from preferential trade agreements in a large market like the European Union, under the Generalised System of Preferences (GSP) and special incentive arrangement for Sustainable Development and Good Governance (GSP+), one requires certificates of origin that many exporters find hard to obtain. Especially in the clothing sector, the rules-of-origin certificates are more of a burden than other requirements relating to technical matters.

Looking at the trade regime since 1995, there is concern that it has not helped raise TFP growth. First, the rise in import protection and its wide dispersion led to greater resource misallocation. This misallocation comes from resources flowing to import substitution and non-tradable goods. Second, the corollary to it is that there is a bias against exports, while the share of Sri Lanka's exports to world trade and the country's GDP have fallen.

Third, due to the emphasis on import substitution as a policy pursued by the Rajapaksa government, there is a greater tendency for the real exchange rate to appreciate, making non-tradable goods more profitable compared to tradable goods. Such activities do not contribute to raising TFP growth. Finally, the government's avowed goal to pursue import substitution in the future is even more disconcerting.

The other aspect of globalisation, increasing FDI, did not happen even after the end of the hostilities in 2009. Regulatory reforms are needed to give greater freedom to individual enterprises to hire and fire personnel and manage their affairs within a credible system of entry, exit and rules of conduct. Certain restrictions continued, despite changes in governments.

Sri Lanka had a rank of 83 out of 189 countries for the World Bank index of the Ease of Doing Business in 2013. The high cost of doing business inhibited FDI. Labour market problems persisted due to inappropriate regulation. The Termination of Employment of Worker Act of 1971 is a case in point. It reduced labour market flexibility and employment. The Revival of Underperforming Enterprises of Underutilised Assets Act No. 43 of 2011 had an inhibiting effect with respect to capital and entrepreneurship. It enabled the arbitrary takeover of businesses, claiming that they were underutilising their capacity with underperforming assets. It does not lead to a healthy investment climate and a vibrant private sector-led economy. This was another reason for the low levels of FDI. Sri Lanka has a poor regulatory framework in place compared to countries like Thailand, Vietnam and Indonesia, and the inflow of FDI is small, even after the end of the war against terrorism.

Government must resist arbitrary interventions in the Private Sector such as proposing salaries with no relationship to productivity and mandating private pension schemes as has been attempted at that time.

Some of the problems of the incentive system with respect to the public sector was as follows:

First, State-Owned Enterprises (SOEs) which account for 11 per cent of GDP are not subject to the same codes of conduct as private firms. They have privileged access to state-owned banks, more efficient customs movement and better access to get in certifications with respect to exports and imports. Of course, only a few of them can export since they are not internationally competitive. When an SOE product is exported, it entailed a subsidy to the importer. To encourage exports without taking into consideration their international competitiveness, these exported products had hidden subsidies provided by the government from the time of their establishment. Second, SOEs have to stranglehold over domestic businesses since they dominate crucial services like electricity, water, petroleum products, gas and air transport. Their hold on the economy has been increasing since 2004. Many activities have been renationalised, such as Sri Lankan Airlines and the Shell takeover of petrol distribution. Also, the creation of a new government-owned airline, Mihin Air and the acquisition of shares of a few major commercial banks had taken place.

Finally, there is no effective way to control SOEs. The parliamentary Committee on Public Expenditure (COPE) tried to bring control over SOEs, but its efforts were limited due to the lack of majority political support for the Committee. Public enterprises can behave badly with impurity with little or no consequences to their management since the system of patronage protects them. One example is the Ceylon Petroleum Corporation, which caused major losses due to hedging.

Two thousand and four marked a clear departure from liberal trade, FDI and flexible labour markets based on ideological grounds. But, even more importantly trade interventions were more associated with the need to raise resources for the war. Many new tariffs and tariff-like instruments called para tariffs were introduced during this time. These new instruments proliferated, making it very difficult to determine the overall tariff structure. In addition, there is greater recourse to use NTMs such as quotas and other quantitative restrictions.

During the 2015–2019 period, the government that came into power was a coalition government composed of the UNP and the SLFP which had significant ideological differences with respect to policies towards globalisation. In this situation, the president who led the SLFP had an anti-globalisation point of view and did not support freer trade. In the next chapter we can see additional factors such as the state of economic understanding during the 1950s, provided the historical context by the Visiting Economists.

Chapter 3

Through Eminent Eyes: A 50-Year Retrospective as a Background to Globalisation

3.1 Introduction

At the behest of the Prime Minister, Mr. S. W. R. D. Bandaranaike, the Director of National Planning, Dr. Gamani Corea, invited seven eminent economists to visit Sri Lanka during the 1957–1958 period and write papers on the economic prospects for Sri Lanka. The idea to extend such an invitation had come to Mr. Bandaranaike from Indian Prime Minister Jawaharlal Nehru who had invited Nicholas Kaldor to advise India on a new tax system.[1] These invited economists were not given any specific terms of reference but only a list of topics as guidance.[2] Their advice and ideas were sought for the preparation of a Ten-Year Plan (1959–1968).[3] The list of topics reveals what the Sri Lankan government wanted to be advised on.

The papers by the eminent visiting economists provide a look into development thinking at the time and their views on prospects for the economic development of Sri Lanka. A review of their work provides a window into the economic "zeitgeist" or the spirit of the time. Their work continues to resonate sixty-plus years later in Sri Lanka with increasing

---

[1] The publication of Dr. Gamani Corea's memoirs has allowed the author to gain new insights into the genesis of the *Papers by Visiting Economists*. Corea (2008).
[2] *Ibid.*
[3] They were not paid fees but only travel expenses and were considered guests of the state.

relevance given the great macroeconomic imbalances, a mountain of debt, a stalled reform programme and recidivism with respect to the role of the private sector, trade and regulatory regime.

This chapter is divided into six sections. Section 3.1 and 3.2 provide the introduction and the biographical sketches and challenges faced by the visiting economists. Section 3.3 provides the background and explains the prevailing economic and policy thinking at the time. Section 3.4 provides the core content of the eminent economists' contribution with a commentary on the different aspects of the content in light of the economic thinking of the later years. Section 3.5 provides a brief account of the economic development in Sri Lanka for the Ten-Year Plan (1959–1968) period, for which the economists' contributions were to be used as inputs. Section 3.6 concludes the chapter.

This chapter finds that the visiting economists provided an antidote to the radical thinking of the time led by leftist parties, the Trotskyite *Lanka Sama Samaja Party* (LSSP), the Communists (CP) and other left of center parties, the *Mahajana Eksath Peramuna* (MEP), who had plans for creating a socialist economy and undoing what was considered a dependent colonial economy. The papers written by the visiting economists provided a reasoned and sober analysis of the economic possibilities of the country. However, given the limited theoretical and empirical work on the state of economic development at the time, their short engagement with the economy and the unanticipated rapid decline in foreign exchange reserves, their ideas and their advice did not stand the test of time.

Within a few years to a decade of the publication of these papers, public road transport was nationalised as were port cargo operations. This was followed by the nationalisation of the largest commercial bank, the Bank of Ceylon, and the creation of publicly owned banks, starting with the People's Bank. Foreign-owned plantations were nationalised in 1975 and many of them were privatised in 2002 given their poor performance under state ownership. A strongly dirigiste economy emerged in the early 1960s. This was more for the economic exigencies of the increasing balance-of-payment deficits, overvalued exchange rates and the need to raise taxes to cover burgeoning welfare expenditures. The nationalisation of banks helped the governments that followed overcome hard budget constraints, which led to a crowding-out effect of the private sector.

The ideological reasons for intervention emerged later when left-led parties joined the left-of-centre MEP and the Sri Lanka Freedom Party (SLFP). The economy became highly controlled and inefficient, contrary to what the eminent economists had anticipated. There was analytical and empirical work that was undertaken in the late 1960s and early 1970s that contested the notion of investment-led factor-augmenting growth, a key feature of the contribution of eminent economists. The decline and eventual demise of the Soviet model of archetype command and control economy led to the abandoning of state planning in nearly all developing countries. Meanwhile, the strong empirical support for the more open economic policies was provided by the success of East Asian countries in the 1970s.

This support gave further backing for the rejection of a planned command economic model of development. The success of China and India since the mid-1990s when they began to follow more open economic policies gave further impetus to the rejection of dirigiste policies. Sri Lanka liberalised its economy in 1977 ahead of many countries but has veered away from that path in recent years.

The contributions of the eminent economists were deficient in three important respects. They neglected political economy aspects in their recommendations, the ethnic strife that became a national problem and the ideological dimension of economic policymaking that prevented a consensus on economic policy (see the chapter on ideology). However, these criticisms derive from 50-year hindsight. It is interesting to speculate as to what a different group of eminent economists would have contributed to the development policy debate and formulation. Milton Friedman and Arnold Harberger would have made a difference in both the debate and the development outcome. Of course, none of them believed in economic planning and they would not have been invited, anyway.

3.2 Brief Biographical Sketches and Challenges

By any standard, this was an eminent group of economists at the top of their profession. They represented a wide spectrum of economic opinions, approaches and policies. John Hicks and Gunnar Myrdal went on to become Nobel Prize laureates in economics, while Joan Robinson, Nicholas Kaldor and Oskar Lange were leading theoreticians making important contributions to the discipline. John Kenneth Galbraith became one of the foremost popul250risers of economics, widening its scope to include both social and organisational issues. Mrs. Ursula Hicks specialised in public finance, particularly, relationships among central, state and local governments.[4] None of them had worked explicitly on economic development before. However, their ideas influenced development policy thinking in later decades through their contributions to economic theory and policymaking, in general, and specific work such as that of Kaldor on taxation in India and that of the Hicks on central and state relationships in Nigeria and Jamaica. Lange laid the theoretical basis for market socialism in which a country could have the efficiency of competitive markets within a socialist political system.[5] Myrdal later went on to become famous for his work *The Asian Drama* where he highlighted issues of governance and corruption that came to the fore in the 1990s. Those concerns resonate with our policies even today.

In terms of the length and scope of the contribution of the papers by the visiting economists, Joan Robinson wielded the most influence followed by Kaldor and Hicks. The specialised papers by Ursula Hicks, Lange, Galbraith and Myrdal had lesser influence. Myrdal's contribution was the most limited. The visitors were of different political hues. The Hicks were leading mainstream (neo-classical) economists from the United Kingdom. Lange was the chairman of the Supreme Constitutional Authority, the equivalent of the head of the state in Poland. Joan Robinson was a British left-winger with a Marxist orientation.[6] Kaldor went on to become a British Labour peer and was a consistent critic of neo-classical economics. Myrdal was a Swedish socialist, well known also for his sociological writing including the state of race relations in the United States.[7] Galbraith was a liberal in the American tradition who described his politics to Prime Minister S. W. R. D. Bandaranaike, had he been Sri Lankan he would have been a socialist (see Corea, 2008).[8]

---

[4] She seemed most prepared for work on Sri Lanka among the member of the group, having advised Dr. Gamani Corea on his D. Phil thesis *The Instability in an Export Economy* (1951) when John Hicks was one of the readers of Dr. Corea's thesis as an examiner.
[5] Lange (1936).
[6] Corea (2008). Joan Robinson was later known as a great admirer of China's collectivism and Mao's leadership. But, her contributions to economic theory were undisputed and highly valued by leading theoreticians including Paul Samuelson who wrote, "Many a times in print and elsewhere, I expressed the considered opinion that the corpus of her work richly deserved a Nobel Prize" (see "Remembering Joan" in Feiwel, 1989).
[7] Myrdal *et al.* (1944). Myrdal was a Nobel-Prize-winning economist.
[8] Corea (2008).

The visiting economists had little work available on the development of "backward areas" as they were called at the time. The available work was mainly that of Lewis (1954) and Nurske (1962), which provided a common basis for thinking about economic development going back to classical economists. Their core analyses and views emanated from classical economists (particularly Ricardo) who focused on the accumulation process, combined with technological change and institutional evolution as the main determinants of steady-state economic growth. They divided the economy into two sectors, one subject to increasing returns called "industry" and the other subject to decreasing returns called "agriculture." The process of growth was one of transferring labour from the decreasing returns sector to the increasing returns sector.[9] The subsequent economic analysis emphasised the role of externalities (Scitovsky, 1954) and economies of scale (Nurske, 1962). Joan Robinson was a strong advocate of capital accumulation as the mainspring of growth and others followed her work.[10] It is not surprising that they emphasised industrialisation as the main solution for the increasing population, for reducing the external instability and for raising the per capita income on a sustained basis. One needs to recall the more formal characterisation of this process by Arthur Lewis.[11]

While the eminent economists had little to go on with respect to economic development theory and practice at the time, they had even less on Sri Lanka. There was the first World Bank report (1952), Ivor Jennings's "The Economy of Sri Lanka" (1948) and a few other pieces that were not distinguished at all.[12] The visiting economists had access to limited data sources at the time. These related to estimates of capital outlays of the government, the import structure, population projections and manpower

---

[9] Adelman and Sunding (1989).
[10] Robinson (1965).
[11] Lewis (1954).
[12] Stein (1954). Stein accepted the argument of the dependency theorists of the time: that export crops were inherently unstable, that their long-term prospects were not good and that the country should be self-sufficient in food; he added, "Ceylonese could not afford to specialise!" which called into question his credentials as an economist. His views were in marked contrast to those of the eminent economists who disabused their readers of these questionable ideas. See also Das Gupta (1949) and Oliver (1956).

resources projections, the first consumer expenditure survey (1952–1953) and the first agricultural plan. It was Joan Robinson who used all these data sources due to which her contribution was the most comprehensive. She also had access to the First Interim Report of the National Planning Commission (1957) that evaluated the Six-Year Investment Programme (1954/1955 to 1959/1960). This report emphasised four major areas of development — the export sector, the dry zone, improvement of productivity in non-estate agriculture and industrialisation. These refrains are found in both the papers by the visiting economists and in the Ten-Year Plan.

There was little interaction among the visitors in preparing these papers, except of course between John Hicks and his wife Ursula Hicks. The economists were expected to work separately; they visited the country at different times, wrote on different topics and had different political views, and there is no evidence that they even saw each other's papers during the preparation of their own.

3.3 The Background to the Papers: The Prevailing Economic and Policy Environment in Sri Lanka[13]

The first post-independence period (1948–1956) can be seen as a continuation of the pre-independence period. Some saw it differently — as a period of transition from the classical export economy that was in existence from the 1920s to a "more development-oriented export economy."[14] However, in a policy sense, it was a continuation, with the same political party remaining in power from 1948 to 1956. The first Six-Year Plan (1947/1948–1952/1953) reflected the intentions of the first independent Sri Lankan government. It contained proposals that had been under discussion in the pre-independence period. While diversification was stated as a goal, there was to be no public sector involvement in the industrialisation of the country.

The intentions of the UNP government in power may have been influenced by a visiting World Bank team in 1951, which suggested that agriculture rather than manufacturing would be more profitable for investment for some time to come. The World Bank team observed that the time was

---

[13] This section is based on Athukorala and Rajapatirana (2000).
[14] This is the term used by Snodgrass (1966).

not ripe for large individual industrial investment projects. However, the government could lay the foundation for future industrial development by conducting a systematic study of raw materials available, and promoting "a wide variety of industrial projects by facilitating the acquisition of technical skills, managerial experience and a habit of industrial development."[15] The report also suggested that the government should not be involved in the direct management of these industries. The World Bank team was critical of the delay in closing down some of the manufacturing enterprises that had been started during the Second World War and also recommended the repealing of the Industrial Product Act of 1949, which had enabled the government to protect domestic handloom textiles — which included towels, sarongs and banians (undershirts) — using a content protection scheme.[16]

Given the emphasis on economic planning in the intellectual climate at the time by the major multilateral donor, the World Bank, which insisted on the preparation of economic plans to provide financial support, the Sri Lankan Government prepared the second Six-Year Plan (1954–1955/1959–1960). This was mainly an investment programme. It included the establishment of medium- and small-sized industries using domestic materials and envisaged the undertaking of these activities by the private sector, following the initial establishment of industries with government support. Towards that end, the government sponsored the Industrial Corporation Act of 1955, which would establish industries using a corporate model and transfer these industries to the private sector in stages, at which time these establishments would come under the Company Law Act as private sector businesses. However, this scheme could not be implemented as the government changed in 1956 when the UNP suffered a resounding loss in the elections.

The 3 years to 1959 did not lead to a significant change in the policy environment, even though there was a radical change in the government from the UNP to the MEP, a coalition led by the SLFP. However, there

---

[15] The World Bank Report on Sri Lanka. (1952). The World Bank, Washington D.C.
[16] It is noteworthy that the UNP government was prepared to introduce a measure of protection with this Act, presumably for fear of unemployment in the handloom sector. The other interesting point here is the type of instrument that was introduced, a content protection scheme. Each time an import item from this group was purchased by a consumer, he or she had to buy a local product of poor quality and thus pay an implicit tariff. There was no incentive to improve quality under such a scheme.

was much preparation to implement new policies aimed at changing the economic structure. These new policies were contained in the Ten-Year Development Plan.[17] The plan itself constituted a radical shift in the government's attitude towards the economy. The industry was no longer to be relegated to the background and the government was to be very much at the forefront of industrial development. After all, the MEP won the elections on a mandate to be radically different from the past, not only in terms of Sinhalese majority-dominated social policies but also in economic policies to change the economic structure, from what was termed as "dependent capitalism" to a different national milieu. The latter aspect found expression in the attempt to bring many economic activities under government control. In addition, the newly independent countries of the region had embraced socialist economic ideals: India had committed itself to that path and Sri Lanka's Marxist parties (the Trotskyite LSSP as well as the CP) influenced national opinion at the time, even though they joined the SLFP-led coalition in the mid-1960s.

These new ideas found expression in the Ten-Year Plan (1958/1959 to 1967/1968). The eminent economists were invited to contribute to the conceptualisation of the plan, establishing a framework and giving it policy content to achieve its principal objectives. Its objectives reflected the new government's aspirations to change the economic structure. The plan signalled a fundamental departure from the earlier period which was a continuation of the pre-independence period. The plan itself contained a strategy that came to be known as import substitution-based industrialisation or inward-oriented strategy. This Ten-Year Plan was the first comprehensive development plan of the country. It dealt with all sectors and went beyond an investment programme to include saving, financing, the structure of incentives, the role of the public sector and policies towards international trade.

3.4 The Core Content of the Eminent Economists' Contribution

The core content of the eminent economists' contributions has been presented by identifying their common elements, and includes an analysis

---

[17] The Government of Ceylon (1958).

of key sectors, policy issues and matters related to planning and organisation.[18]

The visiting economists viewed the rapid growth of the population as a major problem and the primary reason for the increase in output and employment growth. Joan Robinson highlighted the problem with statistics, while the others made more of a qualitative argument. Robinson wrote the often-quoted line that "the country continues to maintain a primitive birth rate and a modernised death rate and the population is increasing explosively."[19] The basis for her view was the population projections prepared by the Department of Census and Statistics.[20] The immediate concern with the rapid population growth was that the economy would be unable to absorb the increasing labour force. The other more important concern was the large social welfare-related expenditure that the government had committed to a decade earlier, including the provision of free education, free health services and subsidised food. Joan Robinson commented about these expenditures that "Ceylon has tasted the fruit before she has planted the tree."[21] She saw the role of the trade unions as limiting the rate of profits by increasing wages that left less investible funds for development. This would not have gone down well with the Marxist parties who were supported by trade unions.[22]

Hicks's main concern with respect to the population was also to provide employment. He noted that development alone could not solve the employment problem. He proposed "other means" such as birth control measures. Myrdal saw the importance of the population problem but argued that it would have an impact on the workforce only after 20 years. He noted that long-run consequences would be grave unless some restrictions were successfully placed on population growth. In that

---

[18] Mrs. Hicks's contribution is not seen by the present author as immediately germane for the general economic development and planning. As such, it has been omitted from this discussion and evaluation.

[19] Interestingly, she was not the first to use this allusion. Stein referred to "an oriental rate of reproduction and a western rate of mortality." See Stein (1954).

[20] Selvaratnam (1956).

[21] Robinson (1965).

[22] *Ibid.* "Ceylon has imported from advanced capitalist countries the ideals of the welfare state and her trade union movement has imported conceptions that belong to a developed economy, whose business is to keep profits in check and secure an acceptable share of national output for workers."

regard, he advised the preparation of public opinion to focus attention on the issue.

What the eminent economists feared about rapid population growth did not materialise. Since the 1980s, there has been a decline in the birth rate that paralleled the decline in the death rate in the 1930s and 1940s. Compared to the views of Economists at that time there was no significant increase in the population growth rate. No one, including the eminent economists, would have foreseen this rapid demographic transition in Sri Lanka.

In addition, modern population research has questioned the validity of the earlier position that population growth is a burden on the economy. The views of Julian Simon, among others, were influential in toning down the "population bomb" rhetoric of the 1970s. They showed that population increase per se was not a cause of underdevelopment and that neither was population a problem with respect to the availability of resources. Many resource-rich and resource-poor countries were economically poor irrespective of the sizes of their populations. Later projections show that Sri Lanka's population would stabilise at around 22 million by 2020.

The main reason for the decline in population growth rate (which was around 1.1 per cent per year in 2020) was income growth, which turned out to be the best "birth control pill," followed by the higher age of marriage and increased levels of female education and urbanisation. The emigration of a significant minority population also helped reduce the population growth rate below the replacement rate. The low labour force participation rate among females continues in the country.

The best indicator of the new direction for the economy can be seen in the new government's approach towards industry. Without exception, all the visiting economists underscored the need for industrialisation. Three strands of their advice supported industrialisation. First, Hicks, Robinson and Kaldor were unequivocal in their advocacy of industrialisation as the main solution to the unemployment problem. They demonstrated that Sri Lanka could not address the problem within the context of the existing economic structure of an agricultural export–import economy. Second, a sustained increase in output growth was thought to require industrialisation. This was based on the economic development thinking of the time, which emphasised the externalities and increasing returns aspects of the industry, in contrast to agriculture. Finally, given their concern about the instability of the country's narrow export base of tea, rubber and coconut — the main exports of the time — industrialisation was a way to diversify the economy and reduce foreign trade-related instability. The MEP government that came into power in 1956 was predisposed towards industrialisation as it saw dependence on export agriculture as a vestige of colonial domination.[23] The visiting economists advocated industrialisation as a solution to the unemployment, slow output growth and income instability problems and this found easy acceptance among the different elements of the ruling coalition given their ideological predisposition.

As a product of the development thinking of the time (conveyed well by the visiting economists), the Ten-Year Plan underscored the commitment of the new MEP government to make a very strong effort to change the economic structure through industrial development. This is found in different aspects of the plan's overall industrial objectives. First, in the Ten-Year Plan, 20 per cent of resources were to be spent on the industry, as compared to 4.7 per cent in the Second Six-Year Investment Programme (1954/1955–1958/1959). Second, tax laws were amended to give strong incentives to the private sector to promote industrialisation.[24] Third, an elaborate package of incentives was offered to industries, which created fewer incentives for agriculture. The programmes led to a movement away from support for agriculture given that the same resources competed for both industry and agriculture activities. Finally, there was also an attempt to give the nationals more opportunities to produce, trade and distribute industrial products through a "Ceylonisation" policy that had begun earlier.

Contrary to what the visiting economists expected, Sri Lanka's successful industrial development was in labour-intensive textile manufacturing for export. The industries they recommended, such as cement, fertiliser, spinning and rubber goods, were not internationally competitive, unlike textiles. However, their recommendations to create infrastructure — power, transport, and communication — has served the country well given that they supported the high growth of the later periods.

---

[23] Athukorala and Jayasuriya (1994) wrote, "Although the SLFP *(the leading party within the MEP)* was not committed ideologically to socialism, it was not averse to adopting socialist rhetoric and promising to nationalise foreign owned plantations and take over many industries."

[24] Government of Sri Lanka, Income Tax Ordinance No. 56, 1957, Section 7a and New Section 44c.

Their recommendations to encourage import substitution in manufacturing proved to be highly expensive in terms of the domestic resource costs of producing these items. Instead of saving foreign exchange, this led to a huge drain on resources once the initial phase of easy import substitution was reached. There was a virtual transfer of resources from the general consumer to highly inefficient producers who sold their goods at high premiums. It is no accident that import substitution-led industrialisation had failed the world over in the 1960s. The high watermark of the import restrictions-based attempt at industrialisation was reached by the mid-1970s when the degree of import and exchange controls made Sri Lanka one of the most restricted economies in the developing world. It was during this period that Sri Lanka experienced the lowest growth in total factor productivity; during the 1966–1974 period, total factor productivity was — 2.99 per cent per year for all manufacturing industries.[25]

It was clear to the visiting economists that an increase in agricultural productivity was the key to the transfer of manpower to the industry. After all, there would be a limit to expanding agricultural output as diminishing returns would set in with the limited availability of land. Without an increase in productivity, the aggregate output would fall, as manpower and other resources were transferred to the industrial sector.[26] In addition, the savings to support investment in industry had to come from agriculture — both plantations and domestic agriculture. The keenness of the political leaders to eliminate the use of chemical fertiliser caused a large problem.

Hicks and Kaldor, who discussed general development strategy, recognised the importance of the plantation economy in raising per capita income in Sri Lanka, compared to its neighbours.[27] Kaldor went on to say that, contrary to the widespread belief prevailing among the leftist politicians at the time, it was further development of the plantation economy that would provide the means for rapid growth. He did not share the general view that came to prevail in the later years of declining terms of trade (a la Prebisch-Singer). Disagreeing with the earlier UNP administration,

---

[25] Athukorala and Rajapatirana (2000).

[26] Hicks (1959) wrote, "It can be concluded pretty safely that if there is no expansion in agricultural output, an expansion of non-agricultural sectors, sufficient to absorb into employment the increase in population that is in prospect, is not practicable" page 11. Papers by Visiting Economists to Ceylon (1959).

[27] Kaldor (1959) remarked, "Ceylon owes its prosperity, in comparison with other countries of the region, to her plantations economy." Papers by Visiting Economists to Ceylon (1959).

all the eminent economists saw waste in the large colonial schemes, particularly those schemes intended to develop food production using irrigation schemes.[28] To them, a rupee invested in plantations would give a higher return than a rupee invested in domestic agriculture. Plantations provided economies of scale and better organisation, and involved a well-developed scientific application of inputs to increase productivity. Domestic agriculture had none of these characteristics. The visiting economists also felt that increased production in domestic agriculture achieved through expensive means would lead to greater consumption and be a strain on the balance of payments. They believed that the goal of food self-sufficiency was ultimately self-defeating.

Joan Robinson offered a different view. While she felt that the labour employed in export agriculture was more productive than the labour employed in opening (increasing the acreage of the land) new land, in the 10-year time horizon, new land could be opened (the acreage has been increased) until industry could absorb more labour and have higher productivity. She felt that there was considerable potential to increase paddy production from existing land. But, she also hoped that other crops could absorb some more labour. To her, the expense of opening new land was mostly in the form of employing labour. She was more sympathetic to opening new land even though productivity would be low in marginal land. Similarly, Lange was also more disposed towards expanding domestic agriculture than Hicks and Kaldor.[29]

Although the National Planning Council had identified the development of the Dry Zone as a priority, the visiting economists did not pay much attention to it. This was perhaps because little information was available to them about the resources and agrarian and physical characteristics of the Dry Zone.

Agriculture did better than industry in productivity growth and providing the food requirements of the population. Emphasis on food requirements was favoured by Joan Robinson. When the UNP came to power in 1965, it began a policy of import substitution in agriculture and there was

---

[28] *Ibid.* "In the long run the employment problem in my view can only be successfully tackled through industrialisation and large-scale construction projects associated with industrial production, rather than by colonisation schemes," p. 26.

[29] Lange (1959), "Though agricultural production by itself cannot solve Ceylon's economic problems ... the development of agricultural production is an indispensable complementary factor of industrial development," p. 77. Papers by Visiting Economists to Ceylon (1959).

appreciable output growth during that period given that there were fewer distortions in the agriculture sector compared to the industry. But, with the first oil shock in 1973 when the MEP came into power, fertiliser, transport and related costs went up. In addition, the government at the time introduced a host of controls, such as forbidding the transportation of rice from surplus to deficit areas, which reduced the returns to rice farmers.

Agriculture was also subject to many other interventions such as food and fertiliser subsidies and institutional reforms including land reforms in 1972. Rice subsidies continued well into the 1980s. When an attempt was made by the UNP government to reduce these subsidies, there was a general strike organised by the LSSP and other leftist parties in 1953, and that effort was abandoned. Domestic agriculture was dominated by rice in which self-sufficiency was sought by all governments. There were periods when high domestic output was achieved with good weather, cheap fertiliser and some success in the application of modern methods of cultivation. However, consumers paid a high cost for self-sufficiency.

In contrast to domestic agriculture, which remained in private hands, plantation agriculture was nationalised in 1975 and privatised in 2002. This full circle was due to shifting governments and ideologies. The 1972 and 1975 land reforms paved the way for this turn of events.

Marxist parties saw nationalisation as the means to achieve a restructured economy.[30] The visiting economists were clear that plantations should not be nationalised in the short run. Kaldor devoted some effort to clarifying the issue. He noted that Sri Lanka's progress towards a socialist state would be gradual and felt that, unless nationalisation was necessary in the interests of development, it was better to provide for growth in the public sector through new developments rather than through the nationalisation of existing enterprises. While he saw some advantages to the partial nationalisation of banks and insurance companies in terms of wielding control over the investment of funds, he did not see an advantage in the nationalisation of estate companies. In addition, he noted that having the nationalisation Sword of Damocles hanging over the estate sector and leaving it to the last made the worst of both worlds. Instead, he proposed a "gentlemen's agreement" with the estate companies, limiting their annual remittances of dividends and the government agreeing not to nationalise estates for the next 20 years. He also proposed that the government

---

[30] Kelegama (2006) noted that nationalisation of foreign owned plantations was suggested before independence by Philip Gunawardena.

establish the principles on which compensation would be paid in the event of nationalisation.

Joan Robinson subscribed to the view that financial and commercial institutions, instead of the estate sector, should be the ones to be nationalised. She was also clear that estates should not be taken over without compensation. She feared that such a move would discourage foreign direct investment (FDI) in the country. However, the Marxist parties saw FDI as an instrument of exploitation with little or no benefit to the country. On the other hand, Lange was afraid that FDI would create foreign economic enclaves.

While the Marxist parties saw nationalisation as a solution for a restructured and non-colonial economy, its promise did not materialise. Instead, changing ownership of the means of production led to huge inefficiencies, large dependence on the fiscal system and increased bureaucratisation and politicisation of decisions at sector and firm levels.[31] The Business Acquisition Act of 1971 increased the threat of nationalisation across many sectors. Kaldor was naïve in thinking that a "gentlemen's agreement" could be worked out in which foreign-owned firms would remit limited amounts of profits from the sector and also continue to invest in plantations. Neither event materialised. The result was the nationalisation of plantations in 1975 and then privatisation or denationalisation in 2002.

With the nationalisation of plantations, there was a significant drop in output and productivity. Policies towards plantations were chaotic with six ministries overseeing the sector.[32] There was also the adverse effect of the reduction of land holdings combined with poor management. Many who were appointed to manage plantations had no background or expertise in planting but were appointed based on political patronage. This situation was rectified to some extent with the privatisation of 2002. As may be recalled, the eminent economists were against "precipitous nationalisations" (Joan Robinson's term). In a decade and a half, plantations were nationalised with compensation (even though there have been questions as to its adequacy). Similar to the nationalisation, privatisation in 2002

---

[31] Kelegama (2006) indicated that the 1971–1977 nationalisation of some sectors was necessary to stem the drain of foreign exchange and to prevent the evasion of controls. This argument is not convincing, since it justifies nationalisation as an answer to foreign exchange problems.

[32] Sanderatne (1995).

was also considered to be problematic by many, both in its approach and implementation.

Joan Robinson had advocated the nationalisation of banks and insurance firms. This was done early, and the results have been mixed at best. It led to an inefficient banking system (in the sense that the resource costs are high given the high intermediation costs). Foreign banks have had free rein and earned huge returns while being only marginally efficient, compared to the Bank of Ceylon and People's Bank, which dominate the financial system, in terms of the size of their reported assets. Worse still, these nationalised banks have been used extensively by politicians for political patronage. The top management of state-owned banks is appointed by the party that wins the elections. The management in turn provides large loans to party supporters as payback. Consequently, until recently, some portions of their portfolios were non-recoverable. State ownership of commercial banks had proved to be problematic even in a developed country with centuries-old institutions, such as France, where President Pompidou denationalised the commercial banks after initially nationalising them. In fact, convincing proof of the rejection of socialism will come when a future government does the same in Sri Lanka.

All the visiting economists dealing with the general economic problems of the country advocated one form of protection or another. Hicks made the mildest recommendation on that score, noting that some form of protection was necessary to encourage industry and advised that tariffs were better than quantitative import controls for that purpose. He noted that protection would raise the return to capital in that activity. However, he warned that rigorous control of imports was an inevitable obstacle to the establishment of new industries as it would only help to maintain old industries. He was averse to stringent exchange controls and noted that they would deter investment when they affected trade.

One reason that Joan Robinson argued for import substitution was the difficulties faced by latecomers competing in the world market. She recommended producing import substitutes and noted that it could be done only with protection. She saw the advantage of small units for export as this would not disrupt the world market.

Kaldor argued for the introduction of a "scientific tariff" (where a non-economic objective is to be achieved by a tariff or tariff structure that minimises costs in terms of real income forgone[33]) and to eschew quantitative

---

[33] Johnson (1960).

restrictions.³⁴ He suggested that the protection granted to selected domestic industries would facilitate the import of capital goods and raw materials for those industries. He found fault with the existing low tariffs and the lack of discrimination by the type of goods imported. But, with the increasing balance-of-payment difficulties in the early 1960s, hardly 2 years after the contributions by the visiting economists, a battery of trade and exchange controls were introduced.³⁵ As such trade regimes do, the system of controls became increasingly more restrictive, and the system of incentives created by these controls became perverse and chaotic.³⁶

The mild form of protection that the eminent economists advocated would have run into difficulties even without the balance-of-payment crisis for a number of reasons that have since been documented in trade policy literature. First, the protection from imports entails bias against exports since both activities compete for the same domestic resources. This was not appreciated in 1958 even though the theoretical foundation for it was established by the now-familiar Lerner Symmetry theorem (which comes into its own as an economy moves towards full employment), which shows that import duty has a tax equivalent on exports. Second, fine-tuning protection through a "scientific tariff" is difficult, given that the precision required in measuring elastic ties of supply and demand has to rely on estimates based on past data in a rapidly changing world. It is even more difficult to create and administer the tariff system since it would be subject to lobbying, rent and revenue-seeking when there is a departure from a uniform tariff. Third, the theory of effective protection had not been developed at that stage, so when the eminent economists advocated low tariffs for final goods and even lower tariffs for inputs and raw materials, they were inadvertently recommending the raising of effective rates of protection.³⁷ Finally, the economy became increasingly more dependent on imports once the easy stages of import

---

[34] It has now been well established that quantitative restrictions lead to a host of problems for countries compared to tariffs, particularly in inducing rent-seeking behaviour and making the economy more rigid such that adjustment to supply-side shocks become more difficult. Both these aspects make quantitative restrictions more harmful than tariffs and entail large welfare losses.

[35] Rajapatirana (1988) and Athukorala and Rajapatirana (2000).

[36] Krueger (1978) documented this phenomenon in her NBER research studies with Bhagwati (1978).

[37] Corden (1966).

substitution were reached. The combination of state-created public monopolies in importing, channelling and administration of imports by the state-owned producer of the competing products led to large inefficiencies and a drain on foreign exchange resources. The introduction of a foreign exchange budget compounded the allocation problem by subjecting minor transactions to stringent controls and wasteful and unacceptably intrusive scrutiny by the Minister of Finance himself.[38]

The visiting economists were specifically invited to provide advice on the design of the Ten-Year Plan and national planning in general. After all, they were to advise the National Planning Council. Lange, Myrdal and, to a lesser extent, Kaldor dealt with the topic of national planning. Their brief was to consider national planning in a mixed economy context — an example was India and not the Soviet Union or the People's Republic of China. Lange and Myrdal were well-known leaders of planning in mixed economies. The Ten-Year Plan was to be a perspective plan, the only such plan prepared in Sri Lanka at that time.[39] Myrdal had commented that it was technically one of the best planning documents prepared by any developing country at the time.[40] Prime Minister S. W. R. D. Bandaranaike was very enthusiastic about the Ten-Year Plan and had remarked that even if his government did not achieve anything else, it would be remembered for the design of the Ten-Year Plan.[41]

The high rate of population growth combined with low productivity was identified as a fundamental problem that had to be addressed. Lange was identified as the leading expert on planning in the group. He emphasised the need to coordinate different development components of the plan in terms of two dimensions, namely, to provide for balanced growth of the different sectors of the national economy with respect to outputs, raw

---

[38] It was quite a sight to see the controller of Foreign Exchange at the Central Bank marching in to see the Minister of Finance with files of individuals who had applied for foreign exchange to import a car from foreign exchange earnings made abroad.

[39] Fernando (1997).

[40] Fernando, L. (1997b). Development planning in Sri Lanka. In W. D. Lakshman (ed.). *Dilemmas of Development: Fifty Years of Economic Change in Sri Lanka*. Colombo: Sri Lanka Economists Association.

[41] Tragically, Mr. Bandaranaike was assassinated in September 1959, and he did not live to see the plan implemented. In the event, it was not implemented since it did not have an operational content, and the change in government in 1965 when the UNP came to power ended what was left of the original plan.

materials and intermediate inputs and to achieve inter-temporal balance such that the development of different sectors would be synchronised. He also referred to matching physical requirements with financial resources. He was for creating "commanding heights," which meant concentrating within the hands of the government the sufficient economic means to carry out the strategy, and argued for creating administrative machinery for implementing the plan. Lange went on to describe and elaborate processes needed to implement the plan with an immediate action programme and different elements needed in agriculture, power and some specific products. Furthermore, Lange described a host of policies relating to trade, finance and the division of responsibilities between the state and the private sector. If Joan Robinson was the main protagonist for economic strategy and related policies, Lange was her counterpart in defining a planning system for the country. Myrdal, on the other hand, argued about the type of plan needed for the country. He proposed a long-term broad-perspective plan covering 10–20 years. It was to be a rolling plan so that it would not create undue rigidities. He suggested that the National Planning Secretariat should have executive authority rather than only an advisory role.

None of the visiting economists questioned the viability or the realism of planning in the country. Successive governments prepared plans despite their ideological differences. However, none was fully implemented.[42] The governments were encouraged by the World Bank and other multilaterals to have a national plan as a prerequisite to having access to aid. It was only much later on that scepticism arose regarding planning. The work of Hayek questioned the theory and the empirics of planning, respectively. Hayek went on to receive a Nobel Prize for his contribution to economic theory that devastated the theory of planning, due to the impossibility of having up-to-date information to carry out a plan.[43] Others questioned the concept, noting that information was simply not available to undertake such an enterprise.[44]

---

[42] Kelegama (2006) noted, "Since 1948 Sri Lanka produced an array of planning documents which often failed to survive their life spans."

[43] Hayek and the Austrian School criticised the Central Planners for "groping in the dark." The mathematical solution proposed by Lange to solve thousands of simultaneous equations not one time but continuously was not feasible. See Hayek (1945).

[44] Stolper (1966).

Many economists in Sri Lanka, however, accepted planning as necessary to increase the rate of economic growth. They had witnessed the high growth rates of the Soviet Union and the initial growth phase of India. Some saw the problem of underdevelopment of the country as stemming from the inability to plan well.[45] Others, particularly those disposed towards free markets, found that planning was not able to deliver growth per se, going on comparative country experience. The high growth experienced by the Soviet Union in the 1920s–1940s was based on factor-augmented growth (or using more labour and capital per unit of output) rather than increasing efficiency (total factor productivity). Such a growth path was not sustainable. Similarly, India's initial planned industrialisation failed to raise the growth rate. It did meet with early success due to import substitution, but that could not be sustained as these industries were not internationally competitive. It was also found that when protected outputs are valued at international prices rather than domestic prices, they had very low and even negative value added.[46] Public ownership of the means of production proved to be incompatible with achieving high growth.

Joan Robinson's idea was that planning would allow a country to keep consumption low during the initial stages of development so that large amounts could be invested to raise the growth rate. It turned out that the Soviet Union kept consumption inordinately low. People suffered as a result. She objected to the Soviet model for this reason and later embraced Maoist China's approach which she felt was less drastic in containing consumption. However, she was wrong in believing that. Mao's China was notoriously neglectful of Chinese agriculture, particularly during the "Great Leap," which emphasised small-scale industry and led to the famine of 1958–1961 that caused the death of some 29.5 million Chinese citizens.[47]

The eminent economists, particularly Lange and Myrdal, advised the NPC on the organisation of planning. They felt that an advisory council without executive authority would not succeed. It was their ideas that led to the increase in planning horizon to 10 years, creating a rolling plan giving the government enough flexibility to change goals and means as new developments took place in the country and the world.

---

[45] Fernando (1997).
[46] Little *et al.* (1970).
[47] Sen (1987).

Reviewing the Ten-Year Plan when it came out in 1959, Professor Indraratne noted that its goals could not be achieved due to some of its questionable assumptions (see the next section for details). He noted that the assumed capital–output ratio was unrealistically low, as was the assumption that terms of trade would remain the same over the next 10 years (it could have meant an average value equal to 1957 terms of trade but with a wide variance).[48] He also questioned the lack of a provision for depreciation of existing and newly created capital in the plan.

The Ten-Year Plan that the eminent economists helped to develop was never implemented due to the assassination of Prime Minister S. W. R. D Bandaranaike, the change in the government when the SLFP lost the election in 1960 and the lack of enthusiasm for it on the part of the UNP that came into power in 1960. One reason that the plan was not fully implemented was the wide ideological differences and lack of a consensus on development strategy among the major political parties and their coalition partners.[49] For the same reasons, it is unlikely that the plan would have succeeded either. The plan itself did not have a viable implementation programme.[50] The next section points out that the plan was not economically viable as a framework, even though it was a consistent and comprehensive document.

Robinson's contribution to the growth and macroeconomic framework was the most important among the contributions of the visiting economists.[51] Although she did not write down a formal model, certain elements of her contribution suggest a well-thought-out framework. She presented it in bits and pieces in different estimates and in somewhat of an accounting framework. Hicks provided some examples by simulating the requirements for an increase in output by 25 per cent and tracing its implications for the economic structure, noting that decreasing returns to agriculture necessitated a change in the economic structure. The overall growth rate to be aimed at was 5.9 per cent per year according

---

[48] Indraratne (1958).
[49] Corea (2008).
[50] Corea (2008) wrote that the plan set out a grand design but that it was not an operational document.
[51] Robinson was very modest and noted that her reflections on economic possibilities were "necessarily hasty and superficial." She made use of the NPC's preliminary estimates but put them together in a way that led to a consistent framework (1959).

to Robinson.[52] It is also clear that many of the elements of the macroeconomic framework are based on Robinson's contribution. Its main strength lies in its consistency rather than a model based on econometrically derived behavioural functions, such as those for consumption, saving, investment, import and export. Nor was it an optimising model, the likes of which were in vogue later in the profession.[53] The main framework that Joan Robinson used in her exercise was to derive a growth rate that would absorb the 1.5 million workers who would be seeking work in the coming 10 years. To employ them, the required increase in income was Rs. 4,000 million, raising national income at constant prices (1957) to Rs. 9,000 million. It was based on an investment rate of over 21 per cent far above the existing rate of 12 per cent. At the end of the period, there was to be an external balance due to increased exports and reduced imports because of import substitution and as well as some external resources that added up to Rs. 690 million.

The following conclusions emerge from the growth and macroeconomic framework in the papers by the eminent economists. First, the framework was built component by component by Robinson with back-of-the-envelope calculations. Second, the baseline figures were taken from the different sources available at the time such as the Agricultural Plan's figures and departmental data that had been gathered by the Planning Secretariat. Third, it would seem that the 5.9 per cent growth rate was developed taking into account the need to absorb 1.5 million workers, a capital–output ratio of 2.6 and a buildup of the level of savings with various taxes and revenue measures. This led to the unusual number of 5.9 per cent rather than 6 per cent or 5 per cent. Fourth, the framework expressly recognised a foreign exchange constraint that was to be handled through import restrictions, import substitution and new exports. Finally, a number of simplifying assumptions were made, such as the constancy of terms of trade, zero depreciation of the capital stock, and success in achieving a cut in imports and a parallel increase in exports to bring about equilibrium. One outcome of the exercise was to show that Sri Lanka would become free of foreign aid by 1968. Unlike the other eminent economists, Robinson worried about inflation if the supply response to the

---

[52] Corea (2008) wrote that while the NPC did not want to provide a particular number for growth, it was Joan Robinson who decided the growth rate for the Ten-Year Plan.
[53] The framework is reminiscent of the World Bank's Revised Minimum Standard Model whose main virtue was its consistency and possibility of working out a range of outcomes under different assumptions.

policies was not forthcoming or if the government was not able to restrain its expenditures in line with the new revenue measures.

The 10-year Plan (1959–1969) of the Government of Ceylon document showed only slight variation from the growth and macroeconomic framework Joan Robinson presented in her essay. The variations were the result of the Plan using actual (1957) base numbers while Robinson rounded them off for estimates. The development plan strategy of import substitution was where there were some for greater import substitution and others for less import substitution. Import substitution by itself does not increase efficiency, but would lead to a less efficient way of producing goods. The key points of the framework were to provide employment opportunities for the 1.4 million labour force (Joan Robinson took this as 1.5 million) that would be added to the economy in 10 years, to diversify the economy and to attain a growth rate of 5.9 per cent per year. With a population growth rate of 3 per cent per year, per capita income would grow by 2.9 per cent and GDP would increase by 88 per cent over the plan period. To generate such a rate of growth, investment had to be raised from 12.9 per cent of GDP in 1957 to 21.1 per cent by 1968. Industrial production (industry, construction and electricity) would more than double and their share in GDP would rise from 12 per cent in 1957 to 23 per cent in 1968. Agriculture's share would fall from 54 per cent to 45 per cent over the plan period.

There were many aspects of the exercise that Robinson presented that could be criticised with the luxury of hindsight and the availability of experience both within and without Sri Lanka. First, it was a simple Harrod-Domar model using fixed coefficients, where the results of a model can go to infinity or zero. In most of the time it is impossible to have a robust plan for the economy as shown by Hayek. It is also clear that the implied model was a single good model to the extent that there were no relative prices between say agriculture and industry, domestic and foreign prices, or between one period and another. Second, she used a comparative static approach of looking at two endpoints. There were no outcomes developed for an interim period. Third, even though the prevailing idea was that terms of trade would deteriorate over time and would also fluctuate widely, she took the terms of trade in 1957 as fixed for her projections for exports, imports and the external balance. Fourth, she used a capital–output ratio of 2.6 even though she expressed doubt about the concept in the first instance. However, by taking such a figure and noting the need for GDP to grow by 5.9 per cent per year, she derived the needed level of savings. And, in true Keynesian spirit, she equated them to ex-ante investments which were to rise from 12.9 per cent in 1957 to 21.1 per cent in 1968 to bring internal equilibrium. Empirical evidence that has arisen over the last 50 years indicates that a typical developing country has a higher Incremental Capital Output Ratio (ICOR) than what she assumed. As such, it would have necessitated a higher level of savings to produce the 5.9 per cent growth rate. Fifth, as venturesome as she was with these estimates, there was little policy content that assigned the outcomes of various aggregates to specific policies. It is now well known that after the initial phase, import substitution-based industrialisation became highly inefficient. Even if the savings could be generated, the growth rate could not be achieved; with this result, the primary goal of increasing employment by 1.4 million persons would not have been realised. Sixth, in her framework, efficiency took a back seat to capital accumulation in true Robinson spirit. Without the proper policy context, efficiencies could not have been achieved. Later research on comparative country performances shows the growth of total factor productivity to be as important a contributor to growth as factor augmentation. Seventh, her worry about inflation proved to be baseless until the 1980s. Finally, her assumption that the country would not need any foreign assistance after 1968 was optimistic, to say the least. The reality turned out to be entirely different.

Lange and Galbraith took the lead in defining the roles, attributes and functions of public sector corporations. Such entities were required, given that the plan anticipated increased state ownership and the takeover and establishment of large-scale public sector enterprises. This approach emanated from what Lange called "a general agreement that public investment and government policy must be a driving force moving forward the national economy."[54] It also reflected the rather dubious view, prevalent at the time, that the private sector was not up to the task of undertaking large operations in the economy consistent with the national plans. The government had moved in the direction of establishing such corporations with the Industrial Corporations Act No. 49 of 1957.

Public corporations were expected to operate like business enterprises with regard to methods of management and accounting, but were distinguished from private enterprises by being agents of the national economic plan. Since Lange was "a market socialist," he advised that public corporations must make profits, that personnel must have proper incentives to perform and that executive decisions must be made by a board comprising both management and workers. Such corporations, Lange contended,

---

[54] Lange (1936).

"must be, by the very nature of the situation, the dynamic forces of industrial development."[55]

Galbraith struck a more cautionary note. He observed that these enterprises often worked badly.[56] He emphasised good management and pride in workmanship, but not necessarily good pay. In addition, he commented on the differences between public enterprises and private enterprises relating to the nature of their decisions, with their low tempo and a high premium on the correctness of decisions. They also required greater technical knowledge than government departments to produce goods that could be sold at a profit. He then laid out the specifics of such an organisation in that it had to have clear rules and a competent board of management that should not be an executive body.

The visiting economists recommended that public sector corporations be at the forefront of changing the economic structure through industrialisation. The State Industrial Corporations Act 49 of 1957 provided the legal framework to reconstitute existing state corporations and establish new corporations to promote the development of large-scale basic industries. During the 1958–1963 period, some 14 state industrial corporations were established in such areas as cement, textiles, sugar, paper, chemicals, ceramics, mineral sands and leather. By 1974, there were 25 state industrial corporations that included steel and oil refining. By 2005, the country had 200 state enterprises/corporations in different sectors of which 75 were commercial and 125 were non-commercial (regulatory, research, promotional and educational) corporations.

The visiting economists recommended the creation of public sector corporations, particularly in the industrial sector. The World Bank's first report on Sri Lanka had recommended that these public sector corporations should become private enterprises once they were on their feet. By and large, they continued to operate with government support. The few that were transferred to the private sector during the UNP regime included the State Distilleries Corporation, the National Paper Corporation, Sri Lanka Tyre and Union Motors.

There were many problems with the public sector corporations from the very beginning. First, it was assumed that these corporations would function smoothly, their management would not be too difficult and that

---

[55] *Ibid.*

[56] Galbraith (1959) added that their "path is strewn with wreckage. Some are congenitally slow, some congenitally costly and a great many have had not earnings but losses."

they would be efficient and generate surpluses for the public sector. The opposite happened. Some of these corporations, such as the steel corporation or the chemicals corporation, should never have been created because the country did not have a comparative advantage in these activities at the time of their creation. They survived for five decades mostly due to government transfers, the monopoly positions they enjoyed when the economy was highly restricted and political patronage.

Second, given what is called the principal–agent problem in economics, the management of public sector corporations was very difficult because the principal (in this case the ministry in charge) had different goals and objectives from the agent (management of the state corporations). Their objectives and functions converged after the politicisation of the management, but they did not help increase efficiency or generate surpluses for the government budget. Instead, they became a significant drain on the fiscal system. With a few exceptions, like the ceramics corporation, they were a drag on the economy.

Third, state corporations also had to operate in a way that was not commercially viable since they had to provide goods at subsidised prices in keeping with the government's objective of providing welfare for a large segment of the population. In particular, in the case of goods that were high in public consumption, such as milk, edible fats and oils, the corporations could not charge market-clearing prices.

Fourth, efficiency was further compromised when the government gave the monopoly of the import of competitive products to the state corporations producing them.[57] Consequently, many corporations charged high prices and at times cross-subsidised between products to reduce losses. Many other bad practices were used by state corporations, such as what could be called content protection. When the State Hardware Corporation made mistakes in ordering parts from abroad, the loss of the mistake was passed on to the consumer, by insisting the consumer to buy an unnecessary part, to bear the loss. Losses and mistakes were passed on to the consumer with impunity.

Finally, if the corporations were as inefficient and rent extracting as they were, why did they survive the 1977 liberalisation? By 1977, they produced 60 per cent of the industrial output of the country and

---

[57] This was called "channelling in the Indian experience" and was a major reason for compounding inefficiency by reducing competition and enjoying monopoly profits. These enterprises did not have the incentive to reduce costs.

continued to produce a large part of industrial output even after the liberalisation of the economy. The answer lies in the political economy aspects of these corporations: They became a powerful source of political patronage. That is, they had grown in influence in the political sphere because both major parties used them for political purposes, such as rewarding their supporters and extracting services during elections (e.g. the Ceylon Transport Board transported voters who supported the government in power). Moreover, some corporations such as the Ceylon Electricity Board had a stronghold on the economy because they were providing essential services, in this case, electricity. Equally, the Ceylon Electricity Board's finances were adversely affected by other corporations not paying their electricity bills, so the inefficiencies were spread around. The state-owned banks (even though they do not come under the State Industrial Corporations Act of 1957) had to follow similar policies, being directed to give subsidised loans to political supporters of the party in power.

To sum up, the eminent economists did not foresee the enormous problems that these state corporations created for the economy at large. They had seen the experience of a few such corporations in Europe and recommended that these alien institutions be transplanted to Sri Lanka without much thought. They could not have known better. It is only with hindsight, supported by 50 years of experience, that one can now conclude that these corporations were a bad idea in the first place. However, the public sentiment in the country even today seems to favour state ownership over private ownership. Without a change in that mindset, these corporations are bound to continue. And, they will continue to be a drag on the economy.

Taken together, the core contribution of the eminent economists could be described as advocating an inward-oriented development strategy. An important element of that strategy was industrialisation behind import restrictions. Such a strategy was later formalised by Prebisch (1959) and earlier by Singer (1950) among others. Their main concern was the alleged secular decline in the terms of trade of primary exporters and unequal partnership in trade and capital transactions between the developing and developed countries. Besides, the land was limited, and increasing the area of cultivation would have led to diminishing returns, hence the move towards industrialisation. Robinson, Myrdal and Lange could be identified as staunch believers in inward-oriented development strategy and Hicks as less of a supporter.

This is understandable given the existing state of knowledge on development issues, international development experience up to that date, the predisposition of developing country leadership at the time towards state intervention and the association of development with industrialisation.[58] In addition, the emerging leadership in developing countries at that time was anti-colonial. Marxists and even nationalists (particularly Nehru) were staunch believers of inward-oriented strategy. Dr. Corea and members of the Planning Secretariat were also adherents of this strategy as seen in their later writings.[59] Dr. Corea's political masters after 1956 were natural supporters of the strategy given that the MEP coalition comprised nationalists and socialists and was ideologically predisposed towards such a strategy.

Socialists — Robinson was one — believed in the "unfailing superiority of socialism for the third world" that derived from the fact that socialist governments have complete control over surplus from production, there is no income from property and the savings problem which plagued capitalist economies is automatically solved.[60] This was the reason why she and others believed that socialist economies grew faster than capitalist economies at that time. The economic aspects of socialism were at the polar end of inward-oriented strategy. The corollary to the belief in these aspects of economic organisation and strategy was the lack of confidence in the market in general and the ability of market prices to allocate resources efficiently and equitably. But, Lange and, to some extent, Robinson were exponents of "market socialism" where prices that equated supply with demand (with marginal costs equated with marginal revenue to maximise the "surplus") in a socialist system would be as efficient as those under a private ownership-based competitive equilibrium.

---

[58] Krueger (1997) in her presidential address to the American Economic Association remarked that development economics in the 1950s was "a mixture of touristic impressions, half-truths and misapplied policy inferences."

[59] Dr. Corea (2008) wrote, "What industrial structure was feasible for a small country the size of Ceylon? At that time around the mid-fifties, industrialisation based on manufactured goods did not seem a realistic option. Foreign markets were highly protected, and the knowledge of technology needed to compete in those markets was lacking." Industrialisation for the domestic market or, in other words, import substitution appeared, therefore, the most feasible option" p. 225.

[60] Adelman and Sunding (1989).

Both empirical work on trade and development and the experience of the East Asian developing countries in the 1970s led to the eclipse of inward-oriented development strategy and gave way to outward-oriented development strategy.[61] Perhaps, Hicks was the closest to this position which included four important elements: (i) an incentive system that reduced bias against exports and no primacy given to import substitution, which led to industrialisation; (ii) a more neutral approach to activities in that resources were to be allocated to the activities that had the highest rate of return and not to predetermined activities based on assumed externalities and increasing returns; (iii) greater use of market prices to allocate resources and limited intervention only to address specific distortions; and (iv) avoidance of macroeconomic instability, by not having large external deficits and inflation. Writing at the time they did, the papers by the visiting economists had only a minor enthusiasm for items (ii) and (iv).[62] This is understandable given there was hardly any theoretical literature to support an outward-oriented strategy at the time. As mentioned earlier, the writings of such persons as were not considered mainstream thoughts.

3.5 Economic Performance during the Ten-Year Plan Period

Because the eminent economists advised the government on economic strategy, policy and organisation for the Ten-Year Plan, it would be useful to review how economic performance turned out during this period, even though the Ten-Year Plan was never formally implemented by any government. It is true, however, that many elements of the plan were followed by the two governments that came into power during the 1959–1968 period. The MEP (with the SLFP as the senior partner) was in power from 1956–1960. Then it lost election in 1960, and won again during the same year. Having won the election they governed the country during the 1960–1965 period. The UNP won the next election and governed during the 1965–1970 period. Thus, the Ten-Year Plan period covered two governments with opposing ideologies and programmes. But, since both faced similar economic situations, their approaches were not too different

---

[61] Little et al. (1970), Bhagwati (1978) and Krueger (1978).
[62] Robinson worried about inflation.

from each other at the time, save for the half-hearted effort by the UNP to partially liberalise the economy in 1968.

The GDP growth rate averaged 4.01 per cent a year for the 1959–1968 period, in contrast to the 5.9 per cent anticipated by the eminent economists and the Ten-Year Plan document. There was a boost to growth in 1968 when the UNP attempted to liberalise the economy, but it did not have enough steam or credibility to sustain growth. The liberalisation measures included some import liberalisation, the devaluation of the Rupee and the adaptation of a dual exchange rate in the form of the Foreign Exchange Entitlement Certificate (FEEC) scheme. The main reasons for the fall in the growth rate were the deteriorating external environment, the inability to raise savings significantly above the 1957 level and a defective policy framework that responded to the poor external environment by increasing restrictions and turning the economy even more towards a command economy. Except for the Hicks, the others would have been more sympathetic to the MEP than to the UNP programme.

The following developments took place with respect to the external environment during this period. First, the terms of trade deteriorated from 307 in 1959 to 210 in 1968 (1990 base = 100).[63] Even though the export volumes increased due to better performance of the plantations sector, this did not suffice to slow down the decline in external reserves, which fell from Special Drawing Rights (SDR) 147.6 million in 1959 to SDR 70.1 million in 1968. This was despite the drastic import and exchange controls introduced in the early 1960s.[64] Consequently, the reserve level fell from 4 months of goods imports in 1959 to 2.1 months of goods imports over the same period. In between, when the UNP government was in power in 1965, it was able to get the World Bank to host an Aid Group for Sri Lanka that temporarily boosted reserves to SDR 85.7 million through increased aid. But, as other liberalisation efforts have shown elsewhere, when they are not credible, they do not lead to a sustained improvement in the external position.

Finally, on the domestic side of the outcome, there were not enough savings to raise the level of investment above the average of 14.5 per cent. Savings were low because GDP growth was low and because welfare expenditure on food subsidies, free health and education was a huge charge on the budget. Meanwhile, economic efficiency suffered from

---

[63] The data for this section are drawn from Kelegama (2006).
[64] Kelegama (2006) cited the ILO (1971) which indicated that "Apart from Burma, Ceylon was the only country in Asia earning less foreign exchange in 1968 than 1958."

increased trade and domestic restrictions. Thus, in contrast to Robinson's exercise, both savings and efficiency (as denoted by a rise in the capital–output ratio) fell, leading to a low growth rate and the inability to provide sufficient employment opportunities for the increasing labour force. Deteriorating external conditions combined with high consumption expenditures induced an overall imbalance, resulting in rising unemployment, low growth and a greatly uncertain economic future. The MEP won the election again in 1970 and made Sri Lanka one of the most controlled and restrictive economies in the developing world over the 7-year period in which it ruled.

3.6 Conclusions

The papers by the visiting economists provided, for the first time in the economic literature on Sri Lanka, well-rounded commentary and analysis of the economic development problems faced by the country. The eminent economists represented the best and brightest group that had ever visited Sri Lanka and studied the economic situation there. To be sure, many other eminent economists visited the country over the years, but no other group had the cachet and the eminence of this group.

Their commentary and analysis helped to postpone, for a few years at least, the country's movement towards a highly controlled and restrictive policy regime. But, the ideas they espoused were not very different from the mainstream thinking of the time. These ideas, such as import substitution, led to industrialisation, giving primacy to the state over the market; moreover, faith in public sector corporations to carry through the transformation from what was called a dependent economy to a modern economy came to be contested over the next two decades. Both the advances in theoretical literature that were to come later, (e.g. public choice theory associated with Buchanan and Tullock and the new institutional economics of North) and empirical experience moved away from the positions held by the eminent economists at the time.[65]

The eminent economists' contribution is significant for a number of reasons. First, they highlighted the population problem that faced the country: a modern death rate and an old-fashioned birth rate that led to rapid population growth. However, over the next two decades, the

---

[65] Buchanan and Tullock (1962), North (1990a).

urgency of the problem waned as birth rates fell as quickly as the death rates had fallen in the 1930s and 1940s. A demographic transition was achieved in a relatively short time. They also highlighted the cost of providing large subsidies that a country at a low level of development could ill afford. Robinson's classic statement that Sri Lanka was "enjoying the fruit before planting the tree" resonates even today. The only feasible change was to target income supplements to particular groups based on means-testing and not provide subsidies indiscriminately.

Their approach to import substitution-led industrialisation and foreign trade restrictions was rendered invalid due to empirical work which shows that when incentives are skewed towards import substitution, it creates large domestic distortions and a bias against exports. Studies by Balassa (1989) *et al.* showed that countries with more open and outward-oriented policies enjoyed higher growth rates and responded more quickly and effectively to disturbances arising in the international market.[66] In the East Asian countries, the incentive regime which was more or less neutral had proven to be successful. In addition, a comparison of regressions in aggregate and by sector showed that growth rates of export industries were higher than those of import substitution industries. In fact, the latter had negative factor productivity in a multi-country sample.[67] A similar result has been seen in the case of Sri Lanka when total factor productivity was negative during the globalisation-unfriendly period of 1970–1977.[68] The success of China and India with their open economy policies with respect to trade and foreign investment since the 1990s gives additional support to the view that import substitution led to industrialisation and it was bound to fail, as it would not lead to greater efficiency through foreign competition. Also, growth in total factor productivity proved to be more potent and sustainable than factor augmentation.[69]

With respect to agriculture, the economists were a bit ambiguous about supporting domestic agriculture but favoured plantations on efficiency grounds. However, it turned out that support for domestic

---

[66] Balassa (1986), World Development Report (1987), Little *et al.* (1970), Krueger (1978), Deepak and Rajapatirana (1989).
[67] Nishimizu and Robinson (1984).
[68] Athukorala and Rajapatirana (2000).
[69] Chenery *et al.* (1986). When national value-added growth was decomposed, it was shown that half the growth was due to improvement in productivity and that the contribution from capital was only 20 per cent and that of labour was 30 per cent.

agriculture would have been more helpful to reduce the rural poverty that persists to this day. The successive UNP governments supported colonisation schemes, neglecting small farmers, and the eminent economists proved to be right in not supporting these large schemes. Both Gal Oya and Mahaweli projects were not economically justified since the cost of producing rice in these areas turned out to be many times the imported price. But, if self-sufficiency was the goal, as it had become, it would have still been economic to support domestic small-farm agriculture and not those based on large irrigation schemes.

Contrary to the recommendation to not nationalise foreign-owned plantations earlier on, the MEP government nationalised them in 1975. The eminent economists only helped to postpone this event. There was a decline in productivity and output growth in the aftermath. This led to the denationalisation in the early 1990s with some gains, but the act itself has been criticised for lack of transparency.

With respect to macroeconomic adjustment and growth, even though the prevailing idea was that terms of trade would deteriorate over time and would also fluctuate widely, the main contributor, Robinson, took the terms of trade in 1957 as fixed for her projections for exports, imports and the external balance, and used a capital–output ratio of 2.6 to project GDP to grow by 5.9 per cent by building up a level of savings with different taxes, tariffs and public sector surpluses. However, by projecting an external account that was to be in balance, there would be no need for foreign aid by 1968. In this regard, the visiting economists envisioned an overly optimistic scenario. That the Planning Secretariat accepted these projections is surprising since a more realistic projection would have had some degree of dependence on foreign assistance. History proved that this particular projection was not realistic, to say the least.

The type of economic organisation the eminent economists recommended, namely, public sector corporations, were not known to deliver high efficiency in their activities, and many of the goals set for them have remained elusive, such as the public sector surplus to add to the national savings. There were many problems with the public sector corporations from the very beginning. Some were established to produce goods for which the country had no comparative advantage even in a dynamic sense. There was also the principal–agent problem because the principal had different goals and objectives from the agent. State-owned corporations also had to operate in a way that was not commercially viable since they had to provide goods at subsidised prices. Efficiency was further compromised when the government gave the monopoly of import of competitive products to the state corporations producing them. Although the corporations remained as inefficient and rent extracting as they were previously, they survived the 1977 liberalisation. They had grown in influence in the political sphere because both major parties used them for political patronage, appointing supporters to key positions in these corporations.

The contributions of the eminent economists were deficient in three important respects and due, in part, to this the economy performed poorly contrary to what they expected.

First, given the state of knowledge at the time, the economists did not consider the political economy aspects of the recommendations they made. They failed to see that the public sector corporations would become an important political instrument to be used by different governments. Similarly, in advocating a so-called scientific tariff, they created opportunities for lobbying and rent-seeking among different producer groups. Nowhere was this more apparent than in the case of the import monopolies that were granted to public sector corporations. It became a burden on the economy over time and continues to be so today, some 50 years later.

Second, like all other analysts at the time, the eminent economists, especially Kaldor, Robinson and Myrdal, ignored the ethnic issue despite their visiting the country immediately after the ethnic violence of May and June 1958. It was most surprising that Myrdal would ignore it, given that he was the celebrated author of the "American Dilemma" in which he documented the plight of American Blacks in the south.[70] It was a significant lapse given that the ethnic problem is now termed a national problem. It is likely that the economists ignored this dimension as something outside their purview.

Finally, the eminent economists ignored the ideological dimension of economic policymaking in Sri Lanka to their peril.[71] This is one reason why their recommendations were more readily acceptable to the left-of-centre politicians. Except for Hicks, their worldview was more sympathetic to the left than to the right. As one analyst pointed out, it was this ideological distance between the left and the right that was responsible for the inability of the country to develop a consensus on economic policy. It is the reason why the country missed out on the early transition to the

---

[70] Myrdal *et al.* (1944).
[71] Rajapatirana (2009).

rapid export-led growth that the East Asian countries experienced since the mid-1960s. Now, it could be said that democracy prevented such a consensus since the East Asian countries were authoritarian. But, this is not a defensible position because both democracies and authoritarian regimes have succeeded and failed to show strong economic performances.

These criticisms emanate from 50 years of hindsight. Nevertheless, it is worth holding the economists' view to today's mirror to see how far the country has come and how far it has to go to join the fast-growing developing economies in the world. This recounting is necessary so that the same mistakes are not repeated. It is interesting to speculate as to what a different group of eminent economists would have contributed to the development policy debate and formulation.[72] Their advice was followed, and it led to resounding economic success — earlier in Taiwan but later in Chile. Of course, none of them believed in economic planning and, as such, they would not have been invited to Sri Lanka in 1957 and 1958 anyway. The visiting economists did not consider ideology an important aspect of economic policymaking while it was an input into policymaking in Sri Lanka. This leads to Chapter 4 on ideology.

---

[72] In a conversation with the author, Harberger mentioned that he was sent to India in 1958 by the Massachusetts Institute of Technology to advise Indian policymakers who, under the influence of the economic thinking of the time that believed in a planned command economy, did not accept his advice. He soon returned to the University of Chicago.

Chapter 4

Ideology and Economic Policymaking: A Framework Applied to Sri Lanka

4.1 Introduction

Economists have not ventured into the field of ideology and policymaking for a good reason. It is a risky enterprise, given the difficulties of conceptualisation and measurement. Yet, it is very likely that ideas and ideology influence economic policies. Elites who fashion economic policy face competing models. They range from more market-oriented approaches to greater government control. Another aspect of different policies is that the diverse impact they have on the different groups. In such circumstances, they have to fall back on a set of beliefs or ideologies.[1] Since standard policy determinants leave a significant unexplained residual, ideology is a good candidate to fill the unexplained part of the policymaking process.[2] While ideas alone cannot lead to policy change (they need agents and institutions to put them into action), it seems that the joint product between interests and ideas can be an important determinant of the range, choice and use of policies. In this chapter, we explore the nexus between ideology and policymaking in Sri Lanka.

For this, we borrow some concepts and approaches from international relations, a field that has ventured into economic policy, particularly through the window of political economy. While the present chapter does not use a political economy approach per se, its influence can be readily

---

[1] Goldstein and Keohane (1993).
[2] Dutt and Mitra (2005).

seen. In essence, ideas provide a value system, a road map for action and a rallying point for political entrepreneurs as well as policymakers. Interest groups that drive policy change may not be able to agree on the precise goals and means they want to pursue.³ Ideology helps to reduce this cognitive dissonance. Thus, to ignore the influence of ideology on policy would be to leave a significant part of the determinants of policymaking unexplained. Ideas are not only a determinant of the current policy but they live on well after their progenitors are long gone. They become embedded in institutions and law and have a multi-generational influence. Keynes, no intellectual slouch, noted that ideas influence policies in a fundamental way.⁴

In this chapter, we do not raise the question of how ideas are formed, but take that as given and raise the issue of how ideas, in whichever manner they have been formed, are either applied or not applied in policymaking.

This chapter contends that ideology influences policymaking through different channels. Ideology imparts its influence as a system of beliefs, as a road map for action in the hands of political entrepreneurs and policymakers, and by specifying cause–effect relationships (clearly in the hands of elites) to reduce the uncertainty of results arising from policy actions. Ideas influence the choice of policy options that a government considers to address economic problems. A given ideological position would lead to some policy options being chosen over others and some options not being considered at all. Some options increase the probability of success when addressing a particular policy issue, while others that clearly do not are chosen given the ideological position of leaders or elites

---

³Bates and Kruger (1993).

⁴Keynes (1936) wrote, "… the ideas of economists and political philosophers, both when they are right and when they are wrong, are more powerful than is commonly understood. Indeed, the world is ruled by little else. Practical men, who believe themselves to be quite exempt from any intellectual influences, are usually the slaves of some defunct economist. Madmen in authority, who hear voices in the air, are distilling their frenzy from some academic scribbler of a few years back. I am sure that the power of vested interests is vastly exaggerated compared with the gradual encroachment of ideas. Not, indeed, immediately, but after a certain interval; for in the field of economic and political philosophy there are not many who are influenced by new theories after they are 25 or 30 years of age, so that the ideas which civil servants and politicians and even agitators apply to current events are not likely to be the newest. But, soon or late, it is ideas, not vested interests, which are dangerous for good or evil."

who support them. Taking into consideration the close relationship between such choices and outcomes, we find no support for the implied null hypothesis that ideas have no influence on policy. On the contrary, they do have an influence, but it is not always easily observable, particularly in median voter politics where political candidates who seek the middle ground do not appear to be associated with either of the distinct tail ends of the ideological distribution. Thus, candidates may move away from the median position with respect to policy once they win the election. This is another reason why it is difficult to identify a clear ideological position *a priori*.

This highly stylised policy paradigm can explain some of the reasons for policy change over time and across countries and regions. For example, during the post-independence era (1948–2012), Sri Lanka experienced four ideology shifts.[5] Following this introduction, Section 4.2 discusses some leading definitions of ideology. Section 4.3 discusses the main policy-making paradigms. Section 4.4 explores the ideas and the policymaking nexus. Section 4.5 examines the comparative ideological experience of Sri Lanka across time. Section 4.6 examines the comparative ideological experience of Sri Lanka across countries. Section 4.7 gives the conclusions.

4.2 What is Ideology: Leading Definitions

As with other definitions, ideology covers a wide spectrum. Well-known thinkers, both in the past and present, have provided their definitions in accordance with their own positions on ideology.

Karl Marx held that ideology is a cloak for vested interests (hence no influence on its own).[6] For him, ideology had no impact on policy. It seems so ironic that someone who has influenced both policymakers and people, in general, could claim that ideology (namely Marxism) has no independent influence on policy. The former Soviet Union, Maoist China and the few remaining socialist states such as Cuba would disagree with the master in this regard. But importantly, he may have reformed

---

[5] India had only one in 1991. Latin America experienced many ideological shifts from the early 1980s to the early 1990s. South Asia reformed slowly compared to Latin America, with significant changes in the 1980s and some reversals in policy positions in the 1990s, which can be interpreted as a regression to the mean in ideological terms.
[6] North (1990a).

capitalism most by making it recognise worker interests in a fundamental way to lead to more harmonious industrial relations. He did not live to see the enormous influence of his ideology on millions of people for over 150 years. Dung Xiao Peng, the reformist Chinese leader who helped to bring about a paradigm shift in China's economic ideology, said, "I do not care whether the cat is black or white, as long as it catches mice," thus embracing pragmatism as a guiding ideology and eschewing the rigid ideology of traditional Marxism.

Max Weber was more open to the view that ideas play a role in politics and by implication in policymaking. He argued that world images created by ideas are like railway tracks on which actions are pushed along by dynamic interests. Thus, Weber, while recognising that policies are influenced by interests, conceded that ideas provide the tracks on which they (policies) proceed. Unlike Marx, Weber was open to the notion that ideas do matter for policy.

Zbigniew Brzezinski, a modern critic of Marxism and one who predicted the collapse of the Soviet Union accurately, held that ideology comprises a doctrinaire part and an action programme.[7] Raj Krishna held that ideology had a set of value commitments, historical generalisations and institutional preferences, and influenced specific policy actions.[8] The context in which this definition was adopted was his analysis of India's ideological evolution from the 1950s to the 1980s. The social anthropologist Clifford Geertz defined ideology as a system of ideas that are embedded in a value system. Douglass North defined ideology as the subjective perceptions (models, theories) to explain the world around them. To generalise, ideology comprises a doctrinaire, belief or value system, and an action programme that can be implemented by political leaders and is embedded in institutions.

Judith Goldstein and Robert Keohane's writing on foreign policy provides an approach that embraces concepts that are readily applicable to a modern-day policy context.[9] In their framework, ideology has three elements: a value system or beliefs which they call a world view, related to

---

[7]Brezinski was the US Secretary of State under President Carter.

[8]The context in which this definition was adopted was his analysis of India's ideological evolution from the 1950s to the 1980s. Raj Krishna believed that the Indian leaders Jawaharlal Nehru and Vallabhbhai Patel, among others, accepted the British Fabian movement that can be regarded today as socialism lite.

[9]Goldstein and Keohane (1993).

a society's culture, religion and identity; principled beliefs that "consist of normative ideas that specify criteria for determining right and wrong"; and causal beliefs or "beliefs about cause-effect relationships that derive authority from the shared consensus of recognised elites from village leaders to scientists and elite institutions." We adopt their framework to develop the ideology and policymaking nexus in economic policymaking in a developing country's context.[10]

4.3 Policymaking Paradigms

The most common political economy paradigm is that economic policy changes are the result of interest group politics. They are led by political entrepreneurs who may co-opt ideas because of conviction or self-interest to win support or stay in power. A further refinement of this paradigm is that economic policy changes involve transaction costs related to coalition creation, negotiation, agreement and implementation: They entail real resource costs.[11] Policy changes are a part of a cost minimisation process in this paradigm. It is a completely rational approach to policymaking where ideas do not influence the policy decision. Ideas are given and are exogenous to policymaking in this paradigm. The rational model of policymaking implies benefit maximisation subject to a cost constraint. The cost would involve political cost (such as the possibility of losing the next election) or, even worse, a calamitous loss of power through a coup or revolution. The refinement of the transaction cost approach is to recognise that such costs can be identified and minimised.

A different paradigm that treats ideas as endogenous is the so-called "reflectionalist" view of policymaking. Ideas enter policymaking, but it has been difficult to analyse the way in which ideas enter the decision-making process. It is also not amenable to hypothesis testing. Some have claimed that such a view of the nexus between policymaking and ideology belongs to the field of psychology rather than the social sciences. Both these approaches are inadequate to explain the policymaking process.

A cautionary note on methodology is warranted at this point. It is extremely difficult to establish a clear link between ideology and policymaking for many reasons such as the difficulties of definition, measurement

---

[10] Ibid.
[11] North (1990b).

and limited feasibility of using statistical methodology. What is generally pursued is a rather heuristic approach that takes into account what is called congruence procedure and process tracing.[12] The former attempts to establish congruence or consistency between given beliefs or ideology deductively to determine whether a causal role was played in making a particular decision. The latter approach of process tracing attempts "to establish how the policymaker's beliefs influenced his receptivity to and assessment of incoming information about the situation, his definition of the situation, identification, and evaluation options and finally the choice of action."[13]

With respect to leadership, assigning an ideological position is clear enough since politicians have to sell a platform that has an implied ideology to win elections.[14] Where endowments are concerned, we can appeal to the Heckscher–Ohlin model to assign *a priori* ideology based on endowments. A labour-abundant country will favour an ideology that is predisposed towards higher wages and employment in competition with capital and land. As far as institutions are concerned, certain institutions have *a priori* dispositions to different ideological positions. For example, an independent central bank supports more conservative macroeconomic policies than a minister of finance who is a member of the cabinet and is not independent. A minister of industry, for instance, is less conservative and would be willing to favour protection and industrial targeting compared to more neutral policies.

What about ideology? Given a country's history, cultural identity and extent of independence or dependence on super-powers, a country will have a predisposition towards certain ideologies, thus explaining the contrast between South Asia and Latin America.[15] What is more interesting is when these factors move differently from their *a priori* positions.

---

[12] Sun-Ki Chai (1998) stated, "An ideology is an interconnected set of beliefs concerning a particular domain of human interaction that is not derived solely from direct observation and logical inference." However, it does allow one to derive a framework that can explore the link between ideology and policymaking in a satisfactory way.

[13] *Ibid.*

[14] As noted, leaders may not always reveal their true ideological position prior to the election. Their policy actions will allow us to categorise their ideological positions.

[15] The former is more conservative in policy change (in any direction), while the latter is more venturesome and less conservative in changing policies (similarly in either direction).

While South Asia is slower to change policy, South America has more frequent policy changes and more unstable policy frameworks.

4.4 A Policy Paradigm

The key question is how ideology enters policy. Further, what is the simplest way to think about it? Borrowing a paradigm used successfully in international relations literature, we recall the definition that ideology is the beliefs held by actors. Of course, ideologies change as similar to policies. Policies are changed due to ideology. We define ideology to include all three of these beliefs (world views, principled beliefs, and cause-effect relationships) in our framework.

World views are based on people's conception of their identities, religion and culture (e.g. Muslim fundamentalists in the Middle East or Hindu extremists in India), not to mention *Jathika Hela Urumaya* (national heritage politics). It is clear that different countries and regions have different world views. Thus, when countries consider a given policy change, the particular worldview will bear on policy decision. Thus, for example, Sri Lanka had a more conservative approach to fiscal policy until the 1990s at least, while Latin America had more expansive fiscal policies.

Principle beliefs are normative ideas that specify criteria for judging right from wrong (e.g. slavery was wrong, minority rights should be protected, and men and women are equal). Ethical judgements differ among countries and regions. For example, women have fewer rights than men in the Middle East compared to Latin America and South Asia. Economic policies that would result in giving greater access to capital to women would be more limited in the Middle East compared to other regions in the world. So, a change in principled beliefs may be needed to provide equal opportunities to women in that region. Similar situations exist for minorities in different parts of the world. In India, Dalits, the so-called scheduled castes or lower castes, have been provided special access to higher education. Thus, the principle beliefs in India have changed irrespective of whether creating such quotas is beneficial to the country or not in the long run.

Causal beliefs are cause–effect relationships which derive authority from shared consensus among elites in society (e.g. fiscal deficits are bad, increases in money growth lead to inflation and trade protection lowers GDP growth over the long run). An example of change in causal beliefs is the situation in Sri Lanka, where large fiscal deficits seem to be accepted as benign. Similarly, the growth of money supply (mostly fiscal in origin) is considered an inevitable corollary to real GDP growth. Changes in causal beliefs imply changes in strategies for the attainment of economic goals. Changes in causal beliefs are more frequent and more rapid than those in world views and principled beliefs. Politicians are able to affect this aspect of ideology more often than the other two aspects.

Political leaders, institutions and a country's resource endowments along with ideological shifts (as indicated by changes in world views, principled beliefs and causal beliefs) are the main factors in policy changes. Of course, this is a highly stylised framework of policy making. Nevertheless, by using this simple framework comprising four factors, it is possible to examine economic policymaking. We do this by harnessing the technique of first differencing. That is, we can look at policy shifts and decide what kind and combination of these four factors were behind a given policy shift.

At times, policy shifts can be completely exogenous where the policymakers had no choice but to adopt new policies in light of an exogenous factor such as an external price shock, a physical shock such as a tsunami or in reaction to an unanticipated event in which the policymakers are pushed into a corner. Then, they have no choice but to adjust their policies. But, even random events operate via the four factors that we identified. One more caveat is in order. While ideology can impart an independent influence on policy, it needs an agent to put it into practice. These agents are political leaders and institutions. In fact, the most potent factor in policy change is leadership.

Changes in principled beliefs take a second place, followed by institutions and last of all endowments. But, even the last mentioned can have an effect if for instance an oil shock is seen as a permanent change in endowments. A simple example is to measure the purchasing power of a sector or the income generated in it through the changes in real oil prices. The purchasing power and the income generated in it will show the extent of the shock which cannot be ignored as requiring policy actions. Labour, for example, will experience a decline in real wages when there is an oil shock. An oil-exporting country, on the other hand, will experience a sudden increase in its endowments, challenging the policymakers to adopt policies that allow the country to absorb the increase in resources well and not lead to bad after-effects, as in the case of countries that have experienced Dutch disease problems.

We can visualise the contribution of each factor to a policy shift in a general way, while specific country circumstances differ. Leadership and some aspects of ideology operate in changing policies in the short run. In particular, leadership is a vital agent to carry ideas. Leadership is associated with particular interests depending on the endowments of a country. For example, landowners will resist policies to change tenure relationships.

Endowments determine long-run effects. They operate via relative prices: Labour-abundant countries have low wages and would be more willing to accept open trade with rich countries where wages are high.[16] Capital and land-abundant poor countries will be less willing to open to world trade since they will resist a decline in land rents and rental of capital. Leadership in non-democracies caters to such narrow interests. One reason why countries with large mineral endowments have remained non-democratic is that the leadership in such cases has incentives to arrogate power over resources and is unwilling to share the power to create and distribute the returns to these resources.[17]

The influence of institutions is long term and more subtle. Certain institutions by the nature of their functions have conservative ideas. For example, central banks tend to be conservative. Conversely, ministries of industry are less conservative as they are charged with the responsibility of promoting industry. In some cases, as in Sri Lanka's case, institutions do not follow a well-assigned pattern because leadership seems more important than institutions in that particular context. Part of the problem arises from the loss of independence of institutions when politics interferes with policymaking in a direct or unfiltered way.

4.5 The Comparative Ideological Experience of Sri Lanka across Time

Sri Lanka provides a good laboratory to test this policy framework. Ideological factors have influenced important decisions with respect to policy making for the last 60 years. There are five clear examples of these instances: (a) President J. R. Jayewardene's decision to undertake

---

[16] This is not the case in some situations where trade unions resist opening the economy to foreign competition without realising that wages could rise as foreign demand for labour-intensive goods increases.

[17] This applies to countries that have large mineral deposits or oil deposits as the elites benefit from rents from these activities, resisting greater opening of the economies to globalisation.

far-reaching economic reforms to liberalise the economy was more the result of an ideological stance than any other consideration. (b) President Chandrika Kumaratunga changed the ideology of the SLFP from an anti-market stance towards a more pro-market stance as she came into power in 1994. (c) The Rajapaksa government embraced protectionist policies with respect to foreign trade by raising tariffs and introducing those policies that were not followed by President Chandrika Kumaratunga. (d) President Rajapkse refused to accept a grant of US$ 480 million for urban transport, establishing land registration, Cadastral Mapping and land ownership. (e) The Gotabaya Rajapaksa administration delayed the decision to go to the IMF which led to a dire economic condition related to debt.

We reckon there were four episodes of examples of a shift in the policy paradigm undertaken by four leaders, which we identify ideology being the dominant factor that were behind policy changes. In the pre-independence period, there was no independent influence of Sri Lankan ideology on a policy that was made by British colonialist. The colonial attitude to globalisation was conditioned by trade, investment and labour movements within the British Empire. Thus, there was free trade within the empire subject to an imperial preference where those outside the empire had to pay a low tariff much like a modern-day common market. Colonial ideology supported large FDIs into the country, encouraged by a hospitable and supportive regulatory regime, resulting in huge inflows of labour from India to work on plantations. Moreover, the existence of a currency board arrangement with a fixed exchange rate and near-automatic adjustment to reserve-level changes assured macroeconomic stability, which also helped British investments flow in large amounts to the country. Thus, the ideological milieu was globalisation-friendly. However, a currency board system cannot work in Sri Lanka today as a critical factor like the downward flexibility of prices does not exist in a country full of price controls and a mountain of debt.

With independence in 1948, the colonial administration was replaced by a Sri Lankan administration within the framework of parliamentary democracy. The UNP came into power in the 1947 election led by D. S. Senanayake. It did not have a different ideology from the colonial administration. Nor did the other UNP-led governments of Dudley Senanayake and Sri John Kotelawala. One slight change in the ideology was the emphasis by the UNP at that time on domestic agriculture, especially the restoration of the ancient irrigation system. But, this did not have any implications for globalisation as agriculture was not promoted through restrictions on trade, FDI or labour movements.

Four changes in the prevailing ideology can be identified in the post-independence period. All of them took place after 1956. The earlier period of 1948–1955 was mainly a continuation of the ideology that prevailed before independence. The governments led by D. S. Senanayake, Dudley Senanayake and John Kotelawala did not offer or signal a change in ideology. There are four changes associated with the leadership of S. W. R. D. Bandaranaike, Sirimavo Bandaranaike, J. R. Jayewardene and Mahinda Rajapaksa.

A definite change in economic ideology arose with the MEP coming into power in 1956 under Prime Minister S. W. R. D. Bandaranaike. It was a watershed in the political milieu of the country, changing from a post-colonial central ideological position to a left-of-centre ideological position. S. W. R. D. Bandaranaike came into power championing the interests of the Sinhala majority, promising to make Sinhala the official language and then delivering on the promise, creating a permanent rift between the Sinhala majority and the Tamil minority. The corollary to his championing of nationalism and the majoritarian rule was the tilt towards self-sufficiency, which is globalisation-unfriendly.

Another aspect of S. W. R. D. Bandaranaike's ideological stance was that he wanted to move the country away from Western capitalist countries but did not want to follow the Soviet model. Consequently, he initiated a spate of payment agreements with the former Soviet Union countries and some Middle Eastern countries. The original idea was to save foreign exchange, particularly US dollars and UK pounds. Under these payment agreements, goods were exchanged with a host of countries including Russia, Poland, Hungary, Egypt, Jordan and the United Arab Emirates. Only the deficit balances were settled by using dollars or pounds. These agreements were not globalisation-friendly in the sense that the choice set for the exporter and importers was not the rest of the world but the countries with which Sri Lanka had agreements with the commonwealth. Also, this does not pass the test of globalisation-friendly policies with respect to trade (restricted by destination), while FDI was limited with hardly any from these countries except to settle outstanding balances in trade with outdated production techniques and machinery (for example, the setting up of steel and tire corporations). Finally, there was no movement of labour in either direction.

With respect to FDI, S. W. R. D. Bandaranaike did not encourage or discourage it as much as ignore it. So, it is no surprise that this element of globalisation was neglected by the Bandaranaike government. FDI flows began to decline during this period. In fact, foreign agency houses (mostly British-dominated firms that managed plantation agriculture) felt threatened by the nationalisation given the stated ideology of the Bandaranaike-led coalition. Prime Minister Bandaranaike requested British navy personnel to leave Trincomalee, one of the leading strategically located ports in South Asia. He espoused neutrality in foreign affairs by developing closer links with the Soviet Block and the Chinese government.

There was no significant change in the labour movement under the Bandaranaike administration in either direction. Inward movement of people for work was not allowed. In fact, even before Bandaranaike government, the UNP had disenfranchised Tamil plantation workers, virtually the first significant legislation of the UNP as it came into power with the 1947 general election. Bandaranaike had little to do with respect to Tamil labour as a result.

Mr. Bandaranaike followed the ideology of Indian leaders closely. It was Prime Minister Nehru who asked him to invite foreign advisers like Kaldor to advise Sri Lanka on tax policy. He was also influenced by Nehru's commitment to economic planning a la the Soviet Union and invited seven eminent economists to advise on the preparation of the Ten-Year Plan for 1958–1967 (see Chapter 3: "Through Eminent Eyes: A Fifty-Year Retrospective as a background to Globalisation"). He felt that it was his most important contribution to the country.

To sum up, the beginning of the S. W. R. D. Bandaranaike government not only created an ideological breach with the past but also influenced ideology over the next 50 years with respect to globalisation and other vital economic matters. All this came out of a mere three-year Prime Ministership, which ended with his assassination in 1959. One can see his influence on Sri Lankan ideology manifest in the later SLFP-led governments starting from the government of Prime Minister Sirimavo Bandaranaike in 1960–1965 and 1970–1977 and extending to President Rajapaksa (2005–2010).

The 1956 defeat of the UNP, which had remained in power since 1948, was a highly significant event for a number of reasons. First, the UNP governments that were in power up to 1956 were a continuation of the colonial regime in terms of politics and economics. By 1924, Sri Lanka began a path towards self-governance. By 1931, under the Donoughmore Constitution, Sri Lanka had a large measure of independence with respect to domestic affairs and policies. With the Soulbury

Commission in 1947, Sri Lanka became an independent sovereign state. The UNP government pretty much carried on the same paradigm as the British with respect to economic, political and social policies. The defeat of the existing paradigm was very much a re-assertion of the Sinhalese majoritarian world views (i.e. reassertion of religion, culture and national identity) that pre-dated the foreign domination of the country. In that sense, the 1956 policy shift was very much ideology driven. S. W. R. D Bandaranaike after 1956, saw an opportunity to mobilise forces that had different world views, principled beliefs and cause–effect relationships from the political elites of the day. The Political elites were Western-educated, English-speaking middle–class people, and more multi-religious and ethnic in outlook compared to the SLFP membership that led to the coalition against the UNP.

Thus, the policy changes that were heralded after 1956 give clues to their ideological origins. They were associated with an ideology that was in contrast to the existing ideology. These policy changes included, among others, the creation of public corporations, greater affinity with the Soviet bloc, as evidenced by the bilateral payment agreements signed with countries of the Soviet bloc, and changes in institutions such as the introduction of the Paddy Lands Act that altered the relationship between landlords and tenant farmers. These changes could be traced at least in part to ideology in its three manifestations — world views, principled beliefs and cause–effect relationships. It is noteworthy that world views did not change as much as they were able to influence a new group of politicians. These politicians were able to influence both principled beliefs and cause–effect relationships.

Since the 1930s, socialist politicians had tried to alter the ideological milieu of the country in opposition to the prevailing colonial rule. But, they failed due to two major reasons. First, they were not in a position to be in power, given that Sri Lanka was not independent. Second, even when it became independent, the socialist ideological influence was not accepted by the larger community. This was because socialist views conflicted with the world view of the majority, particularly the rural masses (both the Sinhalese and the Tamils). Socialist politicians made inroads that may have influenced principled beliefs at the 1953 Hartal (or general strike), but it was not sufficient to allow them to come into power.

The 1956 ideological shift associated with the victory of the Sri Lanka Freedom Party (SLFP) influenced the principled beliefs and cause–effect relationships, leading to the wresting of power from the UNP. The policy change was a result of an ideological change since there was no foreign exchange or macroeconomic crisis at that time to cause a policy shift. In this sense, the analogy is that of a gradual buildup of opposition to the post-colonial policy regime. It was a cumulative process rather than a shift in the tectonic plates of the political system.

Prime Minister Sirimavo Bandaranaike came into power in 1960, riding a wave of sympathy following the assassination of her husband. She was the leader of the SLFP and Prime Minister in 1960–1965 and 1970–1977. During her first term, she more or less followed the ideology of her late husband. In her second term, she was much more radical in her ideology compared to him. Both times, she led two coalition governments with Marxist parties.

The 1970–1977 period under Prime Minister Sirimavo Bandaranaike led to further ideological changes, culminating in the tightening of the Companies Act to take over business activities, the nationalisation of estates and land reform. In her first term, Mrs. Sirimavo Bandaranaike nationalised the leading commercial bank of the time, the Bank of Ceylon, nationalised the American oil distribution companies and withdrew finances from denominational schools (i.e. schools affiliated with a particular religion). It was also during her first term that an import and exchange control regime was introduced in response to the balance-of-payment crisis that began in 1960 due to increased domestic public expenditure, on the one hand, and an adverse movement in the terms of trade, on the other. Mrs. Bandaranaike's ideological stance also contributed to the tightening of the trade and exchange control regime rather than addressing the immediate problem of the overvalued exchange rate. Thus, with respect to trade, she instituted globalisation-unfriendly policies.

The SLFP–Marxist alliance changed the ideological makeup and pushed the majority of the coalition members to the far left. The world view changed, as did the cause–effect relationship, to presage the policy change towards greater intervention in the economy. Part of it can be explained by macroeconomic problems due to the first oil shock (1971–1973), but these are not sufficient to explain the extent of the policy shift. A definite leftist agenda was on the cards but it could not succeed as much as it could have because the Marxist creed was not in accord with the world views of the majority. Since the majority had more respect for private property but not enough of it to prevent the nationalisation of plantations, taking over of private houses and distributing them at will (but partially compensated) and nationalised Foreign-owned plantations in 1975, took over businesses under the Business Undertaking (Acquisition) Act No. 35 of 1971, and constrained firms from dismissing workers under the Termination of Employment of Workmen (Special Provisions) Act No. 45 of 1971. But, it is important to note that the policy changes in the 1970–1977 period were more of a continuation of the policy shift of 1956. It was also the necessary supplement to a political compromise needed to create a coalition with the Marxist parties. Economic policies of this period were very much influenced by the perceived macroeconomic crisis. Research done later (Athukorala and Jayasuriya, 1992) showed that the government overreacted to the crisis and contracted the economy more than necessary to make the adjustments to high oil prices.

With respect to FDI, the nationalisation of US-owned oil-distributing companies earned the wrath of the United States government, which suspended all aid to the country following the passing of the Hickenlooper Amendment in the US Congress in 1962. The nationalisations had sent a strong negative signal to the rest of the world about the intentions of the Sri Lankan government. Consequently, FDI flows declined.

With respect to the labour movement, Mrs. Bandaranaike signed the Bandaranaike–Shastri Pact with India to repatriate plantation labourers with compensation packages (1964). Her government considered it a singular achievement to send back labourers who had contributed so much to the development and maintenance of tea plantations and the country for nearly 75 years.

It was in her second term of 1970–1977 that Mrs. Bandaranaike came out of the shadow of her husband and established her own ideology, to a large extent influenced by her Marxist coalition partners. This period saw the full flowering of her dirigiste far-left ideology. It was during this period that the trade and investment regime became much more inward-oriented, and her policy stance became increasingly globalisation-unfriendly. Sri Lanka became one of the most controlled economies in the developing world and was compared to the Soviet Union in its heyday with respect to trade, investment and labour movement controls. Her Marxist coalition partners wanted to change the polity and the economy of Sri Lanka into a full-fledged socialist economy. She went along with it and became even more far left because of the JVP youth uprising in 1971. The Marxist coalition partners had convinced her that the uprising was the result of not catering enough to the socialist-leaning youth.

Thus, during her premiership, trade controls covered nearly 100 per cent of the imports as did exchange controls. Traditional exports were taxed both through export taxes and through a dual-exchange rate system. In 1970, the ministry of finance carried out a demonetisation exercise recalling high-denomination currencies and replacing new notes to reduce "black money." Nobody could leave the country without an exit permit and a person's ration book had to be surrendered prior to even a short trip. All these acts of increased control of the economy emanated from the far-left ideology Mrs. Bandaranaike acquired in office. Indeed, Mrs. Bandaranaike and her government were the most globalisation-unfriendly governments in post-independence Sri Lanka.

Major policy changes took place in 1977. It was an ideological shift that undid to a large extent the tilt to the left in the previous 7 years. The UNP victory by a large margin provided the opportunity to change policy in a diametrically opposite way. This was possible due to several reasons. First, the earlier SLFP and Marxist party's policies failed in a dramatic way as reflected in per capita GDP growth, the unemployment rate and external balance, given the huge payment deficits that emerged despite tight import controls. Second, the crisis of the cumulative effect of the oil shock provided the opportunity for the UNP to shift the political economy balance in its favour and against the SLFP-led coalition government. Third, Mrs. Bandaranaike's government had extended the term of parliament to 7 years from five without a mandate from the people, without a general election or a referendum. Fourth, the events in India, where Mrs. Gandhi had assumed an authoritarian stance, gave pause to Sri Lankan voters that a similar position could be taken by another SLFP government if elected. Finally, the election itself, which offered a strong mandate for reforms, with 80 per cent of the seats in UNP hands, provided the opportunity to undertake strong reforms.

The ideological factor played a decisive role in the election. The leader of the opposition and later the President, Mr. J. R. Jayewardene, was convinced that Sri Lanka's future lay in a more market-oriented private enterprise system rather than in the commanding heights approach that had been in place during much of the 1960s and 1970s up to his party's victory in 1977. The election was fought on ideological grounds. More than world views, what seems to have mattered in the election was principled beliefs, where the elites endorsed the return to a more market-driven economy and a cause–effect relationship that got much support from the success of the East Asian countries that had grown rapidly while

Sri Lanka had languished in the period from 1960 to 1977. With the election victory, broad-ranging reform changes were undertaken. These changes included a strong liberalisation of the trade regime, the liberalisation of the financial system in allowing interest rates to allocate short-term capital and the suspension of many egregious policies, such as the nationalisation of private enterprises. It is difficult to assign precise values for the three aspects of ideology. It is probably safe to say that two elements dominated the policy changes in the 1977–2004 period: principled beliefs and cause–effect relationships. The former was because of the change in the mindset of the elites who saw that Sri Lanka's experience of the 1970–1977 period was not going to work; the East Asian countries provided a good example to be followed. It is, however, important to emphasise the role of President J. R. Jayewardene, who was a transformational leader and had received an overwhelming mandate in the election to transform the economy.

J. R. Jayewardene came into power with a sweeping majority. He was right of centre and his government was, for the most part, one that had the exact opposite ideology of Mrs. Bandaranaike's government. In 1977 the UNP government undertook one of the most far-reaching liberalisations of the economy in the developing world, second only to that of Chile in 1974. The Chilean government under President Pinochet was not democratically elected, having come to power in a military coup in 1972. In contrast, the UNP government led by J. R. Jayewardene was elected by a huge majority (getting five-sixths of the votes in parliament). He had a strong globalisation-friendly ideology that was demonstrated in the economic policies undertaken during his government.

The trade liberalisation undertaken by his government did away with almost all the import quotas and also eliminated exchange controls, leading to a market-determined exchange rate. It also reduced tariff protection significantly, leading to a more open economy than in the previous 20 years. Variance in protection was reduced so that resource allocation had to be improved. With respect to financial markets, interest rates were liberalised and there was great reliance placed on monetary policy to steer the economy.

With respect to FDI, Prime Minister Jayewardene (later president after 1978) took a strong globalisation-friendly attitude towards creating the Greater Colombo Economic Commission (GCEC) with wide-ranging powers to facilitate FDI. The investment regime was reformed in several ways. GCEC offered many incentives, such as the creation of Free Trade Zones with infrastructure, ten-year tax holidays, duty-free imported inputs and majority ownership by foreigners. Thus, in all these respects, the government was globalisation-friendly. Restrictions on foreign travel and employment were completely removed. However, inward movement of unskilled labour was not allowed, only skilled labourers associated with FDI ventures were allowed to move. He sent emissaries to the USA to encourage its corporations to invest in Sri Lanka. Two major semiconductor corporations, Harris Corporation and Motorola, came to evaluate the situation, but political uncertainty arising out of the July 1983 anti-Tamil riots and the rise of the LTTE discouraged them from investing in Sri Lanka.

While the Jayewardene government was globalisation-friendly, it failed to maintain appropriate macroeconomic policies to allow the forces of globalisation to lead to better resource allocation due to the overheating of the economy from huge public investments. It led to the now well-known Dutch disease phenomenon that appreciated the exchange rate, inflated the economy and led to huge current account deficits in the balance of payments. The macroeconomic instability it engendered began to unravel the economic liberalisation, and the globalisation-friendly ideology of President Jayewardene began to wane. Consequently, the pace of reforms slowed and stopped, to be started by President Premadasa who succeeded President Jayewardene. He was not an enthusiast of economic liberalisation and globalisation-friendly policies. Besides, the war against the LTTE terrorists began to escalate in the late 1980s as did the insurgency of the JVP, making the country unattractive for FDI. Meanwhile, the appreciation of the exchange rate led to a loss of competitiveness of exports and import substitute activities.

While the changing political power led to different economic policies, such was not the case with the government of Chandrika Kumaratunga. There was no ideological shift even in 1994 when Kumaratunga became president. The 1977 policy paradigm continued. She used her leadership to keep things as they were, and she used the existing institutions and the public service to keep most of the policy regimes in place under the UNP. The role of institutions was enhanced after they had been under inordinate political control during her mother's regime.

One important development arising from this period is that the government took a liberal attitude to overseas employment of Sri Lankan citizens. This helped to earn foreign exchange in the late 1990s and the early 2000s and was second only to the amount earned by garment exports. Also, overseas employment's distributive effect on the rural sector was very positive. In 2013, the administration prohibited mothers with children below age five from leaving the country for foreign employment. This was in response to growing concern that the absence of the mothers would lead to high social costs with young children not having the support of both parents.

President Rajapaksa was also a transformational leader. He was not ideologically predisposed to being globalisation-friendly. This can be inferred when one reads the *Mahinda Chintana*. He has to be recognised as a transformational leader mainly because of his political achievement of bringing peace to the country where the LTTE terrorist organisation was soundly defeated and its leadership eliminated. The peace that this brought provided a rare opportunity for the country to benefit from globalisation. There seemed to be an ideological shift by stealth rather than by announcement as witnessed by the halting of the reform agenda, the lack of fiscal discipline and the creeping and non-transparent use of trade controls. There was also no discussion of policy in public forums except to justify some questionable policy outcomes such as inflation, foreign borrowing at commercial interest rates and bloated public expenditures.

After President Rajapaksa came to power in 2005, there was no significant trade reform. What was attempted in June 2010 after the defeat of the LTTE terrorists was not significant. While it reduced some tariffs, it may have even increased effective rates of protection and also the variance in protection that prevented an efficient allocation of resources. But, part of President Rajapaksa's earlier reluctance to consider economic liberalisation, apart from his ideological stance, was that this was not easy to do when there was a civil war going on in the country with only a short respite with the Cease Fire Agreement (CFA) in 2002. This was because the war needed a large amount of resources and a part of it was financed through increased tariffs and tariff-like taxes called para tariffs. There were at least eight such tariffs such as the Value-Added Tax, the Social Responsibility Levy, National Building Tax, Excise duties, and similar para tariffs. In addition, there were special levies on 22 essential imports. While an attempt was made to reduce the burden of these taxes on foreign trade in 2010, it fell short of improving the incentive structure, raising effective protection rates and increasing their variance. Moreover, there was little effort to reduce the bias against exports (Chapter 9, "Export Growth and Appropriate Macroeconomic Policy: A Necessary Nexus"). Consequently, Sri Lanka's share in world exports of the principal commodities declined as did its share in GDP.

Another feature that inhibited great participation in trade was the appreciation of the exchange rate that acted as a tax on exports. The large inflows of foreign loans mainly from China helped keep the exchange rate appreciated, leading to another Dutch disease phenomenon, reminiscent of the 1980s. After delaying the adjustment of the exchange rate for nearly 6 years, the Central Bank devalued the currency by nearly 20 per cent in 2012, following an unusual announcement of the devaluation of the Sri Lanka rupee by 3.0 per cent in the 2011 budget speech. The Central Bank continued to argue that the exchange rate was not overvalued despite higher domestic inflation compared to Sri Lanka's trading partners, rising current account deficits and loss of reserves which was partly reversed in 2009–2012 with the help of a Stand-by Arrangement from the IMF.

The Rajapaksa government was not able to attract FDI in appreciable amounts even 5 years after the end of the civil war, when the US and Europe were recovering from the GFC. One reason was that the government was able to borrow large sums of foreign exchange from official Chinese sources. A situation like that of the UNP government in the 1977–1980 period has arisen from borrowing at higher interest rates. In the earlier periods low-interest loans, with long maturity and grace periods had been available. The Rajapaksa government's attitude towards privatisation also reveals its left-of-centre ideological bias, which is reminiscent of the 1970–1977 period. A globalisation-unfriendly ideology continued to dominate the Rajapaksa government policies.

4.6 Comparative Ideological Experience of Sri Lanka Across Countries

Sri Lanka, India and Bangladesh had similar initial conditions, factor endowments that were labour-intensive, and globalisation-friendly and -unfriendly policies that were driven by the ideologies of different political groups during different periods (refer to Chapter 2).

Inter-country comparisons show similar ideologies which were governed by different administrations. Globalisation-unfriendly policies were followed during the Nehru and Bandaranaike administrations, where both India and Sri Lanka were constrained by inward-looking approaches.

In 1977, Sri Lanka liberalised the economy under the administration of President J. R. Jayewardene and reaped the benefits of a globalisation-friendly period with the consequent trade openness and economic growth.

In the 1990s, India and Bangladesh came under the new ideological thinking of Prime Ministers P. V. Narasimha Rao and Sheikh Hasina, respectively, and saw a period of trade liberalisation that led to steady economic growth.

4.6.1 The Pre-liberalisation and the Post-liberalisation Period in India

India's approach to globalisation can be identified through the analysis of three distinct periods: 1947–1970s, 1991–2014 and 2014 to the present date. India was compelled to go into liberalisation because of the balance-of-payment crisis that it faced at that time which made India seek help from the IMF. The difference between India, Sri Lanka and Bangladesh was that the liberalisation of the latter two was determined by the ideological positions taken by the presidents in power.

The period of 1947–1970 showed the ideological preferences of Prime Minister Nehru, which impacted policy and globalisation indicators such as trade, FDI, and the labour movement. According to Aluwalia,[18] there was a strong bias in favour of strict government control of the economy, which discouraged FDI and imports to the country.

When comparing the approaches towards open policies in trade, it is seen that after independence in 1947 and the separation of India and Pakistan, India used more socialist-inspired policies with extensive regulations that were globalisation-unfriendly. This was when Prime Minister Nehru adopted a model of planning developed by the Indian Planning Commission which formulated 5-year development plans. The 1947–1970 period was characterised by strict regulations and state control through licensing of businesses, "License Raj," heavy protectionism and nationalisation of leading private enterprises. Prime Minister Nehru's government introduced policies that were based on the Soviet model. The restrictive nature and the state dominance of the allocation of resources demonstrate that this period was globalisation-unfriendly.

Consequently, in the post-1970 period, Prime Minister Rajiv Gandhi's administration undertook a clear relaxing of stringent government regulations, licenses and import controls. The policies were more liberal

---

[18] Aluwalia (2018).

compared to those of Prime Minister Indira Gandhi. According to[19] Aluwalia, basic controls still existed, but they were flexible at the margins, which meant that industrial licensing systems existed, with some industries being exempted.

In 1991, with a new Congress government, India saw a rapid adoption of economic reforms, which were mainly implemented to bring about macroeconomic stability that could address the balance-of-payment crisis and reduce the high rate of inflation. In 1991, according to Aluwalia, the foreign reserves of the country reduced to US$1.1 billion, which was equivalent to the payment of two weeks of imports. At this stage, there was support from the IMF and the World Bank to help the economy use liberalising reforms. According to[20] Aluwalia (2016), the IMF programme ended before the expected date and was effective.

The economic reforms that were implemented in 1991 under Prime Minister V. P. Narasimha Rao and then Finance Minister Dr. Manmohan Singh were outward-oriented with more liberalisation policies such as the abolition of the licensing system,[21] divesting the equity holdings of the government in public institutions, and a fiscal policy which ensured that the fiscal deficit and debt were reduced while there were freer imports and exports with the easing of regulations and tariffs. It is clear that the post-1970 period showed a globalisation-friendly policy change.

Prime Minister Manmohan Singh, who ushered in economic reforms during the period 1991–1996 when he was minister of finance, further promoted economic liberalisation in India during his administration. Policies were focused on sustaining economic growth with greater market access and technological change. He also implemented several infrastructure programmes through Public–Private Partnerships and envisaged an average growth rate of 7 per cent during his administration.

India has been growing fast over the last decade and continues to show a similar growth rate during Prime Minister Narendra Modi's regime. He was the former chief minister of Gujarat. His economic reform programme was globalisation-friendly and followed most of the initiatives that were started by the previous government. According to

---

[19] *Ibid.*
[20] Aluwalia (2016).
[21] Aluwalia (2002).

Panagariya,[22] India leapt in a decade from being the 5th largest economy to the 3rd largest economy.

The Indian economic reforms that led to liberalisation have been long term and varied, ranging from employment creation, infrastructure development and sanitisation (Swachh Bharat and Nal Se Jal initiatives) to digitisation (the adoption of Aadhaar, through bank accounts context of telephone transfer) and focusing on poverty reduction. Implementing a unified tax system through the Goods and Services Tax enabled the unification of the complex tax system of the country. However, according to Panagariya, the country has had a reverse liberalisation policy with much focus on import substitution, characterised by high rates of protection through customs duties. This hampers competition in the world market for India's exports.

India was trying to reduce the import bill by building up its domestic capacity and the manufacturing base of the country. Panagariya[23] stated that India is experiencing high growth rates through fast growth in infrastructure development and that this could be improved further by reducing customs duties through a more open and liberal approach.

Mr. Modi's government has shown a globalisation-friendly approach through liberal policies, but its openness can be improved so as to gather further benefits. Also, there are many other economic reforms that would enable India to attract more FDI by reforming the labour market of the country.

4.6.2 The Pre-liberalisation and Post-liberalisation Period in Bangladesh

Bangladesh gained independence in 1971 when the country separated from Pakistan. The main objective of having their own states, were to have political and economic freedom to pursue their own economic policies.

After the 1980s, import duties gradually reduced along with the reduction in the quantitative restrictions of 1985 and the simplified tariff system of 1986.[24] Prime Minister Sheikh Hasina's (1996–2001 and

---

[22] Panagariya (2023a).
[23] Panagariya (2023b).
[24] Athukorala *et al.* (2011).

2009–2023) leadership played an important role in moving from a globalisation-unfriendly policy to globalisation-friendly policies.

In 1990, trade liberalisation was one of the economic reforms that changed the economy towards a more globalisation-friendly policy environment. 8 The support for structural adjustment policies focused more on openness to trade, FDI, an industrial exchange rate policy and privatisation of state-owned enterprises. With liberalisation, the economy grew rapidly by stimulating exports in the manufacturing sectors and through job creation. Many other sectors that were managed by the state were privatised, such as health, banking, education and the new export-processing zones.

4.6.3 *A Comparison of Sri Lanka, India and Bangladesh*

Both India and Bangladesh have been latecomers to economic reforms when compared to Sri Lanka, which conducted reforms in the late 1970s. Economic reforms in both countries started almost a decade later, but continued mainly because of the consistent ideologies towards globalisation-friendly policies that were carried out with the setting up of an economic reform agenda. S. W. R. D. Bandaranaike's period in Sri Lanka was globalisation-unfriendly that led to low growth rates till 1977. Even though there were many initiatives that opened the economy to the world, they did not continue unlike in the administrations of Prime Ministers Singh and Modi, where we saw a steady economic growth path since the 1990s with a progressive reform agenda that led to digitisation and improvement of financial literacy in the informal sectors of India.

A similar trend was seen in Bangladesh where Prime Minister Hasina's leadership since 2009 led to a reform agenda focused on the improvement of female labour participation through education, improved access to low-cost internet and large-scale mobile penetration. This increased economic activity and reduced poverty.

It was more the ideological position of Prime Minister J.R. Jayawardena which led to the liberalisation in Sri Lanka. India too liberalised the economy due to the ideological position of Prime Minister V. P. Narasimha Rao and the implementation of the programme by then Finance Minister Dr. Manmohan Singh. In the case of Bangladesh also, Prime Minister Hasina was in favour of liberalisation as the rising growth rates of the East Asian economies provided examples to follow. Ideologies played an important role in all three countries, more so in

Bangladesh and Sri Lanka and less so in India. India was compelled to move towards globalisation-friendly policies because of the support it sought from the IMF during its balance-of-payment crisis. All three countries saw a direct increase in growth rates following liberalisation.

4.7 Conclusion

The ideological factor had an important impact on policymaking in Sri Lanka, India and Bangladesh. This is revealed through the ideological positions taken by the presidents and prime ministers of these countries. Another important factor that influenced policymaking in Sri Lanka to some extent was the impact of multinational financial institutions like the World Bank and the IMF as will be discussed in the following two chapters.

Chapter 5

The Impact of International Financial Institutions on Globalisation: World Bank's Analysis in the 1970s and 1980s

5.1 Introduction

One aspect of globalisation in developing countries which has not been discussed earlier is the role of international financial institutions. As countries became integrated across the world through trade, FDI and labour movements, economic analysis (including microeconomic analysis) and financial support were needed through international institutions such as the World Bank and the IMF. The World Bank deals with development and the IMF deals with issues related to stabilisation.

This chapter offers a contrast to the chapter "Through Eminent Eyes: A Fifty-year Retrospective as a Background to Globalisation" (Chapter 3), which examined the economic issues that Sri Lanka faced in the late 1950s. The contrast arises not only from the eminence of the economists who visited the country in the late 1950s but also because they had no agenda to lend money and no official status. They came at the invitation of the Director of Planning, Dr. Gamani Corea, on behalf of Prime Minister S. W. R. D. Bandaranaike and were not paid for their work.[1]

This chapter also indicates how economic analysis changed over time. In the late 1980s and early 1990s, a more incentive-based economic

---

[1] This chapter had its origins in an internal review of the World Bank's economic work.

framework and analysis was applied, only to be at least partially abandoned in the first decade after 2005 where many other issues were examined by the World Bank staff, including the environment, women's issues and institutional issues. Some of the "bread and butter" of macroeconomic and incentive-related issues were "crowded out" by the new issues.

The World Bank's country economic work, which is mostly economic analysis, is intended to identify and analyse key economic issues to provide a basis for the World Bank to carry out a policy dialogue with a country, inform other donors of development priorities and underpin the World Bank's lending operations. This chapter postulates that high-quality economic analysis must be the basis of the World Bank's policy dialogue and lending and that the quality of this analysis ultimately determines the quality of support the World Bank can give to countries in both policy advice and loans to foster economic development. Whatever the status of the informal dialogue with a country in respect of particular policies and projects, this chapter assumes that the main issues, and policy actions to address these issues, must be identified clearly and included in the country's economic analysis so as to inform the country, the World Bank's senior management and the aid community of key economic issues, their relative importance and policy action to address these issues.

Subject to the above-mentioned postulates, this chapter evaluates the economic work on Sri Lanka at that time (for details, see Appendix A). It is largely confined to economic reports rather than sector reports. The purpose of this evaluation is to look at the strengths and weaknesses of the economy as a case study on which some generalisations can be made. This chapter evaluates the economic analysis done on Sri Lanka in the 1970–1985 period. Appendix B of this chapter has a summary of the economic and sector reports.

Section 5.2 discusses the key economic issues faced by the country based on Sri Lankan and other sources largely external to the World Bank. Section 5.3 then examines the World Bank's economic analysis with the main purpose of establishing the issues identified, the priorities attached to the issues and whether they were analysed with sufficient perspective and depth to meet the objectives of the World Bank's economic analysis. Section 5.4 summarises the main findings of the evaluation, recognising the main strengths and deficiencies in economic analysis on Sri Lanka during this period.

5.2 Economic Issues Faced by Sri Lanka in the 1970–1985 Period

5.2.1 *Background*

In Sri Lanka, the period from independence in 1948 to 1960 was characterised by an open economy, one which achieved a higher standard of living and quality of life than most other South Asian or East Asian countries. At independence Sri Lanka's per capita income was the third highest in the region, after Japan and Malaysia. Life expectancy at birth was 54 years compared to Japan's 57.5 years. Primary and secondary school enrolment was 54 per cent, very high for a developing country.

Sri Lanka was a relatively rich country in 1960, with a per capita income of $152, twice that of India ($68), higher than Thailand ($97) and close to that of Korea ($154). Hla Myint showed that Kravis's adjusted figures for per capita income of $961 in 1960 were higher than those in all the countries mentioned here, save Japan where GDP growth averaged 5 per cent per year. This progress was based on an export economy producing tea, rubber, and coconuts that was organised as plantations, using relatively abundant land, immigrant labour and foreign entrepreneurship. Coexisting with this liberal policy environment was a system of social expenditure introduced during the Second World War to provide subsidised education, health and food. By 1960, educational, life expectancy and nutritional standards in Sri Lanka were higher than in all other Asian countries except Japan. As long as the level of these expenditures remained low, there was no adverse impact on production and growth.

The 1960–1970 decade witnessed a very distinct change in the Sri Lankan economy. First, compared to the earlier decade, world commodity prices declined. Second, the burden of social expenditures became heavy, as social programmes expanded (following the 1956 elections that brought into power nationalist–socialist leaders), while export-based revenues fell. Third, economic interventions became pervasive, due to a changing political philosophy as well as attempts to capture more income from the plantation sector. For example, a battery of trade and exchange rate controls was introduced in the 1960–1961 period, which remained in effect until 1977. Domestic restrictions were pervasive and included investment licensing, controls of interest rates and credit ceilings, and various forms of interventions in the labour market through minimum wages, restrictions and social security legislation. The public sector expanded rapidly, from a few state enterprises in 1960 to more than 100 in 1970. These were concentrated in the industrial sector, producing import substitution goods under a high protective wall.[2]

By 1970, the economy had come to be characterised by slow growth, as a result of the distorted policies and subsidies introduced in the previous decade, and began to rapidly command more than 8 per cent of GDP in 1970. In order to finance these expenditures, the export sector was taxed heavily. As expected, high unemployment ensued due to the twin effects of limits to import substitution being reached in a small market and subsidising capital leading to distortionary effects on the allocation of resources in the country, through the fixed exchange rate and interest rates.

5.2.2 *The 1970–1977 Period*

The interventions in the economy further multiplied during the 1970–1977 period. First, the trade regime became even more stringent as quantitative restrictions (QRs) were reintroduced after a brief (1968–1969) liberalisation episode. Second, tax policies began to bite harder since public revenues (based mostly on external trade) were inadequate to finance growing social expenditures. Ceilings were put on personal incomes to keep them low. Third, public control of economic activity extended beyond the industrial sector in the form of the nationalisation of the plantation sector, a sector that had been the mainspring of growth in the economy for more than a century and a half. Various private enterprises were also nationalised as essential services.

The external environment also changed with the first oil shock (1973–1975). Because of the progressive compression of imports, the economy lost its flexibility. Policymakers justified the controls on the basis of a worsening external environment. Social expenditures were reduced sporadically in 1973 as their burden had become excessive. However, these attempts failed and had little prospect of being carried through as they

---

[2] See Rajapatirana (1988), Deepak and Rajapatirana (1989) and Athukorala and Rajapatirana (2000).

were neither based on conviction nor based on a well-thought-out programme.

On the eve of the 1977 liberalisation, the Sri Lankan economy could be characterised in the following manner: an expanded, largely publicly owned industrial sector based on import substitution had, by and large, encroached upon the export economy; and an increasingly stringent trade regime had emerged with greater recourse to QRs than in any previous period of Sri Lanka's economic history. The plantation sector was in a depressed state, having been taxed through various means to finance the burgeoning social expenditures and, since 1960, affected by the losses of public enterprises. Moreover, in 1975, plantations were nationalised. The increasingly poor growth performance, arising from large and pervasive distortions of inadequate national savings and inflation caused by the Central Bank-financed budget deficits, further accentuated the symptoms of an economy in crisis.

The fundamental issues at that time were as follows:

(i) There emerged a highly distorted economy, arising out of controls introduced in trade, investment, labour markets and finance, necessitating the reduction of these distortions to resume growth.
(ii) There was an inability to support the exploding social expenditures on food, health and education. Reductions of these expenditures were a prerequisite to raise savings. The targeted use of subsidies was necessary if the objective was to provide a safety net to the poor.
(iii) Arising out of the distortions and insufficient savings were low rates of GDP growth (2.1 per cent for the 1970–1977 period), high unemployment (24 per cent of the labour force by 1977) and many scarcities.[3]
(iv) Large external shocks arose from oil price increases.[4] The resilience of the economy to shocks had to be increased by allowing greater flexibility in labour, capital and exchange markets.

---

[3] Myint (1985) quoted Surjit Bhalla who estimated that Kravis's adjusted figures imply a negative GDP growth of 1.2 per cent for the 1960–1978 period (see Bhalla and Glewwe 1985).

[4] Bela Balassa and Desmond McCarthy estimated that the combined external shock on Sri Lanka arising out of adverse terms of trade, high interest rates and reduced demand for exports was 25 per cent of GNP in the 1979–1981 period as compared with an average of

5.2.3 *The 1978–1985 Period*

This period stands in sharp contrast to the 1970–1977 period. A major effort was made to reduce price distortions with the start of trade liberalisation in 1977. By 1977, Sri Lanka had no choice but to liberalise the economy. Nearly two decades of progressively stringent government controls had imposed high costs on the economy. The trade liberalisation undertaken in 1977 was thus a radical departure from the status quo.

An impressive list of measures was adopted starting in November 1977. The Sri Lankan Rupee was devalued by 46.2 per cent against the US dollar and was unified at the higher rate, which had prevailed under the previous dual rate. A floating rate was then adopted. Most QRs were replaced with tariffs. Price controls were removed except for a few "essential" consumer goods.

Measures to attract foreign private investments were adopted, including changes in regulations governing the repatriation of profits and foreign investment licensing.

At the same time, domestic bank interest rates were allowed to increase sharply, removing the Central Bank-administered interest rate ceilings that had been in effect for all types of commercial bank deposits and loans. The government also permitted the entry of additional foreign banks to foster competition with domestic commercial banks. Entry of foreign banks had been restricted since 1961.

The procurement price of rice was raised by 21 per cent. At the same time, a number of food subsidies were removed along with the advent of liberalisation. These included subsidies for rice and the introduction of a food stamp programme in which the number of subsidy recipients was sharply reduced and the total costs of subsidies were cut. Food subsidies in 1977 accounted for 23.6 per cent of government revenues and 6.3 per cent of the GDP. By 1981, food stamps accounted for 10.5 per cent of revenues and 1.9 per cent of the GDP. Reduced subsidies were targeted at the poorer half of the population. This was coupled with rising prices, reflecting the import costs of rice and flour, for those not eligible for the subsidies.

The liberalisation, while a major step in improving resource allocation, left an unfinished agenda. The measures discussed previously needed

---

6 per cent for developing countries. See "Adjustment Policies in Developing Countries," World Bank, Policy Papers, July 1984.

to be carried forward in a number of respects to complete the original plan of liberalisation. The unfinished agenda included a reduction in the variance of ineffective protective rates, which had led to a neutral trade regime along with the maintenance of the real effective exchange rate so as to continue the promotion of cost competitiveness. Also required was the liberalisation of the domestic capital market, the freeing up of capital transactions and the removal of a number of existing constraints on private direct investments. Labour market rigidities needed to be reduced. It had become very rigid due to such labour legislation as minimum wages, limits to firing employees and social security laws. Finally, the size of the public sector remained large and important.

Despite this unfinished agenda, by most standards, the 2 years following liberalisation were eminently successful, with the economy rebounding with GDP growth rates of 8.2 and 6.3 per cents in 1978 and 1979, respectively, and continuing to grow at 5.8 per cent in 1980. GDP growth averaged 6 per cent a year during the 1978–1985 period. The unemployment rate was halved to 12 per cent of the labour force by 1983.

By 1980, however, signs were already beginning to appear that the economic situation was bound to worsen. Three factors stand out from the economic developments in the 1978–1985 period.

The first was the undertaking of a number of "lead" projects — the Accelerated Mahaweli Programme (a multi-purpose river basin project) and the housing and urban renewal programmes. These projects, which were coupled with steadily responding private investments, raised the total investment rate to 33.8 per cent of the GDP at current market prices in 1980 compared to 14.4 per cent in 1977.[5] The Mahaweli project alone accounted for 44 per cent of public investment in the 1982–1984 period. Public expenditures also began to increase as the reductions in expenditures brought about by the reduction of food subsidies were more than offset by transfers to public enterprises that continued to incur losses. This substantial increase in expenditures was largely financed by foreign borrowings. Domestic savings declined as increased private savings were more than offset by negative public savings. The real growth of consumption and investment exceeded the growth of aggregate output

---

[5]The river basin development scheme was designed to provide irrigation and power. It is referred to as an accelerated programme since the original scheme that was planned to be completed in 30 years was reduced to only 8 years.

during the 1979–1983 period.[6] Linked to the very ambitious public investments programme was a huge capital inflow.

Second, by 1980, the second oil price hike had taken place and the international economy was going into a recession. Adverse terms of trade combined with reduced volumes of exports (the latter mostly due to supply constraints on the tree crop sector) worsened the trade balance. In part, the increased capital inflow which led to an appreciation of the real exchange rate (Dutch disease phenomenon) induced an adverse trade balance, while the increased price of oil imports after 1979, and the recession which followed, played a significant role in the deterioration of the balance of payments. Investment goods related to the Accelerated Mahaweli project dominated the composition of imports.

Finally, domestically and foreign-induced macroeconomic shocks (i.e. the accelerated public investments and world recession), revisionist thinking among some members of the government and the reassertion of the penchant of the bureaucracy for control led to a number of setbacks to liberalisation. The real exchange rate appreciated, reversing the gain in competitiveness achieved through the devaluation. Inflation exceeded 26 per cent in 1980, and a huge current account deficit opened up, exceeding 16 per cent of the GDP. Various *ad hoc* measures were introduced to limit imports, which increased the level of and variance in protection. In addition, credit, ceilings and differential interest rates were reintroduced.

The macroeconomic imbalances which emerged in 1980 continued up to 1985. During the 1980–1985 period, some attempts were made to control aggregate demand arising out of a runaway public investment programme. Public expenditures were reduced. The huge capital inflow also slowed down. The current account deficit was reduced to 0.9 per cent of the GDP by 1984. However, the economy was no longer in macroeconomic balance with high inflation and an unsustainable current account deficit, while the incentive structure had deteriorated since 1978.

Three major issues stand out in the 1977–1985 period:

(i) Macroeconomic stabilisation was needed following runaway expansion in the public expenditure programme.
(ii) Completing the unfinished agenda of trade liberalisation and needed improvements in the regulatory regime.

---

[6] Consumption in real terms grew at an average annual rate of 7.5 per cent during the 1978–1983 period, while investment grew by 9.7 per cent over the same period.

(iii) Increasing the flexibility of the economy to withstand external shocks by removing obstacles to the adjustment process; obstacles that arise from labour and capital market rigidities and administrative regulations.

To sum up, the salient economic challenges of the 1970–1977 period were improving resource allocation and reducing large public expenditures. This is in contrast to the 1978–1985 period in which the key issues were restoring macroeconomic stability and continuity along the path of liberalisation of the economy.

5.3 World Bank's Economic Work on Sri Lanka

This section examines whether the World Bank's economic work had addressed the key issues facing the Sri Lankan economy (as identified in Section 5.2) and whether the issues were analysed with sufficient perspective and depth to meet the objectives of the World Bank's economic and sector work. This is followed by a discussion of more specific strengths and weaknesses in the reports.

5.3.1 *Economic Work: 1970–1977*

The dominant issues of the 1970–1977 period, ranked in the order of their importance, were pervasive distortions in both goods and factor markets, insufficient savings arising from large consumer subsidies and the lack of flexibility in an economy that had been put in a straightjacket of controls.

In contrast, the World Bank's economic reports dealt mostly with the insufficient savings issues, related to public savings. The 1973 report, for example, analysed the 1972 fiscal performance in detail.[7] It emphasised reduced growth of current expenditures arising from greater control of such expenditures by the Treasury, the reduction in military expenditures (with the ending of the 1971 insurgency) and the shift from the procurement of rice from the domestic market to imports.[8] The 10 per cent increase in public revenue achieved that year was welcomed.

---

[7] *"Economic Outlook for Sri Lanka"* January 23, 1973.
[8] Since the import prices of rice were kept low with an overvalued exchange rate, Sri Lanka had a curious situation when a reduction in domestic procurement due to a drought or other crop failure improved budgetary performance!

The report concluded that public investment was the key to economic development. Two reasons were cited for this view: the political structure (Mrs. Bandaranaike's socialist government was in power during this period) and the perception of poor prospects for private investments.[9] The report acquiesced with the prevailing view of the World Bank that ownership did not matter for economic performance!

What was conspicuously absent in these reports, particularly in the case of the 1973, 1975 and 1977 reports, was the limited attention paid to efficiency and the elimination of distortions. Appropriate price policies to encourage agricultural production were recommended and the increase in export duties was recognised as "increasing the imbalance in price incentives between production for the domestic and foreign market." However, contrary to this concern, the report then went on to comment that the import surcharges imposed to raise revenues would also increase the availability of foreign exchange. Thus, even when looking at the revenue side of existing controls, the reports did not take up the incentive aspect of the controls. In other words, in these reports, efficiency considerations took a back seat to resource mobilisation in the public sector.

Another example of the relative absence of efficiency considerations was seen in the treatment of the external sector during this period. A continuing theme in the reports related to the declining terms of trade.[10] The reports recommend the diversification of exports without regarding efficiency considerations. The 1976 economic report categorically stated that Sri Lankans' economic difficulties emanated from "structural overdependence" on a few primary commodities. Diversification was seen as the necessary structural adjustment, when in fact tea, rubber and coconut exports had been the mainstay of the export-led growth of the country. What was also missed in these reports was that these exports were hardly given a chance to contribute to growth. Export incomes were very heavily taxed due to a narrow tax base through high export duties on all three

---

[9]The 1975 CEM considered the private sector as an "element" in development while emphasising the importance of public sector investments.

[10]Economic reports from 1973, 1974, 1976, 1977 and 1978 uncritically commented on declining terms of trade without the qualification that in 1970–1971, terms of trade were at a peak and the decline in the barter terms of trade does not by itself imply worsening welfare.

crops. These taxes amounted to nearly a quarter of the total revenues.[11] For instance, the marginal tax rate on the FOB price of tea was close to 50 per cent, not including the taxes implied in the dual exchange rate. As a result of this taxation, tree crop output declined by 1.12 per cent per year between the 1969–1971 and 1976–1978 periods.[12] The share of the key crop exports in total exports declined from 77.9 per cent in 1970–1977 to 46.2 per cent in 1982.

Moreover, these traditional exports were at a disadvantage due to the high import protection given especially to manufacturers. For example, the effective rate of protection for the manufacturers as a group was 38 per cent in 1981 (no estimates are available before this time).[13] Even assuming that traditional exports were not subject to border taxes, this would still represent a serious disadvantage. However, given that these exports were subject to at least a 25 per cent export tax, the disadvantage of the tariff structure is even higher than that implied by the ERP estimate for manufactures. It is important to realise that by 1981 most import tariffs were reduced so that the levels of effective protection accorded to imports, and therefore the bias against these exports, were even higher during the 1970–1977 period. The trade bias index for traditional exports was 0.64 compared to 1.24 for manufacturing in 1970. By 1977, the bias increased to 0.59 for traditional exports compared to 1.59 for manufactures.[14]

These exports were further disadvantaged by the dual exchange rate system which acted as a powerful tax subsidy system.[15] The system implied a 55 per cent tax on traditional exports compared to non-traditional exports or non-essential imports.

It is, therefore, no surprise that Sri Lanka's shares in the world markets for these exports progressively declined (Table 5.1).

---

[11] The 1977 report states, "substantial efforts have been made to diversify the economy but they have been inadequate to offset the efforts of various diversities." These diversities are recognised as adverse terms of trade and droughts.
[12] Bertrand (1985).
[13] Cuthbertson and Khan (1981).
[14] The trade bias index is the ratio of the nominal effective exchange rate for exports to nominal effective exchange rate for imports. See Cuthbertson (1985). Athukorala and Jayasuriya (1993).
[15] The Foreign Exchange Entitlement Scheme introduced in 1968 granted a 55 per cent higher exchange rate for non-traditional exports, compared to traditional exports. The percentage was later increased to 65 per cent.

Table 5.1. Share of Sri Lanka's Tree Crop Exports in World Exports

Year	Tea	Rubber	Coconut
1970	28.2	5.5	9.4
1979	20.7	3.9	3

Source: IMF. Direction of Trade (1982).

This decrease in market share was the result of the high taxation of these exports through income and export taxes, the bias arising from import restrictions and the dual exchange rate during the 1968–1977 period. Yet, the World Bank reports were exhorting the Sri Lankans to diversify, when in fact the "structural weakness" arose from the heavy taxation rather than anything inherently wrong with the exports. In other words, the World Bank reports were advocating that more should be done to promote so-called non-traditional exports, while the main reason for the decline in traditional exports was insufficient incentives.[16] The surprise is not that these exports performed poorly, but that they performed at all! Moreover, no diversification could come without overall growth, and overall growth was stilted by existing policy-induced distortions. Unfortunately, diversification was seen as a goal when in fact it would have been a natural outcome of growth in the economy.

The neglect of the efficiency issues is also seen in the treatment of the analysis of the dual exchange rate system. The 1975 economic report, for example, welcomed the additional public revenues arising from the system. Only limited attention was paid by the World Bank reports to the misallocation of resources arising out of the dual exchange rate system.[17]

Regarding imports, the World Bank reports extolled the country's import substitution drive in food crops, although the reports did also warn against import substitution in industry, the latter, however, with some moderation. The arguments used to support import substitution in food arose from "food security" considerations and the alleged saving of foreign exchange through the import substitution in food to import capital

---

[16] As late as 1981, a World Bank report stated, "The tree crops remained the Achilles heel of Sri Lanka's development acting as a strong drag on output, export and government revenues." 1981 CEM, paragraph 1.04.

[17] Sri Lanka, Country Economic Memorandum (CEM), Report No. 1425-CE, 1977.

and raw materials (sic).[18] For example, the reduction of rice imports in total rice consumption was welcomed in the 1975 report. However, no attention was paid to the cost or efficiency considerations stemming from this import substitution.[19] This uncritical acclaim for import substitution in food crops goes on even in the World Bank reports of the 1980s.[20]

By their continued concern about the adequacy of savings, the World Bank reports seemed to have ranked this as the primary issue in the 1970–1977 period. However, no attempt was made to highlight private sector savings or conditions necessary to raise these savings at the given level of income. The country had a poor savings record due to a number of reasons. The first reason was the enormously repressed financial system. Real interest rates remained negative and the real value of financial assets declined throughout this period.[21] Second, the majority of public corporations incurred losses during this period which were made good by government transfers. Such transfers to public corporations amounted to 5–6 per cent of public current expenditures, not to mention the initial capital costs borne by the government. Third, other policies such as the already mentioned ceilings on personal income took their toll on private sector savings. Fourth, throughout the 1970–1977 period, the private sector was under threat of imposition of various new restrictions, nationalisations and public acquisition of urban property.[22] Under these circumstances,

---

[18] 1975 CEM.

[19] Trent Bertrand had estimated that the supply price of rice in Sri Lanka was Rs. 79 per bushel in 1984, adjusting for the large fertiliser subsidy. This compares with the supply price of Rs. 25 per bushel in Burma. Even after adjusting for transport costs, subsidies in Burma for fertiliser and its overvalued exchange rate, the marginal cost of producing rice was much higher in Sri Lanka than in Burma. In Mahaweli Basin areas where irrigation was heavily subsidised, the supply price of rice would have been around Rs. 330 per bushel in the median areas and Rs. 500 per bushel in the high cost areas: "Food Self-Sufficiency in Asia," WDR 1985.

[20] The 1983 CEM welcomed the increased self-sufficiency in rice from 33 per cent in the 1970–1977 period to 12 per cent in the 1970–1977 period to the 12 per cent in 1978–1983 period.

[21] Khatkhate (1982).

[22] For example, after a large part of the tree crop (plantations sector) was nationalised, the 1976 World Bank report concluded that with the nationalisation, the previous uncertainties in the tree crop sector would be removed and that would pave the way for higher growth of the sector. The World Bank at the time had no appreciation of the private sector's role in the economy.

private savings were constrained. No account of these circumstances was analysed when the World Bank reports highlighted the need for increasing national savings.

The first important issue is the incompatibility attempting to complete the liberalisation of the economy at the same time increasing public expenditure that associated with the Mahaweli project. The second important issue is to take measures to stabilise the economy because at that time public expenditure was increasing due to Mahaweli project. The issues of Macroeconomic stability have been discussed below.

The third important issue that was relevant for this period was increasing the flexibility of the labour and capital markets, given that the oil price hikes had necessitated an adjustment in the economy. Given the stated distortions, the country would have had to adjust its relative prices even if the oil price hike had not taken place. In respect to the labour market, many rigidities prevailed. Minimum wages were enforced. This was in response to a highly potent trade union movement that had aligned itself with different political parties. Regulations regarding hiring and firing employees had also robbed the labour market of much flexibility. As a consequence of high real wages in the formal sector and various distortions (overvalued exchange rates and negative real interest rates), unemployment was high, amounting to 24 per cent of the labour force. The World Banks reports noted the high unemployment but stopped short of making recommendations to reduce or eliminate labour market distortions.[23] Also, some World Bank reports recommended alternative ways of creating employment through the promotion of tourism, non-traditional exports and export-oriented manufacturing. There was by implication the uncritical acceptance of Sri Lanka's attempt to increase domestic value added, especially the attempt to create employment through such interventions as licensing industries based on their employment impact. The importance of these markets for the adjustment of the economy was not appreciated. Instead, the World Bank reports considered adjustment as changing the structure of production away from traditional exports. Thus, what was not realised was the importance of these markets as a means of adjustment. Rather, the World Bank reports concentrated on the possible outcome, that of changing the structure of production. This is not to say that the World Bank reports were not unaware of labour market issues. For example, the 1977 Economic Report recommended that "effects of

---

[23] The 1972 Economic Report noted that high real wages were a problem.

wage-price policies on profits and productivity should be analysed and extensive distortions rectified." But, the heart of the macroeconomic adjustment of real wages, exchange rates, real interest rates and removal of quantitative controls was not appreciated in the World Bank reports.

To sum up, the World Bank's economic and sector work during the 1970–1977 period highlighted public sector savings issues over the issues of improving resource allocation or increasing the flexibility of factor markets. There was little analytical effort to link reduced savings and the distorted incentive structure. There was no adequate evidence produced about the allocation of resources in the World Bank reports regarding, either in comparing world prices to domestic prices, movements in the real exchange rates, the real interest rate or any measures of real wages and productivity over time. Much was made of "structural weaknesses," but this was identified with the country's specialisation in three export commodities.

5.3.2 *Economic and Sector Work: 1978–1985*

The important issues of 1978–1985 were macroeconomic stability, completing the unfinished agenda of the 1977 liberalisation and the continuing need to increase the flexibility of the capital and labour markets which had become rigid due to two decades of controls.

With respect to the macroeconomic stability issue, a number of questions arise: (i) When was this recognised as an important issue? (ii) What effort was made to analyse the issue? (iii) What were the policy recommendations made in the reports to restore macroeconomic stability?

Clearly, the macroeconomic issue was the most dominant one for the period as evidenced by the huge expansion in public expenditures, the large current account deficit, the high inflation and the substantial capital inflow. The World Bank reports began to pay attention to this imbalance only in 1981. Despite the discussion of the Mahaweli project with the government since 1978, in which it was known that the government was planning on compressing a 30-year project to 8 years (originally intended to be reduced to 6 years), the World Bank reports did not address this issue until 1981. As discussed previously, 44 per cent of all public investment was planned for the Mahaweli project between 1979 and 1981. The pressure on aggregate demand arose from the huge public expenditure related to the Mahaweli Scheme. (Especially since project aid for Mahaweli was agreed upon at the Sri Lanka Aid Group meeting in addition to other funds which were to be mobilised through the members of the Aid Group).

Apart from the macroeconomic instability that the project and the second oil shock engendered, there were genuine questions regarding the viability of the project on the basis of proper economic analysis.[24] Some would question the estimated 10 per cent rate of return on such a huge project given that there were enormous returns to be gained from the rehabilitation of an economy that was run down over the past two decades.[25] Estimates of the costs of producing rice in the Mahaweli areas did not leave much to be desired in the way of high rates of return for rice cultivation, which was a major thrust of the project.[26] In addition, there were the accompanying macroeconomic costs, including high inflation, the consequent appreciation of the real exchange rate and the recourse to foreign borrowing that would be non-optimal if the rate of return consideration was as just mentioned, if the capital inflows were permanent and there was no concern for current account deficit or the appreciation of the exchange rate.[27]

The second question with respect to macroeconomic instability is about the efforts made to analyse this issue. The 1981 economic reports traced the origin of the macroeconomic instability to the budget deficits. More specifically, the reports emphasised the "weakening of expenditure control." Since typically the focus of the World Bank reports had been on the government budget, this was thus not a departure from the earlier analytical efforts. Also, there was no appreciation of the connection between the budget deficits, the savings and investment gap in the private

---

[24] The World Bank after an initial agreement to support the project had some second thoughts, when a World Bank-financed study of the project (NEDECO report) recommended a slower rate of implementation than what the government envisaged. Also, the 1981 World Bank report commented that donors had made commitments before project costs had been properly estimated.

[25] One interpretation why the World Bank supported the project is that it was manoeuvred into it by the Government of Sri Lanka. See Levy (1989).

[26] *Ibid.* Trent Bertrand.

[27] Deepak Lal has argued that the usual signs of macroeconomic crisis present in Sri Lanka's context, i.e. a large current account deficit and a public sector deficit, is misleading given the capital inflow. The appreciation of the real exchange rate was the *means* by which the capital inflow was absorbed into the economy. See "The Real Exchange Rate, Capital flows and Inflation 1970–1982) World Bank, July 1985.

sector, and the current account deficit. In fact, there were many instances when the reports referred to the external and internal balances as if they were unconnected. The 1981 report argued that the government policy "should aim at first reducing the current account deficit, second reducing the budget deficit and third the private sector saving–investment gap."[28]

On the issue of the analysis of macroeconomic instability, the 1982 report expressed concern that the budget deficit would "leak into imports." (The report estimated that 40 per cent of public expenditures would appear as demand for imports.) The report did not appreciate the fact that increased demand for non-traded goods would be more damaging to the economy than the "leak into imports," which in this case would have acted as a safety value through the loss of reserves rather than permanently distorting the cost structure.[29]

The first question should have been the compatibility to completing the economic liberalisation while at the same time, increasing public expenditure arising from the Mahaweli Project. Bank reports analysed the macroeconomic issues belatedly. The macroeconomic imbalances were not anticipated. For instance, the 1980 economic report described Sri Lanka's development strategy as a "twin strategy of economic liberalisation and a program of increased public investment" without seeing the contradiction in such an approach. As such, the reversal of the gains from the liberalisation was not seen until as late as 1983 while the potential for a worsening macroeconomic situation was already present in 1978 with the plants installed to undertake the accelerated Mahaweli project. Moreover, a macroeconomic imbalance was inevitable under the circumstances, even if the world economy had not gone into a recession as it did.

This leads to the third question that was raised in respect of the macroeconomic imbalance regarding the policy recommendations made in the economic reports to restore equilibrium. The 1981–1985 reports (without exception) argue for a reduction in budget deficits. However, the argument continues to be made that public revenue efforts must be increased despite the adverse effects of the fast growth of public sector expenditures. These expanded expenditures had crowded out private sector activities and reduced their profitability through an overvalued exchange rate and high costs. No attempt was made to indicate that expenditure cuts

---

[28] The fundamental macroeconomic identity that these gaps sum to zero is not appreciated. See Dornbusch (1980).
[29] The Dutch disease literature studies this case well (see Neary and Corden (1982)).

would be optimal at the margin compared to revenue increase to reduce the public sector deficit.

The 1981 report argued that measures to reduce the current account deficit could include "direct" measures on trade such as curbing non-essential imports and indirect measures to cut aggregate demand. The same report advocated measures to promote specific exports (industrial exports, spices and other minor crops) to raise export earnings. Little was said about efficiency.

None of the reports of this period made links between the overvalued exchange rate and domestic inflation, whereas the exchange rate was used to keep domestic inflation rates low. The currency appreciation accomplished this at the expense of loss of reserves. Consequently, imports had to be financed through commercial borrowings.

The World Bank reports did not anticipate macroeconomic instability, but it was recognised as an important issue in 1981. It was, however, not clearly or rigorously analysed to bring out a set of appropriate policy recommendations.

The policy recommendations made ran counter to liberalisation as part of the recommendations advocated curbing non-essential imports and promoting specific exports to "earn more exchange." Aggregate demand policies were recommended but not sufficiently developed apart from the recommendations relating to the budget deficit.

The second issue of importance during this period was that of completing the unfinished agenda of the 1977 liberalisation and thus reducing further distortions in the economy. While there was no explicit reference to completing the agenda of liberalisation, there were efforts to examine the incentive structure in greater detail than before.

The industrial sector report of 1984 commented at length on the incentive structure, covering the trade regime, the domestic tax structure, operations of public corporations and the problems relating to financial intermediation. That report examined the trade regime in some detail, commenting on the negative impacts of various tax, licensing and subsidy policies that distorted prices and ran counter to the liberalisation attempt. Some of these conclusions re-emerged in the 1985 economic report, especially in comments on the tariff reforms introduced with the 1985 budget. These measures included the reduction in overall levels of nominal protection, reducing its variance and reducing the levels of export taxes on traditional exports. The 1985 economic report took up the remaining distortions in the trade regime, particularly the 35 exemptions granted in the tariff reforms to continue the protection of public enterprises. Part of the reason why the trade regime was examined in detail was due to some work commissioned in 1979 to conduct a study on effective rates of protection. Thus, in the 1978–1985 period, there was a close examination of the incentive system compared to the 1970–1977 period.

The final issue of importance in the 1978–1985 period related to the need to increase the flexibility of factor markets by removing some of the rigidities introduced into these markets through labour laws and capital market interventions. These were not taken up in economic and sector work, rendering the World Bank's recommendations less useful, especially when the World Bank reports continued to exhort the government to undertake "structural adjustment." Thus, there was little analysis of the labour market except for a couple of research-financed studies.[30]

The analysis of financial and capital markets is even more inadequate compared to the labour market. This is despite the ramifications arising out of the growing debt and capital inflows. As mentioned earlier, a chapter in the 1984 industrial report did look at financial intermediation, but this was only a beginning and was inadequate to underpin the macroeconomic advice the World Bank was expected to give. Little is known, at least analytically, about the equity and capital markets except that they remained regulated. The World Bank reports broadly touched on this subject matter. This remained a part of the unfinished agenda. Meanwhile, given the emerging macroeconomic situation, the monetary policy became tight. The 1985 report noted that this policy had reduced private investment without noting that liquidity restraints are more binding on the private sector than the public sector. The structure of discount rates has been further manipulated by increasing the variance in the rates for the purpose of credit allocation. The World Bank reports did not take up these issues in the adjustment context, while the International Monetary Fund does this in the context of the monetary policy.

To sum up, the World Bank's economic and sector work in the 1978–1985 period, in which macro stability issues dominated the economy,

---

[30] Two studies were associated with the work initiated by the Development Research Department: Raja Korale's study on employment and Gary Fields's study on labour markets, both of which are in the draft stages. However, they fall short of a good description of the labour market and the way it works, especially given the existing labour laws.

identified the problem, but belatedly. The analysis of this situation left much to be desired, as did the policy prescriptions, some of which advocated import controls. The World Bank's economic policies during this period looked more closely at the incentive structure compared to the 1970–1977 period; however, many areas remained unexplored, such as those relating to differential interest rates, real exchange rates and capital market regulations. Finally, the World Bank's economic analysis did little, if anything, to study labour and capital markets to analyse macroeconomic adjustment.

5.4 Nature of Economic and Sector Work in Sri Lanka

As for a majority of developing countries, the World Bank's economic reports were the most informative and up-to-date commentary on the Sri Lankan economy. These reports commanded a wide audience among the policymakers of the country and the donor community. Economic reports were produced every year to service the Sri Lanka Aid Group, while sector reports were produced at the rate of one every sixteen months. Thus, for the period 1970–1985, there were fifteen reports in terms of the most up-to-date and comprehensive commentaries on short-term development in the economy.[31]

The commentaries on public finance issues in the reports were particularly noteworthy. Public revenues and expenditures were comprehensively analysed highlighting public transfers and drawing important distinctions among various categories of expenditures and revenues. In 1981, a comprehensive analysis of public expenditures was undertaken on the basis of which the government made sharp cuts in its expenditure programmes.

Finally, there has been discernible improvement in the quality of the most recent economic reports as they have been able to draw on high-quality sector work that had been undertaken since 1981 in respect of industrial incentives and agricultural sector incentives. More was being

---

[31] The International Monetary Fund's Reviews of Economic Developments had a narrow coverage while their analytical quality with respect to macroeconomic issues tends to be on average higher than that of the World Bank reports.

said about the incentives structure than before. But, from the late 1990s onwards, the World Bank economic work again began to neglect incentive issues. For example, since 2013, incentive reforms have been on the backburner and, it would thwart the efforts to maintain a GDP growth rate of over 6 per cent during President Mahinda Rajapakse's period (2005–2015), while the medium- to long-term strategy aimed at doubling per capita income to US$ 4,000 by 2016. This could not have had taken place because of the mis-allocation of resources and the absence incentive reforms.

(a) Inability to identify dominant issues
The basic deficiency of the World Bank reports on Sri Lanka during the period involved their inability to identify the dominant issues in time and to provide policy advice on the basis of the issues identified. For instance, the dominant issue of the 1970–1977 period was the highly distorted incentive structure. The dominant issue of the 1978–1985 period was the macroeconomic imbalance arising out of large public expenditures on the so-called "lead projects."

The World Bank reports of the 1970–1977 period were concerned with macroeconomic issues of inadequate public savings although there was no serious macroeconomic imbalance through most of the period. Conversely, the World Bank reports began to focus on the incentive structure after 1977 when the economic liberalisation had made fundamental policy changes to improve the incentive structure. It was only in 1981 that the World Bank reports began to highlight the macroeconomic imbalance issue when in fact it was discernible as early as 1979 and could have been anticipated in 1978.

(b) Insufficient analysis of issues identified
The major deficiency in this area is the relative neglect of efficiency considerations in the analyses of public policy. Thus, the reports uncritically accepted and advocated the diversification of the economy as a policy goal when in fact growth of traditional exports had been stifled by export taxes, a dual exchange rate and import restrictions. In the same vein, increases in public investments up to 1981 had been praised without concern for the return to public investment compared to private investment when the latter had been crowded out due to credit constraints, investment licensing procedures and remaining exchange controls.

Similarly, private savings behaviour was not analysed when the reports were emphasising "domestic resource mobilisation." For example, an inquiry as to why exports declined or private savings were inadequate would have alerted the authors to begin looking at the underlying incentive structure. A very glaring deficiency was the lack of economic analysis in sector reports save for two or three such reports. Finally, there was hardly any analysis of labour and capital markets, which play an important role in macroeconomic adjustment.

(c) Incorrect analysis

Under this category, many deficiencies can be cited.

Clearly, basic macroeconomic identities have been misunderstood. As described in Section 5.2, many reports had either not understood or not explored the connection between the current account deficit and the saving–investment gap. These were treated as though they were unconnected. Indeed, the 1981 report said that the priorities for policy action were to eliminate the current account deficit first, the public sector deficit second and the private sector saving–investment gap third!

Achievement of rice self-sufficiency was praised when there had been horrendous costs associated with it. Trent Bertrand estimated that the cost of domestic production of rice in Sri Lanka in the Mahaweli project areas was sixfold compared to importing rice from Burma at that time.

The argument for export diversification was similarly based on a false premise, namely in confusing a mean–variance issue. Indeed the 1984 CEM made the argument for diversification out of tea when tea export revenues had increased rapidly, without noting that stabilisation of export incomes was a macroeconomic issue. The country had always enjoyed a comparative advantage in tea which was the basis of its high mean income. To conclude that tree crops remained the "Achilles heel of Sri Lanka development" was a gross error. Incentive studies in 1981 clearly indicated the comparative advantage for producing tea. Ironically, these studies had been financed by the World Bank.

The World Bank reports on the public sector deficits mentioned inadequate financial resources rather than the deleterious effects arising out of inflationary financed deficits and the permanent increase in the cost structure when non-traded goods prices increased. The World Bank reports were concerned about the "leak into imports" of 40 per cent of increased public expenditure rather than the more serious damage arising out of an appreciated exchange rate. In fact, a leak into imports would act as a safety valve by letting reserves go down rather than making costs go up!

(d) Improper and opaque policy prescriptions

Improper policy prescriptions were inevitable if indeed (b) inadequate analysis and (c) incorrect analyses were present. The improper policy prescriptions related to specific areas rather than the general policy prescriptions such as getting prices right, reducing budget deficits, reducing controls and maintaining positive real interest rates.

One of the basic problems encountered in policy prescriptions in Sri Lanka reports was that there was no clear identification of policy actions that followed the analysis. Various suggestions for some policy change or the other were interspersed within the descriptive text, so the reader was hard pressed to find clear prescriptions of policy. One was left with the impression that the authors of the reports either lacked conviction or had no well-specified model in their minds as to how things worked. They seemed to bend backward and avoid being prescriptive.

Specific areas in which clearly wrong policies had been recommended were found in a number of reports as follows:

- To impose import restrictions on non-essential goods as a means of correcting the balance-of-payment deficits.
- To undertake specific measures to promote exports by identifying winners, especially among non-traditional exports.
- To raise revenues to close budget deficits when the returns to public investment had been known to be low.
- To deliberately increase domestic value added for employment creation.

Each of these prescriptions led to reductions in efficiency and was self-defeating macroeconomically as indicated in Section 4C.

(e) Lack of continuity and perspective

As mentioned earlier, the economic analysis of Sri Lanka largely confined itself to a commentary on current problems. As such, there was little continuity in the reports. There was no tracking of issues or analysis of events up to a given point. One reason why there seemed to be such a concentration on current events was that the main purpose of the economic reports seemed to be to serve the aid group, especially for recommending levels of aid. Even for this, however, little was reported on the evolution of the issues identified in earlier reports. For example, when commenting on declining terms of trade, there was no reference to the peak level in the past. In 1 year, for example, great concern was expressed about public enterprise performance; in the next year, there was hardly any mention of the concern. There was also no follow-up on what happened to the policy recommendations made earlier.

There was no obligation while writing the economic reports to provide at least a medium-term historical account of the evolution of the economy. Data and statistics, at least in the appendices, had about a 10-year history. But, there was little reference to their changes over time in the text or relating these statistics to the analysis in the text.

While the historical perspective was limited, there was also no perspective into the future. To be sure, there were 5-year projections. These projects dealt mostly with the balance of payments as required to make aid recommendations. Moreover, the projections lacked a policy context because the projected gaps would change very much with changes in the policy environment. Finally, there were no underlying assumptions spelled out in the projections. They were included under the heading of "World Bank estimate," and no basis for such estimates was provided.

(f) Unnecessary length and diffusion

The economic reports tended to be long, with some exceeding 120 pages. Out of the 15 economic reports written during the 1970–1980 period, only one was less than 40 pages — it was an "updating report." The reports provided a wide variety of information, especially focusing on current issues. They contained information ranging from national income, developments in sectors, government revenue and expenditure to the balance of payments — the standard information — to public enterprise financial performance, data relating to specific sectors (especially if a sector report had been recently completed) and some particular information on public investment plans and non-traditional exports.

The information base was wide and sound. The information in the World Bank report should be gathered to begin an analysis, rather than be treated as results of a good analytical effort.

The reports were scattered as to their policy focus or prescription. There was no statement of the important fundamental issues for the medium term and a clear analysis of these issues in a deliberate way to produce policy prescriptions. Of course, the quality of the reports varied over time. There was some improvement over time, but much could have been done to reduce the size and increase the focus of the economic reports.

5.5 Conclusion

Looking into the 1990s and the period 2000–2011, there has been less emphasis on economy-wide reports. As noted, in the first decade after the year 2000, many other issues were examined by the World Bank staff, including the environment, women's issues and institutional issues. Some of the "bread and butter" of macroeconomic and incentive-related issues were "crowded out" by the new issues. Most of the macroeconomic work was relegated to the International Monetary Fund, which was appropriate. However, both these institutions had little interest beyond the medium term since their work was largely to back up their lending for development and balance-of-payment support. At times, the IMF went beyond the balance-of-payment support to provide longer-term finance in the form of Extended Fund Facilities. There is little evidence that these operations supported incentive reforms. A fair statement is that the jury is still out on their achievements. Unfortunately, internal reviews undertaken by both these institutions lacked credibility both internally and externally.

Appendix A

Tables 5.1A–5.4A were based on economic reports reviewed for the study. No attempt has been made to expand the data beyond World Bank sources, which of course ultimately come from the countries themselves.

Table 5.1A. Historical Data; Rates of Change (Constant Prices)

Indicator	1979	1980	1981	1982	1983	1984
Real GDP	6.3	5.8	5.8	5.0	5.0	5.0
Fixed Investment	29.9	16.0	−6.2	6.3	0.5	−6.1
Total Investment	32.0	22.5	−11.7	5.7	−1.0	−5.1
Consumption	2.3	7.0	4.8	9.8	5.1	2.7
Public	−2.7	−3.0	−8.5	22.5	−1.5	−7.9
Private	2.9	8.2	6.2	8.7	5.8	4.2
Savings	34.5	−0.3	11.3	−20.5	4.2	19.0
Exports	13.7	3.6	10.0	4.5	−2.0	13.2
Imports	19.1	19.1	−7.0	14.7	−2.9	−0.9
Rupee Deflators (1982=100)						
Gross Domestic Product	61.5	73.8	89.2	100.0	115.9	138.5
Imports (G+NFS)	66.4	84.7	98.8	100.0	105.8	111.0
Exports (G+NFS)	77.5	90.8	99.7	100.0	120.2	148.0
Total Expenditures	59.6	74.5	90.2	100.0	114.0	130.5
Government Consumption	63.0	77.0	93.4	100.0	113.4	128.0
Private Consumption	63.0	77.0	93.4	100.0	113.4	128.0
Fixed Investment	50.5	68.5	81.5	100.0	115.9	138.5
Changes in Stocks	50.5	68.5	81.5	100.0	112.3	144.2

Source: The World Bank, Sri Lanka: Recent Economic Developments and Policies for Growth, (Report No. 5628-CE), May 14, 1985, Table 2.

Table 5.2A. Structure of the Economy

Sector	1978	1979	1980	1981	1982	1983	1984
Agriculture	30.5	26.9.	27.6	27.7	27.0	27.1	28.0
Mining	1.8	1.9	2.0	2.0	2.7	2.5	2.3
Manufacturing	20.0	19.1	17.7	16.2	14.7	13.7	14.4
Construction	4.8	6.5	8.9	8.8	8.6	8.7	8.1
Services	42.9	45.6	43.8	45.3	47.3	48.0	47.2

Source: The World Bank, Sri Lanka: Recent Economic Developments and Policies for Growth, (Report No. 5628-CE), May 14, 1985, Table 2.1.

Table 5.3A. Macroeconomic Balance (as a percentage of GDP)

	1978	1979	1980	1981	1982	1983	1984
Current Account Deficit (Foreign Savings)	4.5	11.1	19.8	13.8	15.2	12.4	3.7
Private Sector							
Investment	13.6	18.6	25.3	23.0	25.4	24.2	21.7
Fixed	12.8	18.0	24.3	22.5	25.2	24.3	21.6
Change in Stocks	0.8	0.6	1.0	0.5	0.2	−0.1	0.1
Savings	16.8	14.3	17.6	15.7	16.8	16.2	18.9
Investment–Savings	−3.2	4.3	7.7	7.3	8.6	8.0	2.8
Public Sector							
Investment	6.4	7.2	8.6	4.8	5.2	4.6	4.4
Fixed	7.2	7.3	7.1	4.9	5.1	4.7	4.4
Change in Stocks	−0.8	−0.1	1.5	−0.1	0.1	−0.1	—
Savings	−1.3	0.4	−3.5	−1.7	−1.4	0.2	3.5
Revenue	27.4	24.3	21.1	19.1	17.8	19.5	22.7
Expenditure	28.7	23.9	24.6	20.8	19.2	19.3	19.2
Investment–Savings	7.7	6.8	12.1	6.5	6.6	4.4	0.9
Public and Private							
Investment–Savings	4.5	11.1	19.8	13.8	15.2	12.4	3.7

Source: The International Monetary Fund, Sri Lanka: Recent Economic Developments and Policies for Growth, (Report No. SM/85/112), April 25, 1985, Table 2.

Table 5.4A. Financial Indicators (as a percentage of GDP)

	1978	1979	1980	1981	1982	1983	1984
Money	13.8	14.6	14.0	11.7	11.7	12.0	10.9
Money Plus Quasi Money	25.3	28.6	29.6	28.6	30.2	30.2	28.1
Domestic Credit							
Net Credit to Government	4.4	5.7	13.7	15.2	17.2	14.5	9.5
Credit to Private	20.7	21.2	24.4	24.4	24.9	25.7	22.9
Net International Reserves	7.7	7.7	0.9	0.1	−0.5	−0.4	4.8
Government Deficit	−13.7	−13.8	−23.1	−15.6	−17.3	−13.3	−10.2

Source: The World Bank, Sri Lanka: Recent Economic Developments and Policies for Growth, (Report No. 5628-CE), May 14, 1985, Table 6.02.

Appendix B

World Bank Reports on Sri Lanka, 1970–1985 (a selective list)

COUNTRY ECONOMIC REPORTS

The 1973 Economic Outlook (January 1973)
The report mainly discussed the 1973 budget. The use of the Foreign Exchange Entitlement Certificate (a form of general import surcharge) as a new revenue measure was analysed. The report also looked at other budgetary issues, such as withdrawal of the free rice ration from income taxpayers, changes in excise duty, other indirect taxes, profits from the sugar monopoly and other expenditure measures. In addition, Chapter I looked at trends in production and growth, Chapter II considered government finance and Chapter III covered the overall balance-of-payment situation for 1982.

Recent Economic Developments and Current Prospects (April 1974)
Reviewing economic developments in 1973, the report concluded that events were dominated by the serious balance-of-payment situation, caused by a sharp downward movement in the terms of trade. It stated that incentives must be provided to producers to achieve a higher level of agricultural production, exports must be accelerated, public finances must be placed on a viable footing and an adequate level of public capital formation must be attained. Moreover, it stated that Sri Lanka should be able to continue to support social objectives while pursuing economic goals, largely by concentrating on the agricultural sector.

Recent Economic Developments and Current Prospects (February 1975)
This report claimed that problems over the prior 4 years were due to several domestic and external factors, including savings in the public sector which were hindered by an inability to generate a surplus and by continuing uncertainty in the private sector over the future role of large entrepreneurs in the society; a severe drought also affected the economy. Increased capital formation and the availability of capital goods, raw materials and consumer goods, which required expanding the exports and/or foreign assistance as well as progress in import substitution, were considered essential.

Country Economic Memorandum (March 1976)
This report stated that the Sri Lankan economy had endured long-term difficulties arising from structural overdependence on a few primary commodities combined with steadily deteriorating terms of trade. At the same time, economic policies had placed heavy emphasis on the welfare and redistributive objectives with corresponding resource requirements which had constrained the growth in productivity. Capital formation had been inadequate. The urgent structural adjustments required were the subject of this report. Expanded agricultural production was considered essential, and efforts to promote manufactured exports were to be furthered.

Country Economic Memorandum (February 1977)
The report stated that Sri Lanka's chronic economic difficulties were due to the structural overdependence on three primary export commodities and a political commitment to far-reaching welfare and redistributive objectives not matched by sufficient growth in output. However, a build-up in external reserves in 1976 made the 1977 external payments position more manageable. A programme of action was recommended to stimulate production, especially in agriculture, through investments that were less capital-intensive and with short gestation periods. Also, industrial exports and tourism were to be promoted vigorously to diversify the export base.

Development Issues and Prospects (March 1978)
Social gains, according to the report, had been jeopardised by poor economic performance in the 1970s. Inadequate development expenditure and a misallocation of resources within the productive sectors had contributed to economic stagnation. Policy measures and investments must be taken to stimulate the more rapid growth of output, savings, import-substitution, and exports of which the economy was capable. Prospects for growth were stated to depend heavily on import liberalisation and agricultural output, as well as an increase in the rate of investment.

Key Development Issues in the 1980s (May 1980)
After reviewing the government's programme of economic reforms, the report looked at two areas where further action was needed: the medium-term public investment programme and agricultural producer incentives. A review of mobilisation and allocation decisions was claimed to be necessary, according to the report. The adequacy of agricultural incentives

was crucial to the success of the government's strategy. These included prices for paddy, import policies related to many minor field crops, export taxation policies and returns from fertiliser use.

Policies and Prospects for Economic Adjustment (May 1981)
The report examined the government's economic programme of 1980, noting that measures had proven to be insufficient. The main stabilisation tasks were to involve (i) reducing the current account deficit in the balance of payments, (ii) reducing the level of the government's overall budget deficit and (iii) reducing the increasing gap between private investment and the domestic private savings available to finance this investment. Decreasing capital expenditures was stated to be essential to adjustment. A critical sector was energy. Improvement of the balance of payments in the medium term would have required the development of non-traditional exports.

Country Economic Report (May 1982)
The report reviewed developments since 1977 and discussed the requirements and policy options for the restoration of the adjustment momentum achieved in 1981, with special emphasis on budgetary policies, which had contributed to the main source of instability, and on the need to keep the use of non-concessional finance to prudent levels. The report also focused on the longer-term requirements of a successful economic adjustment programme including policies to strengthen the directly productive sectors, especially exports. In addition, the immediate balance-of-payment outlook was reviewed and estimates were provided of Sri Lanka's aid requirements for the next 2 years.

An Interim Assessment of Experience and Priorities (May 1983)
This report included a macroeconomic review of Sri Lanka's experience since liberalisation. The developments in 1982 were reviewed from the medium-term perspective; there was a more detailed discussion of the need for better financial management in the public sector and improved trade and industrialisation policies; and a review was conducted of the status of the existing aid pipeline and balance-of-payments prospects. Significant progress in Sri Lanka's liberalisation strategy had been made. But, financial imbalance in the budget had led to high inflation and a

widening deficit in the balance of payments, while industrial and export growth remained low.

Recent Economic Developments, Prospects and Policies (May 1984)
Despite improvements in the economy, the report stated that the size of the budget and current account deficits remained excessive. These imbalances symbolised underlying structural weaknesses, which included a low-yielding public revenue system in the face of an ambitious and long-gestating public investment programme, as well as distortions in the incentives framework for production and trade. This report considered the short-term stabilisation task and the requisite measures for structural reforms in budgetary practices, and in the incentives and institutions of the key sectors of agriculture, industry and energy. It also presented a medium-term balance-of-payment outlook for the country.

Recent Economic Development and Policies for Growth (May 1985)
The report stated that the substantial 5 per cent real GDP growth rate during 1984 was due in large part to unusually high tea export prices. At the same time, long-term growth trends in several major sectors of the economy had remained low. This, according to the report, underscored the continued vulnerability of the Sri Lankan economy to fluctuations in tea earnings with the need to develop new areas of growth if living standards were to continue to rise. The primary focus of the report was on those policy changes in the overall incentive framework which were needed for continued growth. Emphasis was placed on sector-wide policies in agriculture and industry. The report concluded by emphasising the vital role of the aid community in the achievement of Sri Lanka's development objectives.

SECTOR REPORTS

Agricultural Sector Brief (June 1972)
The report stated that an agricultural strategy must achieve an acceptable compromise between often conflicting social and economic objectives. The three essential elements of a realistic agriculture structure for Sri Lanka were stated to be the expansion of tree crop production, correction of price distortions to allow efficient resource use and adjustment of

the investment balance to reflect socioeconomic priorities. Projects and programmes of a quick disbursing nature were claimed to be needed to generate future savings and provide future employment opportunities.

Agricultural Sector Survey (February 1973)
Diversification of the sector was a major development goal and better performance of the food sector was required to meet the growing food requirements. The following areas had considerable to have potential for development: (i) replanting of tea with high-yield material and improved cultural practices; (ii) improving cultural and tapping practices and processing quality of rubber; (iii) paying increased attention to coconut production; (iv) improved coordination of farm services and input supply for food crops; and (v) better land use and research and extension services.

Agricultural Policy and Programme Review (February 1975)
The report stated that Sri Lanka's agricultural policies aimed to increase self-sufficiency in food production, diversify crop production, expand employment opportunities and improve rural living conditions and social services. Additional measures were recommended in the report: (i) reduction of the subsidy on fertiliser; (ii) expansion of extension programmes: (iii) assessment of draft and mechanical power needs; (iv) improvements in land use; (v) improvement of farm credit programmes; (vi) evaluation of taxation, levies and subsidy systems; and (vii) provision of more foreign exchange.

Issues and Prospects for Industrial Development (September 1979)
Although Sri Lanka had a long history of industrialisation, it was, according to the report, nevertheless, under-industrialised relative to countries in a similar economic position. The real growth of about 10 per cent per annum in industrial value added would be achievable over the medium term, according to the report, provided that (i) further adjustments were made in the system of trade and fiscal incentives; (ii) there was adequate industrial finance and more priority was placed on the expansion of sub-sectors in which Sri Lanka had comparative advantage, especially labour-intensive industries; and (iii) government planning and implementation capabilities were strengthened. Additionally, industrial development was required to shift away from import substitution towards export promotion.

Telecommunications Sector Memorandum (November 1979)
The report indicated that customer-related functions and manual operations were highly over-centralised. Institutional improvements over a wide spectrum of managerial and operational activities were needed. Existing services were seriously deficient in both quality and quantity. Access to service was poor. Integrated development of the sector with sustained investment was necessary to overcome the current serious deficiencies in telecommunications services.

Power Sector Memorandum (May 1980)
The report recommended that (i) the World Bank follow up a restructuring of the Ceylon Electricity Board (CEB) tariffs in line with the results of the ongoing tariff study; (ii) the efficiency of CEB operations be reviewed regularly; (iii) institutional cooperation at high levels and as a formal process be encouraged; (iv) the World Bank implement consistent and comprehensive long-range system planning as a long-term objective; (v) the World Bank encourage the use of appropriate selection criteria for rural electrification schemes; and (vi) the World Bank consider a project for financial assistance.

Forestry Sector Review (September 1980)
Lack of data and trained staff, according to the report, inhibited efforts to develop the sector. The proposed programme focused on these two issues. The recommended planning programme required (i) the implementation of a land use study; (ii) inventory of forest resources; (iii) assessment of the contribution of non-forest resources; (iv) assessment of the present and future requirements of services wood products; (v) assessment of the industrial processing capability; (vi) intensification of forest research and extension; and (vii) development of a national master plan.

Education Sector Memorandum (October 1981)
The report examined how public demand for education over the last two decades had caused a steady decline in quality throughout the education system. In addition, there was needed considerable variation in educational opportunities between rural and urban areas, and between different social groups for the formation and functioning of school clusters; the design, implementation and cost of an evaluation and monitoring system; and the detailed functioning of educational institutions.

Domestic Consulting Industry (April 1982)

The report examined the three categories of the 122 domestically owned consulting firms — architecture, accounting and management, and engineering. The government's continuing policy of maintaining in-house capacity was stated to have had a dampening effect on the growth and development of the consulting services industry. Significant benefits, the report claimed, would derive from the greater use of local consultant capabilities. Specific actions to relieve constraints were suggested.

Issues and Options in the Energy Sector (May 1982)

High oil import bills and power shortages, according to the report, had made energy a major national concern. Efforts to promote energy conservation were to be complemented by rationalisation of an energy pricing policy. Inadequate planning and delays in decision-making and programme implementation were largely held responsible for the energy problems of the time. Surmounting these problems would have required a substantial strengthening of the weak and fragmented institutional structure for energy management and planning.

Water Supply and Sanitation Sector Study (June 1984)

This report outlined the findings of a mission. It concluded that among the major factors which would determine the degree of achievement of goals were the implementation capability of the Water Supply and Drainage Board, the capacity of the local construction industry and the available financing from local and foreign sources. The report also discussed the use of appropriate technology, the rehabilitation of existing installations, an appropriate programme of preventive maintenance, upgrading distribution facilities and the improvement of coordination between the various institutions associated with the water supply and sanitation sector.

Urban Sector Report (June 1984)

The report asserted that urban problems of the time were manageable, subject to certain policy shifts in favour of strong efforts to improve the financial and managerial performance of local governments and utility agencies. The purpose of the review was to identify measures that would help (i) increase domestic resource mobilisation; (ii) improve the efficiency and effectiveness of resource mobilisation for land, infrastructure and service delivery; and (iii) improve and strengthen institutions for urban management and training.

Selected Issues of Industrial and Trade Policies in Sri Lanka (January 1984)
This report analysed the policy environment which prevailed during the 1977–1982 period. It reviewed in detail the policies introduced in 1977, concentrating on three areas of particular relevance to industrial development: trade policies, the assessment of public enterprises, and the policies and institutions of financial intermediation with emphasis on the effects of financial regulation on manufacturing. The report recommended a reduction in the level and variance of the tariff structure and the maintenance of a competitive real exchange to ensure the competitiveness of traded sectors. The most important industrial policy interventions were the Business Turnover Tax (BTT), the income tax holidays and investment licensing. Regarding manufacturing public enterprises, the report required the government to find ways to reduce its financial claims on the budget. And, among policy recommendations on financial intermediation, the report suggested that the government hand over to commercial banks the responsibility of setting interest rates.

Other Sector Reports included the following: Dairy Sector Review (April 1983); Tree Crop Sector Review (March 1984); Transport Sector Memorandum (March 1984); Population and Health Sector Report (September 1984); Education and Training Sector Memorandum (May 1985); Power Sub-Sector Review (June 1985); and Agricultural Sector Review (July 1985).

Chapter 6

The Role of International Financial Institutions in Globalisation: The International Monetary Fund (IMF) and Its Role in Sri Lanka

6.1 Introduction

After the Second World War, as developing countries remained poor, there was a move from reconstruction to development with decolonisation taking place in the developing world. Since it was difficult to raise long-term capital at that time, the World Bank was created so that the developing countries would have access to capital.

6.2 The IMF

The IMF was created to help with short-term balance-of-payment problems. A question arises as to why Sri Lanka asked for help on so many occasions (16 times) and why Sri Lanka failed to seek assistance for the 17th time. The answer is that Sri Lankan governments chose to neglect remedial measures to overcome the crisis by not addressing the IMF's suggestions to reform fiscal and monetary policies. There was an underlying ideological bias with those who were in power, whose advisors advocated for a "Home grown solution."

6.3 Sri Lanka and the IMF

Since 1950, there had been large fiscal deficits and high inflation in Sri Lanka like in most Latin American and African countries that were seeking the IMF's help. The IMF and the World Bank provided funds at a concessionary rate, but the countries continued to have imbalances. Some could argue that there was a moral hazard involved. Sri Lanka had these imbalances due to excessive domestic spending, government and external deficits due to a combination of excess expenditure over total revenues and appreciated exchange rate, domestic imbalance and a balance-of-payment deficit not covered by capital inflows.

Sri Lanka got assistance in the form of a Stand-by Agreement (SBA) and through extended fund facilities. Like in the case of many other developing countries, Sri Lanka did not like the conditions that were set by the IMF, which were considered too stringent, given the size of the deficits and inappropriate interest rates. In the case of Sri Lanka, there were special considerations after 2019, when the newly elected President of the Country who had got 69 per cent of the vote was advised by the newly appointed Governor of the Central Bank, who was ideologically not keen to borrow from the IMF. The second governor did not want to go to the IMF because of the IMF's intrusive monitoring. It was revealed that Sri Lanka could have avoided much of the difficulties that arose in 2020 in the balance of payments had it gone to the IMF earlier. As a consequence, the Central Bank began to print money at a significant scale, which led to a tremendous jump in the inflation rate of up to 70 per cent. It seemed that these two governors believed in the so-called modern monetary theory, which states that an increase in money supply does not have a significant impact on inflation. The first governor was seeking an alternative "home-grown" model to deal with Sri Lanka's economic problems.

To complicate matters, the resultant economic crisis led to a political crisis. A majority of the voters in the country who gave Gotabaya Rajapaksa a large majority reversed their views. According to the constitution, Ranil Wickremesinghe was elected by the parliament as the new president to replace Gotabaya Rajapaksa who resigned.

The IMF proposed seven aspects that needed to be addressed to make the economy more stable. If Sri Lanka followed the fiscal, monetary and incentive policies proposed by the IMF, it would be able to reduce the magnitude of the crisis. Stabilisation programmes proposed by the IMF would provide reassurance to the creditors that Sri Lanka was on a reasonable path of recovery to repay at least a part of the debt. This process of going to the IMF, after being qualified for the EFF (Extended Fund Facility) program, would lead to getting access to financial markets following an upgrading of the country's credit worthiness and raising the assurance of repayment of debt over time.

The World Bank "repurposed" its lending programmes to address Sri Lanka's situation. The World Bank could help with funds as well as providing some analysis of issues to be reconciled, such as public expenditure reviews and incentive reform programmes for the medium and long terms.

Given its role, the IMF deals with issues that are akin to an emergency room in a hospital, with immediate attention given to patients who seek help in the immediate and short runs. Given the nature of its role, IMF involvements, while short, have a crucial role to play in assisting countries that are in crisis return to better economic health.

The IMF provides funds through its stand-by programmes, extended fund facility programmes and monitoring programmes. All these devices have been used by Sri Lanka. These programmes provide advice and funds. Each country's situation is different. Country officials led by the Central Bank and the Ministry of Finance participate in the design of programmes (as some detractors have claimed, there is no one package for all countries as Joe Stiglitz stated), and it is not a one-sided programme dictated by IMF officials. The amount of the credit depends on the quota of the country and is determined by reference to the national income of the country and the country's access to the world financial market. When a country is in a situation of an external imbalance due to an external shock or domestically caused monetary or credit expansion, IMF programmes are designed to address them and get the country back to economic health.

Unlike the World Bank, (see Chapter 5) funds from the IMF programmes go directly to the Central Bank. The IMF funds facilities vary according to income groups of the countries. The IMF provides funding for interest rates that are below commercial rates. For the IMF's Extended Fund Facilities, the cost of borrowing is generally linked to its market-based interest rate. Total quotas are increased depending on the demand for funds by the world market, and the quotas are reviewed at regular intervals (generally no more than 5 years apart).

Since the 1980s, the World Bank and the IMF have worked together to improve conditions in developing countries. A structural adjustment programme of the World Bank requires an IMF programme as a prerequisite. This joint effort has been successful. In many instances, experts from both institutions work together in the field.

In the late 1990s, the IMF had problems in East Asia, mainly due to a misdiagnosis of private sector-led expansionary policies, as it diagnosed the problem as a fiscal problem. However, reforms of the institution and joint work helped to raise the level of analysis and adjustment programmes. The IMF also began to pay greater attention to the cost of adjustment of countries undertaking its programmes. Now, a typical IMF programme will have a safety net, with proper timing and sequencing and new elements brought in that help out with smoother adjustments.

Over the 1965–2020 period, Sri Lanka had undertaken 16 programmes (See Table 6.1). Some saw these programmes as unsuited as they encouraged countries to run to the IMF for help in every crisis. The

Table 6.1. Sri Lanka: History of Lending Commitments with the IMF as of September 30, 2018 (in thousands of SDRs)

Facility	Date of Arrangement	Expiration Date	Amount Agreed	Amount Drawn	Amount Outstanding
Extended Fund Facility	Jun 03, 2016	Jun 02, 2019	1,070,780	715,230	715,230
Stand-by Arrangement	Jul 24, 2009	Jul 23, 2012	1,653,600	1,653,600	0
Extended Credit Facility	Apr 18, 2003	Apr 17, 2006	269,000	38,390	0
Extended Fund Facility	Apr 18, 2003	Apr 17, 2006	144,400	20,670	0
Stand-by Arrangement	Apr 20, 2001	Sep 19, 2002	200,000	200,000	0
Extended Credit Facility	Sep 13, 1991	Jul 31, 1995	336,000	280,000	0
Structural Adjustment Facility Commitment	Mar 09, 1988	Mar 08, 1991	156,170	156,170	0
Stand-by Arrangement	Sep 14, 1983	Jul 31, 1984	100,000	50,000	0
Extended Fund Facility	Jan 01, 1979	Dec 31, 1981	260,300	260,300	0
Stand-by Arrangement	Dec 02, 1977	Dec 01, 1978	93,000	93,000	0
Stand-by Arrangement	Apr 30, 1974	Apr 29, 1975	24,500	7,000	0
Stand-by Arrangement	Mar 18, 1971	Mar 17, 1972	24,500	24,500	0
Stand-by Arrangement	Aug 12, 1969	Aug 11, 1970	19,500	19,500	0
Stand-by Arrangement	May 06, 1968	May 05, 1969	19,500	19,500	0
Stand-by Arrangement	Jun 15, 1966	Jun 14, 1967	25,000	25,000	0
Stand-by Arrangement	Jun 15, 1965	Jun 14, 1966	30,000	22,500	0
Total			4,426,250	3,585,360	715,230

Source: The IMF official website, accessed on the April 14, 2022.

left of centre groups complained that client countries seem to have delegated reforms and adjustments to the IMF, instead of taking full responsibility to come out of a self-created crisis.

However, as most officials in developing countries know, the IMF has worldwide experience with different countries and circumstances. There is some room for error when the IMF analysis deals with countries with different policies and institutional environments. While there is scope for error given the diversity of countries, there have been few errors. In the case of Sri Lanka, there were no errors in the last 55 years. There was an error in 1953 which was the recommendation by the IMF to cut down subsidised rice rations. Since that time, the IMF programmes have elements of protecting the poor from higher prices.

One can also see that there have been accommodations for countries to move their reform agenda at a politically feasible pace.

6.4 Sri Lanka-Specific IMF Programmes

There was a strong request for help from the IMF both from the private sector and the public officials, given the dire circumstances of the country. The country was in trouble with very high foreign debt repayments and slowed down GDP growth, partly due to lockdowns to minimise the rate of infections of COVID-19. But, there had been a strong protest against Sri Lanka seeking help from the IMF within the governing party during the Gotabaya Rajapaksa period.

One complaint is that the IMF has strong conditions, which to some extent is true. But, any lender has to assess the risks of having a programme at this difficult juncture. Many independent evaluators of IMF lending have found that its recommendations for reforms and conditions have been fair, with no bias in either direction (too far right or too far left). One example of the independence of the IMF board is that it extended funds to Iran during the Iranian crisis when a new religious leader Khomeini became the president of Iran.

While the IMF extended a special emergency facility to help countries deal with COVID-19, Sri Lanka may have been reluctant to accept the offer. Nearly 100 countries availed themselves of the facility. As seen in other instances analysed in this book, ideology trumped economics. It is for the same reason that the government of Sri Lanka did not accept the $480 million grant from the Millennium Challenge Corporation (MCC) in the USA to improve urban transport and help create a land market through the determination of land ownership through a cadastral survey (incidentally, the entire programme was developed with the participation of Sri Lankan experts).

A question arose among economists as to why the Sri Lankan government was reluctant to go to the IMF when it had been to the IMF on sixteen earlier occasions as shown in Table 6.1.

The government has gone for negotiations with the IMF from 2021–2022, as the country was in a severe economic crisis with high limited funds to repay creditors. Without an IMF program the country would not be able to have an organised restructuring of debt. Also, without the IMF crisis the dire financial crisis would have become worse. And the country would have to undergo a disorganised default. Latin American experience with debt in the 1980s showed that, with unstructured debt, it will take a long time for a country to get back to its position before the crisis. With the new administration led by the new President Ranil Wickremesinghe, an IMF programme was negotiated and a debt restructuring programme was initiated, supported by independent financial and legal experts under an IMF–EFF (Extended Fund Facility) programme.

6.5 Conclusion

The reluctance to go to the IMF for help, the vast amount of money being printed with scant attention to likely inflation and a belief in the untested modern monetary theory, which claims that increases in money supply do not affect inflation, have contributed to the worsening of the crisis. Had Sri Lanka gone to the IMF in 2021, the country would have been in a more comfortable position to deal with the debt overhang. Currency swaps were used in exchange for domestic currency without strict fixed terms. It also would have been a situation in which Sri Lanka would need not have taken recourse to sign debt swaps which were a non-transparent process where various inducements to the partner countries are agreed as currency swap. In Chapter 7, we see that ideology played an important role in the pursuit of industrial policy versus having a policy towards industry. People with a left-of-centre ideology prefer industry policies rather than a neutral policy towards industry, where policies were chosen based on the decisions made by people who prefer picking winners rather than allowing prices to be determined in the market (see Chapter 4).

Chapter 7

Industrial Policy Versus Policy Towards Industry Debate: The Sri Lanka Case

7.1 Introduction

Policy debates inform the public. They should provide at least two sides to an issue. Even more importantly, they should provide grist for policy-making. One exception is the case between industrial policy and neutral policy towards industry related to Sri Lanka. Sri Lanka moved from neutral policies to industrial policies in the late 1950s without a debate. The government of the day simply adopted industrial policies due to the prevailing ideology and economic circumstances (the deteriorating balance-of-payment situation), with state-owned enterprises as the instrument. Similarly, in the 1977 reform package, the government of the day switched to a more neutral policy towards industry partly due to ideology and partly due to the failure of the industrial policy. Again, there was no debate. In the early 1990s, Sri Lankan economists made the case for industrial policy and the debate began. This time, the focus shifted to the private sector to carry out industrial policy, unlike on the previous occasion. But, there has not been a proper debate. The present chapter examines the new case for industrial policy today. It is hoped that it would provide a little balance and two sides to the debate.

Industrial policy means policies aimed at raising the share of a particular component of output, most commonly the share of manufacturing output in GDP in the case of Sri Lanka. This could be done by raising productivity (output per unit of input) and value added by diverting resources to the sector or activity. It could be in manufacturing, exports or any other component of GDP or activity that is considered to have strong growth potential. This leads to the claim that public support is needed for a particular dynamic activity or sector. The main rationale for such intervention is that if it is left to the market or, as is commonly done, to the private sector, such an activity will not come about and be a future source of output growth. Thus, industrial policy implies targeting or selective intervention in a particular sector or activity. It is based on the infant industry argument. There is, of course, a strong case for infant industry intervention in economic theory going back to the time of List and Hamilton. Sri Lankan economists have by and large espoused this argument as being necessary for the country to achieve high rates of growth in manufacturing output and exports and to match the performance of East Asian economies.[1] Putting these two positions together, a majority of Sri Lankan economists have denigrated the industrial achievements of the country to date.

A policy towards industry means an approach that does not, in general, target any particular activity as a public policy but maintains a neutral stance towards all activities through uniform incentives. But, a neutral policy towards industry does not mean an abdication of the government's role. It means that the government has an onerous role to play in promoting growth, but it is done at a more general level where intervention in any particular activity is the exception, rather than the rule. Under this policy stance, the public policy addresses only those distortions that prevent the emergence of a viable long-term industry or activity. Thus, these two types of policy stances can be described as a selective intervention in the economy in contrast to the pursuit of neutral policies in general. The government provides a trade regime that is neutral towards activities and produces for the domestic market, where the foreign market has stable macroeconomic policies and exchange rates, with legal and regulatory frameworks allowing easy entry and exit from different sectors or activities. With a few exceptions, it lets the market make the decisions as to where to invest.

Some Sri Lankan analysts have attempted to distinguish between trade policy and industrial policy. When trade policies are deliberately articulated to favour one particular activity over others, it becomes an instrument of industrial policy. However, it is well known that trade policy

---

[1] Bhagwati and Ramaswami (1963).

is not the appropriate instrument to address domestic distortions. It leads to an unnecessary consumption cost (and under some circumstances to a production cost) and can be avoided by using a domestic subsidy for the intervention. Of course, if the purpose is to discourage the expansion of an activity or a particular output that has negative externalities (such as the production of a pollutant), then the appropriate policy is a targeted domestic tax. This chapter does not consider interventions on optimal tariff or strategic trade theory grounds given the small-country assumption for Sri Lanka. Sri Lanka has no monopoly or oligopoly power to influence foreign demand or supply.

The debate between industrial policy and policy towards industry assumes special significance in Sri Lanka for several reasons. First, by and large, it has been a one-sided debate. A majority of Sri Lankan economists have favoured industrial policy over neutral policy towards industry. Second, many who advocate selective interventions to raise manufacturing output and exports have not made a rigorous attempt to examine the validity of the arguments on either side, but have taken market failure as a given fact and one that leads to industrial policy.[2] Most often, neutral policies have been denigrated by Sri Lankan economists as those that would not lead to rapid industrialisation. They are characterised as "market fundamentalist," "neo-classical" in approach or, what some have called, "a low-growth trajectory." Often, neutral policies are attacked as an element of the "Washington consensus" even though economic policies could originate anywhere in the world, and they have. In fact, those countries that have achieved great economic success do not owe a penny to any particular capital city except their own.

Those who favour a neutral policy towards industry accuse the other side of "picking winners" and being "statists" who prefer maintaining the dominance of the public sector beyond its comparative advantage or simply being unable to let go of control of various aspects and activities of the economy due to a particular political ideology or bureaucratic interest to extract rents from a control regime. They are also accused of ignoring what has happened in the world in the last two decades when there has been greater use of market-based allocation of resources from Beijing to Moscow and from Delhi to Kampala. Third, the debate assumes special significance because Sri Lanka's manufacturing output growth has slowed since the late 1990s and a reassessment of Sri Lanka's strategy

---

[2] Athukorala and Rajapatirana (2000).

to achieve high growth has been suggested. Fourth, with large and new foreign assistance available, there would be a reassessment of economic policy. Finally, while a majority of Sri Lankan economists have argued for industrial policy, policymakers have not followed their advice, especially after the 1977 liberalisation of the economy.[3]

In particular, this chapter attempts to keep the "noisy" elements out of the discussion, so that one can look at the issues per se and not characterise each position or denigrate the opposite side. Such an approach will examine the debate in terms of the issues and will not focus on any particular individual or group. This is done in the interest of saving space and is not meant to deny any credit or assign any blame to any author or authors.

To anticipate the conclusion, the chapter finds that the risks and costs associated with industrial policy have not been sufficiently recognised in the Sri Lankan debate. The interpretation of the main ingredient of the success of East Asian countries is not industrial policy but having proper economic fundamentals. The 1997–2000 East Asian crises were in part due to the attempt to use financial policies as an instrument of industrial policy and the neglect of macroeconomic fundamentals. This chapter presents an alternative to industrial policy, namely, having neutral policies towards industry but intervening in particular activities when it is justified on proper infant industry grounds. Government intervention would also require an institutional setup to ensure that the determination and implementation of such an intervention would minimise the costs and avoid capture by vested interests.

This chapter is organised as follows: After the introduction (Section 7.1), Section 7.2 examines the main elements of the case for industrial policy, which is based on the infant industry argument. Section 7.3 evaluates the case put forward for industrial policy based on the East Asian countries' experience, especially following the crisis faced by those countries during the 1997–2000 period. Section 7.4 examines Sri Lanka's manufacturing export experience to consider whether one would be better informed by looking at experience rather than conjectures as to what would have happened if one type of policy was followed rather than the other. Section 7.5 provides the conclusions.

---

[3] Athukorala and Rajapatirana (2000).

7.2 The Case for Industrial Policy

As mentioned, industrial policy derives its theoretical support from the infant industry argument. The infant industry argument is very respectable in neo-classical economics and has been examined by the leading economists of the day such as Johnson (1965), Kemp (1960), Grubel (1966) and Corden (1974 and 1994), and Krueger and Tuncer (1982). In contrast, Lall (1990) and Wade (1990) advocate industrial policy both on grounds of their heterodox position on economic theory and their interpretation of the East Asian experience. They were later supported by Stiglitz (1989) in his critique of globalisation.[4]

The main elements of the infant industry argument can be summarised in four propositions[5]: (a) New industries and activities have high costs compared to foreign enterprises and they require some time to become competitive. (b) It is not profitable for any new firm to enter that industry without assistance because a firm that is willing to invest in technology, labour training and similar learning activities cannot appropriate the benefits of that investment to itself. (c) With assistance from the government, the firm may be able to become competitive in the future and be able to turn out net profits following initial losses which will justify the initial investment. (d) Assistance is required for a temporary period after which costs would fall and it would enable the firm to compete with foreign firms without further public assistance.

Sri Lankan economists have argued that there are a host of reasons why the initial costs of firms would be high such as "supply-side market failures" in both product and factor markets, the limited ability to create technological capability, the absence of necessary labour and managerial skills, weak backward and forward linkage creation, and the weakness of the institutions that could promote industry.[6] Individual entrepreneurs overestimate the costs and risks and underestimate the benefits from their investment in this milieu. The Sri Lankan economists cited in this chapter see market failures and the absence of markets as leading to a weak

---

[4] Stiglitz is perhaps the exception because his espousal of industrial policy arises mostly on grounds of the pure theory of information. He holds that markets do not carry information efficiently and markets are altogether absent in some instances. He uses this view to interpret the East Asian Experience (1996).
[5] Krueger and Tuncer (1982).
[6] Athukorala and Rajapatirana (2000).

industrial performance all around and the country's inability to duplicate the success of East Asian countries, according to their interpretation of the ingredients of East Asian countries' industrial success.

It is necessary to examine the arguments for intervention on infant industry grounds and to see what elements support the case for industrial policy. With reference to (a), high costs of new industries would arise from the reasons given by those who advocate industrial policy. But, while agreeing that the initial costs of industries may be high for a variety of reasons, industrial policy cannot be the sweeping answer that has been put forward by a majority of Sri Lankan economists. To be sure, developing countries like Sri Lanka will have high costs of capital and weak institutions that raise transaction costs, causing the initial costs of establishment and operation to rise. The main contention of those who advocate industrial policy is that these deficiencies have to be addressed by targeting these activities for public support on a wide scale. This would imply a subsidy of some type to the firm or activity, either to raise the profitability of the industry through raising domestic output prices (through a guaranteed price to the producer or protection) or to reduce costs through subsidising the particular factor of production or input if it is overpriced due to distortion (such as a monopoly in the supply of the input). It could be a subsidy to capital or skilled labour or some intermediate input. However, the optimal intervention theory holds that the intervention has to go to the origin of the distortion directly. It is well known that trade protection is not the answer in the presence of domestic distortions, since it leads to a lower welfare outcome than an optimum subsidy.[7] A targeted subsidy to address the high cost is superior to trade protection since the former does not involve a consumption cost. But, it could involve costs in terms of the producer surplus in the manner in which the subsidy is financed (e.g. raising taxes on other efficient producers). It is essential that there is a time element involved in the process to give it the required dynamic character because over time costs decline and profitability increases. The initial high costs must fall over time for the industry or activity to become profitable. However, it is important to make the point that the initial cost disadvantage is temporary and not a permanent state of affairs. If the latter were the case, the country has no static or dynamic comparative advantage in the production of the item, so no amount of

---

[7] Corden (1994) was a pioneer in the ranking of trade interventions since 1957. This work was followed by others including Johnson (1965) and Bhagwati and Ramaswami (1963).

subsidy will help to overcome the cost disadvantage. The infant supported then becomes a geriatric ward needing permanent sustenance.

With respect to (b), the presence of an externality, it is essential that the benefits of investments are not internal to the firm but to the industry. This means that a private entrepreneur would not be able to recover the investment costs from future profits because the benefits of his investment (such as training labour or acquiring technological capability) could not be appropriated by that entrepreneur. If the benefits are internal to the firm, it can make initial losses but recover them over time, and in fact it can become a profitable venture without public support. In this sense, these losses are an investment. And, like any investment, it must have a high rate of return compared to other investments.[8] Thus, it is essential that there is an externality, namely, that the firm that invests cannot appropriate the increased returns to it because other firms (in the industry) that benefit from it (such as a lowering cost) keep the benefit to themselves.

With respect to (c), it is necessary that industrial policy-based assistance leads to the creation of returns over and above that which would be possible if there were no intervention. What is even more important is that the return to the activity must rise above all other activities for it to be optimal. Otherwise, the resources used to support one activity imply an opportunity cost to other activities. Thus, if manufacturing and export activities are supported for reasons of raising a particular component of the GDP, it must be such that there is no reduction in output of other activities beyond a reasonable period of support. In other words, the return generated to the supported activity, must be over and above other activities. The real reason for the promotion is to raise GDP and its growth rate rather than some particular component of the GDP. Thus, measuring success as equal to an increase in exports due to the promotion of exports is not the appropriate way to measure success. The simple test is to see whether support for an activity raises overall GDP, or in a dynamic sense raises the GDP growth rate.

---

[8] A simple test is whether, over time, the present value of the benefits (appropriately discounted) exceeds the losses, including the investment (similarly discounted), that are to accrue over the lifetime of the investment. This is necessary but not sufficient. The returns must be better than any other investment that could be undertaken for it to be sufficient. Otherwise, the intervention is not optimal.

Finally, with respect to (d), the issue of the time period of support needed for an infant to grow up has to be determined. What is the cutoff period for support? It should be intuitively clear that all activities requiring support may not have the same period and extent of support, because cost structures, degrees of learning, the extents of market power and technological capabilities differ. This then leads to the issue of how to determine what activities to support, what form the support must take and for what period support is needed. These are intrinsically difficult questions.

These generic requirements for viable industrial policy are more demanding than commonly recognised in the Sri Lankan debate on industrial policy.

Moreover, other considerations not mentioned here come into play, making the advocacy of industrial policy a questionable proposition. These considerations also arise from the received theory of policy intervention. They may sound easy on the surface but are eminently difficult to implement in fact. These considerations are as follows: (i) The choice of which activities to support in the sense that the activity has a long-term dynamic comparative advantage is not as easy to determine. Why would bureaucrats have better knowledge of products and markets than those in the market themselves and those whose decisions as to where to invest are subject to their own individual risk evaluations? These investors would be careful in choosing the investment in the first place. The exceptions to this rule are few and hard to come by. (ii) What is the optimal form of intervention given that the received theory tells us that the policy must be targeted at the particular deficiency or distortion that prevents a country from realising greater returns to its resources from supporting a particular activity? (iii) For what period is support needed and could it be fixed in advance? (iv) What is the exit policy from support in the absence of a fixed period when a highly political choice is involved in giving or taking away support? The latter is more difficult given that the political processes are not often capable of withdrawing support once it is given, since groups or coalitions are built to preserve the support. (v) It is not the case that bureaucrats and administrators are neutral actors in allocating support; they could be seeking rent themselves through rent seeking activities according to public choice theory.[9] (vi) It is also not clear if the

---

[9] It is extraordinary that Stiglitz does not recognize that the success of East Asian economies arose from creating markets at home and penetrating new markets abroad. There is a possibility that industry policy could lead to rent seeking.

firms that receive public support will put it to the use for which it was requested. This is a difficult area to monitor due to the principal–agent problem encountered in decision-making for optimal outcomes. The public is the principal and the bureaucrats are the agents. It is rarely the case that their interests coincide even among presumably the world's best bureaucrats as one saw in the case of the East Asian countries. (vii) The firms that receive support will pursue lobbying to maintain that support. It may also be rational for the firms receiving support to not invest but window-dress to satisfy some bureaucratic performance criterion. As Baldwin (1969) noted, it is not even clear if firms will make the appropriate investment of the funds they receive in public support.[10] Their incentive to maximise profits would prevail over making some uncertain long-term investment. If the investment in knowledge that industrial policy has supported is easily duplicable by other firms, then the returns will fall, and firms will be reluctant to invest even if public funds were to be available. (viii) Finally, private markets can create mechanisms to preserve the knowledge to ensure returns to such investment through technology agreements with foreign firms that have the technology protected by patents. Alternatively, domestic firms (if there are a small number of firms involved in the industry) can come to an agreement to use technology on a cost-sharing basis. Thus, an externality is internalised through the use of the market.[11]

In Sri Lanka, the record of the various public enterprises that received huge, targeted subsidies is hardly encouraging. They became veritable geriatric wards rather than infants who grew up to adulthood to fend for themselves. This must have a sobering effect on those who advocate industrial policy for Sri Lanka. They must be careful to recognise the difficulties in formulating, implementing and monitoring industrial policies. They would of course argue that the support of public enterprises was wrong because even a prima facie example for the infant industry could not be made in those cases. But, the fact is that nobody tried. It was a political decision based on ideology at the time when the governments of the day followed the model of state ownership as a panacea for handling all manner of perceived social evils. These enterprises wasted public resources on a tremendous scale which adversely impacted both GDP

---

[10] Baldwin (1969).

[11] Coase (1960) made this point, and it was the basis for the extension of externality issues in the work of Buchanan and Stubblebine (1962).

growth and equity. However, the proponents of modern-day industrial policy would argue that support for the private sector would be more viable on grounds that private enterprises will have to pass market tests ultimately, even if they were to receive handsome subsidies initially. Thus, those who say that Sri Lanka should follow the East Asian model are implicitly making that argument. That case is examined in Section 7.3.

7.3 East Asian Countries' Experiences and their Relevance for Industrial Policy in Sri Lanka

A large majority of Sri Lankan economists emphasise the role of industrial policy (i.e. the use of selective intervention to promote manufacturing exports) as the main ingredient that led to the stellar performance of East Asian countries. This demands careful analysis to establish what worked and what did not if these countries are to serve as a model for Sri Lanka.

The debate has become even more important due to the 1997–2000 East Asian crisis. The crisis that began in Thailand spread to Malaysia, Indonesia and the four Tigers (Singapore, Taiwan, Hong Kong and South Korea). While Hong Kong, Taiwan and Singapore experienced much reduced GDP growth compared to their past, these countries did not face a crisis. South Korea, Indonesia and Thailand, on the other hand, underwent tremendous economic crises. Some countries lost more than 10 per cent of their GDP in a single year. Even before the crisis, there had been doubts about the nature of the performance of these countries and a vast majority of the mainstream (orthodox) economists were sceptical about the role of industrial policy as the main reason for their success. Following the crisis, even greater doubts began to emerge on whether the approach was viable. East Asian countries have been held in such esteem that the World Bank called their performance "the East Asian Miracle" and compiled evidence of the manifestation of the miracle and the elements that were responsible for it (World Bank, 1993). This view came to be challenged even before the East Asian crisis. Some began to doubt whether there was even a miracle after all. Moreover, it is noteworthy that these economies have recovered remarkably well, some 5 years after the crisis. The main antidote to the crisis that led to the recovery has been more neutral policies towards industry, eschewing selective interventions through industrial policy.

By any objective standard, East Asian countries have performed better than any other group of developing countries. They have achieved the highest rates of GDP growth during the period 1967–1997, averaging some 7.5 per cent per year. They had high GDP growth, associated employment growth and the most rapid growth in exports of any group of countries. South Korea was able to raise its real exports at the pace of more than 20 per cent per year. Taiwan has a similar or near similar record. Despite reduced demand for exports during world recessions in the early 1970s and early 1980s, Hong Kong was able to increase its exports at double-digit rates.

With exports, imports also increased and East Asian economies became more open economies. There were low levels of protection all around, save for a few areas. Over time, these countries became more integrated with the world economy. Following the crisis, these countries resolved to open their economies even more.

(a) Interpretation by Different Schools

As is to be expected, analysts from different camps give their interpretation of the success of East Asian countries.

At an international level, two broad schools can be identified for analytical purposes, as supporting one view or the other. (a) The conventional school's interpretation, associated with Bhagwati (1978), Krueger (1978), Little (1981), Sachs and Warner (1993), Dollar (1995), and Lawrence and Weinstein (1999) among others, was that the East Asian countries began to grow faster following a period of economic reforms in the mid-1960s when these countries began to use neutral and more market-driven policies rather than administrative mechanisms to allocate resources. This school, contrary to the opinion of some economists in Sri Lanka, did not associate the success of the East Asian countries with laissez-faire policies. Nor was there a Washington Consensus at the time.[12] Except for Hong Kong, all other countries intervened in the markets in one way or another. But, these interventions were less than in their past. They intervened to move towards neutral policies.[13]

With respect to the trade regime, in particular, the East Asian countries' interventions led to more or less neutral incentives for producing for

---

[12] The term "Washington Consensus" was coined by John Williamson in the mid-1980s following the debt crisis in Latin America. Later, he retracted the term and remarked that it was neither Washington based nor was there a consensus to speak of.

[13] Deepak and Rajapatirana (1989) showed that trade incentives were closer to neutrality in the case of South Korea compared to India, using the Little–Mirlees type of accounting prices (ratio of shadow prices to market prices).

the domestic and export markets. They maintained good fundamentals, such as sound fiscal policies and avoidance of inflation, and allowed only mild financial repression. This view is the mainstream view, not only because of the avowed leadership of the main contenders in the economic profession but also due to the vast amount of empirical work they had undertaken themselves and inspired others to undertake. Little (1981), who pioneered the examination of the link between trade and development, held that the presumed increase in productivity from industrial policy, even if it were true, would be necessary but not a sufficient condition for success, since the returns to intervention must be high enough to offset the cost of intervention. And, it also has to be shown that the private sector was incapable of undertaking the investments needed in the first place, as discussed in Section 7.2, in order to justify industrial policy. Furthermore, Little believed that there is no empirical evidence to show that the East Asian countries were able to realise high rates of social return from industrial policies. The purported evidence is anecdotal and not empirically well established, Wade (1990) and Lall (1990)).

While agreeing that East Asian countries have achieved stellar success, Krugman (1997), Young (1995), and Kim and Lau (1996) showed that there was no miracle in East Asia, but that it was the result of increased use of resources, both labour and capital, and not increased efficiency. They also made the important observation that East Asian countries were different in their growth experience compared to Japan in the 1950s and 1960s, even though it is claimed that the countries followed the Japanese approach. For one thing, compared to Japan, the four Tigers, except Hong Kong, had low (and sometimes negative) total factor productivity (TFP) growth. For another, the highest TFP was observed in Hong Kong, a country that did not follow the industrial policy intervention model of Japan.[14] And further, slowing growth in such cases is inevitable when growth is not due to increasing efficiency but increased use of factors. They offered the example of the slowdown in Japan from 1987–1997 as confirmation of their point of view. Japanese growth had to come to an end, as its TFP growth levelled off. In addition, it was found that East Asian countries were well behind the technological frontier reached by the advanced industrial countries, even though they were able to reach

---

[14] See the Asian Miracle (World Bank, 1993). The Hong Kong TFP growth data kept the Miracle Study from tilting towards support for industrial policy.

high levels of technical efficiency.[15] Thus, industrial policy did not meet one of the strongest cases made for it by its proponents.

In contrast to the conventional view, the supporters of industrial policy (Wade, Stiglitz and Lall — referred to in Section 7.2) claimed that the East Asian countries were successful in reaching high levels of efficiency and also in reaching the technological frontier. The success of the East Asian countries was more due to "getting the prices wrong" through industrial policy interventions and "governing the market" (in the words of Wade). Their evidence is much less systematic than the neutral policy towards industry that is the conventional school's view. The industrial policy school's evidence tends to be anecdotal, using mostly South Korean and Taiwanese data. She treated it as an unqualified success prior to the crisis. It is noteworthy that this claim has never been examined in terms of the analytical requirements for the infant industry presented in Section 7.2. There are some oblique references to East Asians countries but their main argument is based on their interpretation of empirical evidence from East Asia. In sharp contrast, the conventional view, of the policy towards the industry, holds that these countries succeeded not because of industrial policy but in spite of it (Little's words).

As is to be expected, industrial policy advocates do not attribute the failure of the countries in the late 1990s as arising from anything to do with the failure of industrial policy. However, the subjugation of the financial market to implement industrial policy through directed credit led to the loss of financial discipline, weak commercial banks, macroeconomic disequilibrium and huge moral hazards and financial collapse.

(b) Industrial Policy Issue and East Asian Countries' Performance
The industrial policy school gained ground in the 1980s in the debate on the factors responsible for the success of East Asian economies, i.e. prior to the East Asian crisis. Their main point of contention was that, in addition to getting the fundamentals right, the East Asian countries selectively intervened in the economy through industrial policy in order to depart from the neutral incentives. Those who espoused this view argued that the

---

[15] Technical efficiency is reached when the frontier (the production possibility curve determined by the given level of technology) is achieved. The technological frontier lies outside the production possibility curve determined by the world state of technology. Sustained growth involves a technological change to move the technology frontier forward.

success of these economies confirmed the importance of dynamic factors such as the learning effects, externalities and that by substituting for the market a country can achieve success in industrialisation. Some claimed that the success of East Asian economies was not due to neutral incentives but to factors that are yet to be understood well.

Wade contended that what they described as the neo-classical position was not relevant to developing countries given that the concern should not be with static but dynamic comparative advantage.[16] Sanjaya Lall, another advocate of industrial policy, influenced the majority of the Sri Lankan economists who contended that industrial policy intervention was the reason for the success of East Asian countries. Kelegama and Wignaraja (1991), Wignaraja (1991), Vidanapathirana (1993), Abeyratne (1997) and Rodrigo (2001) argued for industrial policy in Sri Lanka.

Following Lall, the Sri Lankan economists based their position on the need to promote technology in Sri Lanka through industrial policy. However, they did not deny that incentives were important for industrialisation. They claimed that government intervention was necessary to lead firms in developing countries like Sri Lanka to acquire technological capability. According to their view, East Asian countries succeeded due to building technological capability through industrial policy. They claimed that economic liberalisation had to be supported by industrial policy, which meant that they did not support neutral incentives. Accordingly, they believed that the trade regime should have different rates of protection to reflect different degrees of support for different activities. Some went to the extent of recommending quantitative restrictions to achieve this degree of dispersion of incentives.[17]

Other Asian countries except for Hong Kong and Singapore (at least, up to a point) provided extra incentives to the export sector through duty

---

[16] Keynes provided the best explanation of neo-classical economics in his introduction to the Cambridge Economics Handbooks series. He called it a method or a way of examining issues and not a given body of thought. Thus, what is alleged to be neo-classical is the use of the marginal economic analysis method or the main toolbox of economists. Like value, costs and returns, economic decisions are made at a margin.

[17] But, it is now well known that QRs lead to chaotic incentive structures, encourage rent-seeking and break the link between domestic and foreign prices in ways that make macro-economic management difficult by introducing structural rigidities.

drawbacks, duty exemptions, bonded warehouses, export promotion zones, tax concessions, direct transfers and subsidised credit, comprising a plethora of special incentives. Bhagwati (1986) stated that these efforts of some countries aimed to create an "ultra-export bias." The bias is measured by the excess domestic currency received by producers in exporting activities compared to producers in import-substituting activities. Some analysts argued that exports have special externalities (such as non-pecuniary externalities in which long-run supply curves would fall as the industry expands) and their promotion could enhance productivity (Wesphal, 1978). Others have argued for them on pure "learning-by-doing grounds." Whatever the rationale for these policies, it is clear that East Asian countries did follow a mercantilist strategy of valuing export growth over import growth at the earlier stages of opening their economies. A definite sequencing was followed; exports were promoted before imports were liberalised. The issue is whether this was the appropriate policy in terms of maximising the growth rate of GDP, which is the final test of success, and not maximising a specific component of output, as described in Section 7.2.

East Asian countries' interventions included trade policies (both protective tariffs and export subsidies), tax incentives, credit subsidies, direct transfers and moral suasion. Many of these countries established programmes to accelerate advanced industries. Financial market policies played a decisive role in these interventions in the case of Korea, Indonesia, Thailand and to some extent Taiwan. Mild financial repression that resulted from the low deposit rates and ceilings on lending rates in the early years was not considered to be harmful. There was also the theoretical justification for intervention in financial markets (Stiglitz and Weiss, 1981) based on asymmetric information-related issues between lenders and borrowers that created moral hazards and adverse selection. These attributes of the financial market were said to preclude the market forces from allocating financial resources optimally.[18]

---

[18] One theoretical objection to Stiglitz and Weiss (1981) is that their model applies to a single game in a game-theoretic world and does not apply to repeated games where the parties learn through subsequent rounds. Thus, a commercial bank may not be able to monitor borrower behaviour in the first round of the "lending game," but would certainly learn to evaluate risks well in a particular market and among particular borrowers. In that case, the Stiglitz–Weiss model fails to show the non-optimality of financial markets.

(c) Emphasis on Exports and Postponing Import liberalisation

Some analysts have identified the slow growth of productivity in East Asian countries as arising from industrial policy that led to the slow rate of import liberalisation. Rapid import liberalisation would have helped in two ways. It would have helped to create a competitive environment for domestic producers, on the one hand, and acted as an effective conduit for acquiring technology to move to the technology frontier, on the other. A study by Lawrence and Weinstein (1999) showed that productivity growth is closely associated with import liberalisation. They found that East Asian countries were successful in exports because imports associated with these exports allowed them to increase productivity. Thus, exporting was the result of the productivity increase and not the other way around. Looking at GDP and exports and import growth in Japan over some 40 years, they concluded that Japan could have grown even faster had it liberalised its imports faster. They came to the same conclusion on South Korea.

Exporters were provided "free trade status," while import growth was kept low. However, the system relied on highly efficient administrative mechanisms and tolerant international competitors who did not challenge the export subsidies used to offset the bias against exports arising from import restrictions. There are inherent difficulties in offsetting the bias both in terms of the administrative arrangements and the lack of tolerance for export subsidies in the world today. These factors tend to prevent sequencing export promotion before import liberalisation. Moreover, other empirical work (Panagariya, 2000) showed that exports of countries that provided export subsidies have not grown faster than countries that did not provide export subsidies.

Coordination failures, incomplete markets and asymmetric information issues could well lead to departures from optimal resource allocation under the price mechanism. Government interventions, in this case, were consistent with optimal policy. There were risks and difficulties that arose in the East Asian countries leading to questions on whether the interventions were optimal per se or whether the bureaucrats who were entrusted with substituting for the market were capable of carrying them out without resisting the incentives to seek rents. Public Choice Theory (Buchanan and Tullock, 1962) sounded a sceptical note on the reliance on bureaucrats to act optimally. They could intervene in such ways either to make a personal financial gain or increase the power of bureaucracy for its own purposes. In any event, most would agree that the interventions in East Asia turned out to be excessive and harmful, particularly in the financial sector. Some would argue that it was the financial sector that led to the undoing of the strong performance of the East Asian economies and that there was nothing wrong with interventions in the real sector per se (Ito, 2001). But, this dichotomy is somewhat strained, artificial and not possible to sustain in real-world policymaking, as financial sector problems can, and did, have serious effects on the real sector and vice versa.

(d) Results of Industrial policy
Beason and Weinstein (1996) found that subsidies granted to different industries were negatively correlated with their efficiency in Japan, which is regarded as the paragon of the success of the industrial policy. They showed that the industries that were found to be least productive received the highest subsidies per unit of their value added. Moreover, earlier research had also shown that the selection of industries on infant industry grounds was not an easy task even if the bureaucracy was not seeking rents. Karl Zinsmeister wrote that "many of its strongest businesses — such as home electronics, cameras, robotics, precision equipment, pianos, bicycles, watches and calculators, numerically controlled machine tools, and ceramics — were developed without help from Ministry of International Trade and Industry (MITI) or other agencies."[19] Perhaps, the highly praised bureaucracies of East Asia resisted the temptation to seek rent. But, it became clear during the crisis in East Asia that this assumption was no longer valid. There was a capture of the bureaucracy by politicians and industrialists. The most acute cases were seen in Indonesia, Thailand and South Korea where there was rampant corruption and misuse of funds arising from a symbiotic relationship among three groups (bureaucrats, industrialists and politicians). The success of bureaucracies in Japan and the early period of the South Korean performance may have been the exception rather than the rule. Moreover, this approach led a few families to dominate particular industrial activities, as was the case in South Korea and Indonesia. It led to the growth of monopoly and the lack of contestability in goods and credit markets. The capture of bureaucracy by industrialists and politicians has been found in the allocation of subsidies of various kinds. Instead of promoting contests among the different groups, the bureaucracy entered the contests, leading to corruption on a wide scale.

---

[19] Zinsmeister (1993).

One important lesson from the East Asian experience is that the industrial policymaking process can be easily captured and corrupted, as was in the case in South Korea. It would not only entail heavy costs at the firm level but also have economy-wide and large macroeconomic effects that would operate via the credit and banking systems, as happened in South Korea, Thailand and Indonesia.

A study by Howard Pack (2000), which carefully documented the experiences of Japan and South Korea, found that industrial policy's contribution to the industrial success of these countries was small at best and advocated neutral policies towards the industry for developing countries.[20] His findings are important for two reasons. First, in the past, Pack was a strong advocate of industrial policy, but following the East Asian crisis he re-examined the case to come to the present conclusion. Second, his analysis was done carefully, using four counterfactual calculations to examine the case for industrial policy based on TFP estimates. He found that only one-third of one per cent of growth in the two countries could be attributed to industrial policy. While this is not trivial, it is hardly the secret to success. In addition, the conduct of industrial policy requires an exceptionally capable and non-corrupt bureaucracy and the political ability to withdraw support from non-performing firms. One finds that the risks of using industrial policies when these conditions are not present outweigh their expected benefits.

(e) Relevance for Sri Lanka

The present discussion leads to a number of conclusions regarding the lessons for Sri Lanka from the experience of East Asian countries:
(i) No one has established the case rigorously for East Asian countries' use of industrial policy on infant grounds as described in Section 7.2.
(ii) The stellar performance of East Asian countries can be ascribed to getting the fundamentals right and not to industrial policy per se. What little empirical evidence exists supports that position. The findings of Krugman, Young, and Kim and Lau showed that there was no stellar TFP growth, but that overall GDP growth was based on factor augmentation, attributable to high savings and investments, supported by a stable macroeconomic environment, strong property rights and political stability, at least up to the time of the 1997–2000 crisis. (iii) The pursuit of export promotion at the expense of import liberalisation turned out to

---

[20] Pack (2000)

be less successful than realised earlier, as found by Lawrence and Weinstein (1999). (iv) The crisis calls into question the viability of the industrial policies that led to weak financial systems, overdependence on bureaucratic decisions-making, leading to large moral hazards, and the ultimate collapse of the financial system, weakened by decades of lack of scrutiny and failure to meet basic prudential and regulatory standards. (v) Industrial policies in other countries have fared worse than those of India, Argentina and Turkey, which provide a strong counterfactual test of East Asia's experience. Unlike East Asian countries, these countries did not have good fundamental economic policies. (vi) The contribution from industrial policy has been modest by Pack's estimate and should be contrasted with the risk of capture and rent-seeking. It must be precluded as a viable option for Sri Lanka. (vii) Finally, the recovery in East Asian countries has been good, largely due to the reversal from industrial policy in the direction of more neutral policies towards industry.

7.4 Sri Lanka's Manufacture Export Experience

Sri Lanka's manufacturing export experience has been the main bone of contention for those who advocate for industrial policy. The experience is denigrated strongly by them on several grounds. It is for this reason, the best way to examine the veracity of the case of industry policy versus Policy towards industry is to look at actual experience.

(a) Manufacturing Export Performance

Two broad periods could serve to show contrasts in manufacturing export performance: the period 1960–1977 when Sri Lanka was a highly inward-oriented economy and the period from 1978 onward when, following the economic liberalisation beginning in 1977, it became a more outward-oriented economy.

During the first period, manufacturing export growth was low, some 3–5 per cent per year in current dollars, and its share was only 5 per cent of merchandise exports. During the latter 1978–1995 period, manufacturing exports grew by 32 per cent per year in current dollars. Their share rose to 70 per cent of total merchandise exports. By 2009, they accounted for 75 per cent of total exports. The value of manufacturing exports increased from a mere $5 million to over $5.3 billion in current US dollars by 2009.

During the 1980–1995 period, Sri Lanka was among the top five low-income countries with respect to average growth in export earnings from manufacturing exports and was increasing its share of manufacturing in total merchandise exports. The labour-intensive factor content of Sri Lankan exports rose from a low 2.6 per cent in the 1962–1977 period to nearly 60 per cent during 1990–1995 and it may have risen in the remaining years to 2002.[21] There was a corresponding decline in the share of land or resource-intensive factor content in exports over the same period from 96 per cent to 32 per cent by 1990–1995. It may have fallen below 32 per cent by 2002. The important point here is that with the economic liberalisation and related movement towards more neutral policies, the economy responded strongly not only in terms of the rate of growth of exports but also in its composition to reflect the country's comparative advantage in labour-intensive manufacturing.

In addition, with a return to more neutral policies during the latter period, the bias against exports was reduced. The overall efficiency of the economy improved. This is indicated by the total manufacturing TFP growth. TFP growth was negative during the periods 1966–1974 and 1977–1981. It became positive during the 1981–1988 period and rose to a remarkable 9.17 during 1988–1993.[22] Similar high TFP growth is observed when manufacturing, excluding textiles and clothing, is considered. Many Sri Lankan economists consider the concentration on textiles and clothing as a weak characteristic of Sri Lanka's manufacturing experience due to the low value added in the activity and increased competition from China once MFA quotas are rescinded following the Textile and Clothing Agreement of the Uruguay Round. But, specialisation is what leads to gains from trade, and commodity composition changes over time, as comparative advantage changes.

Despite the success of Sri Lanka's manufacturing exports as seen in the above-mentioned performance, a majority of Sri Lankan economists found this performance wanting in many respects. A variety of criticisms were levelled against this performance by those who *espouse industrial policy*.

---

[21] Athukorala and Rajapatirana (2000).
[22] *Ibid.*

(b) Criticisms of Sri Lanka's manufacturing export performance

First, the growth rates achieved by Sri Lanka were seen as wanting in comparison to the East Asian countries. The latter grew faster on a sustained basis over some special periods in their development. Second, the value added in Sri Lanka's manufacturing exports is considered to be low and hence is described as "shallow industrialisation" by the advocates of industrial policy. Third, it is said that there were no strong forward or backward linkages in the manufacturing sector. Fourth, the commodity composition of Sri Lanka's exports is said to be narrow. Fifth, industrialisation has only resulted in a low rate of labour absorption. Finally, Sri Lanka's exports have a low technological component compared to the East Asian countries.

(c) Evaluation of the criticisms

Several issues arise from these criticisms and the advocacy of industrial policy as the antidote to the alleged poor performance as mentioned in the following:

(i) As seen in Section 7.2, by looking at one component of GDP, namely, manufacturing exports, one cannot pass judgement on the success or failure of a policy towards industry even though the advocates of industrial policy argue in that vein. The proper criterion should be whether the policy raised the GDP level and its growth rate. Increasing manufacturing exports is not equivalent to maximising national income. It is possible to raise manufacturing exports by various means through subsidies and other special incentives, but that is not equivalent to raising overall efficiency or improving welfare. Besides, such a policy is not sustainable and will not be tolerated by trading partners in the current international trading environment.

(ii) Increasing exports by keeping import controls (as suggested by those who advocate industrial policy and claim that Sri Lanka liberalised too rapidly) has many flaws. It would increase the bias against exports and lead to an appreciation of the exchange rate. Empirical evidence from Japan and South Korea (see Lawrence and Weinstein, 1999) shows that these countries could have grown even faster had they liberalised their imports along with the export promotion measures they adopted in the 1960s and 1970s.

(iii) The idea of linkages, both forward and backward, is flawed. It ignores incentives faced by the producers. In other words, maximising domestic value added as advocated by industrial policy proponents could lead to lower levels of efficiency and competitiveness and reduce Sri Lanka's share in world trade. A simple example would illustrate this point. If a country uses imported inputs but the government insists that those should be domestically produced, it would hurt the competitiveness of the activity. There is no guarantee that these inputs would be produced at low costs domestically when compared to the costs of imports. Besides, since imported inputs tend to be produced with more capital-intensive technology, this would amount to a substitution of capital for labour and would go against the country's comparative advantage. In fact, countries' comparative advantage is determined in terms of value adding and not producing the whole value chain in the country. During the import substitution phase (1960–1977), Sri Lanka attempted this strategy with disastrous results.

(iv) There is little or no economics involved in the advocacy of raising the level of technology. Investment in technology is like any other investment. The investor in technology has to look at costs and returns. In doing so, the investor adopts the most viable technology unless he or she faces constraints in the choice of technology. To insist that technology upgrading has to be attempted through industrial policy is to argue on non-economic grounds. Thus, for example, the school which claims to be the "neo-technology school" (Lall *et al.*) is valuing technology for its own sake. The bottom line is that if the use of "low-level" technology is due to a distortion, then a correction is appropriate. But, that need not be industrial policy. When one applies the infant industry argument to this situation, there is no general justification for technology being upgraded through public intervention.[23] There is, of course, another alternative to industrial policy-based technology upgrading, which is to remove any barriers to foreign direct investment, so technology

---

[23] It behoves the advocates of technology capability to ask the question of why textiles and garments were able to upgrade their technology while others were not able or willing to do so.

upgrading takes place in a viable way. This is what has happened in the textiles and garments sector.

(v) The commodity composition of Sri Lanka's exports reflects the country's comparative advantage. In fact, this has changed from resource-intensive to more labour-intensive goods as the economic policy became more neutral. It could have happened faster had policy reforms not been delayed until 1977.

(vi) The charge that labour absorption was low cannot be sustained given that employment increased rapidly following economic liberalisation and also because the factor content of exports changed to more labour-intensive products. In any case, the conjecture that industrial policies could have led to higher labour absorption is not demonstrated by anyone. It is merely a matter of conjecture.

(vii) Sri Lanka's export performance is not as poor as it is made out to be by industrial policy enthusiasts. It has been achieved under adverse circumstances. First, there has been a continued bias against exports despite the 1977 liberalisation (Ratnayake, 1988; Abeyratne, 1997). Second, during most of the post-liberalisation period, the exchange rate remained appreciated, adding to the bias, with some respite following the adoption of a floating exchange rate. Third, there were substantial macroeconomic imbalances in the early 1980s due to the undertaking of accelerated Mahaweli and other lead projects. That led to a Dutch disease problem. Other activities were put at a disadvantage including manufacturing. Fourth, there were two periods of political uncertainty: the JVP uprising in 1989 and the ethnic conflict that plagued the country since 1983. This was hardly the environment to foster high export and GDP growth.

(viii) Finally, the blanket advocacy of industrial policy neglects the political economy problems associated with such a policy in Sri Lanka. It could be easily captured by different interest groups including state-owned enterprises due to widespread political patronage and would also open the door to wide-scale rent-seeking. One very important reason for neutral policies towards industry is precisely to avoid a situation where different activities are provided with different incentives. Departing from neutrality invites lobbying efforts to attempt to capture rents through this process. In addition to embracing industry policy, and adding protection, both these aspects will make the country less competitive with the rest of the world.[24]

(d) An Alternative to Industrial Policy

Evidence from East Asia's and Sri Lanka's own experience and theoretical reasons suggests that a neutral policy towards the industry is more likely to maximise national income than industrial policy. Changing the composition of GDP does not ensure higher GDP growth by itself, only higher efficiency leads to higher growth. This chapter focused on manufacturing exports to highlight the main issues in the debate on industrial policy versus neutral policy towards industry since it is the arena in which a majority of Sri Lankan economists have advocated industrial policy.

As stated at the outset, there are specific cases in which selective interventions are needed when there are sizable distortions, such as capital and labour market distortions, constraints to profit-maximising technology (as against adopting sophisticated technology for its own sake) and lack of complementary investments. Here, the issue is to address the distortion directly by appropriate policy measures. By and large, neutral policy towards industry along with getting the fundamentals right (sound macroeconomic policy, stable prices wages and exchange rates, well-established property rights) will go a long way to provide the proper environment for strong GDP growth with industrial output as an important component of it.

But, this may not be sufficient and that is why some specific interventions may be necessary. The important point is that the answer is not industrial policy. Thus, for example, where there are capital market distortions such as the lack of appropriate collateral for entrepreneurs to finance their investment, the intervention would be focused on the specific nature of the distortion. The absence of an efficient mortgage instrument or the limited ability to use movable property as collateral could lead to constraints on capital. Another example is one in which an entrepreneur finds that he or she has no access to the technology needed for an activity. The answer would be to remove barriers to foreign direct investments and let cost-sharing arrangements take place among entrepreneurs in the activity.

---

[24] Bhagwati and Ramaswami (1963).

In the case of a labour market problem such as the inability to retain workers once they are trained, the answer is to have an apprentice period in which the entrepreneur can finance the cost of the training through appropriate wages that leads to the recovery of training cost and subsequently pays high wages to attract the best talent. Many Sri Lankan firms are known to do this with success. In the event that there is still an inability to appropriate the training costs, public policy could intervene by providing a tax credit or a direct subsidy for labour training on a cost-sharing basis. The infant industry argument provides for theoretically sound and practically enforceable arrangements such as these. The conditions that could be provided under this type of assistance are discussed in the following.

Finally, many of the reasons that were given in Section 7.2 for intervention must satisfy certain criteria to avoid replacing one distortion with another and making matters worse in the bargain.

The appropriate way to formulate the intervention is to ensure that the following conditions are met: (i) Domestic distortions that have been identified as warranting interventions should not be addressed through trade policies. The proper antidote is a domestic subsidy because it avoids the consumption loss associated with protection. (ii) The subsidy should be appropriately targeted and not be a blanket subsidy. (iii) Such a subsidy should be the exception (that is a departure from neutral incentives) rather than the rule. (iv) It is necessary to isolate the evaluation of the need for subsidy or policy measure from any line ministry or group that has a vested interest in the subsidy or policy change. The evaluation could be done by an independent body such as a public commission.[25] (v) The work of such a body must be done in the public domain and be subject to transparency. A request for assistance must be heard and the decision must be made public. All interested parties could be invited to give evidence of why the particular intervention is necessary or not. (vi) All assistance must have a sunset provision with no possibility of extension beyond the initial support and the same party cannot ask for support for the same purpose again. (vii) Special funds could be administered to support

---

[25] Australia has such an institution called the Productivity Commission. It reports to the prime minister, but remains independent in its evaluation. Some of the best economists in the country work with the Commission as consultants or staff members to advise on the formulation of appropriate policies. Note that the word industry that was used before was dropped to signal the work of the Commission.

activities such as provision for small- and medium-scale enterprises with fixed resources based on the same above-mentioned principles for one-time grants.

7.5 Conclusions

Sri Lankan economists have argued for industrial policy on the following grounds: "supply-side market failures" in both product and factor markets, the limited ability to create technological capability, the absence of necessary skills and managerial skills, weak linkage creation and the weakness of institutions that could promote industry.

The case for intervention through industrial policy on infant industry grounds is more stringent than commonly recognised by a majority of Sri Lankan economists due to the following points: (i) The identification of activities to support, on the basis of long-term dynamic comparative advantage, is not easy. (ii) The determination of the optimal form of intervention is similarly not easy. (iii) The period of support needed cannot be fixed in advance. (iv) Bureaucrats and administrators are not neutral actors in allocating support, as they could be seeking rent. (v) Firms that receive public support may not put it to the use for which it was requested. This is a difficult area to monitor due to the principal–agent problem. (vi) The firms that receive support will pursue lobbying to maintain that support as long as possible. (vii) Finally, private markets can provide the proper mechanism to acquire knowledge through patents and technology arrangements with foreign firms that have the technology protected from patents. Alternatively, domestic firms (if there are a small number of firms involved in the industry) can come to an arrangement to use technology on a cost-sharing basis.

A number of conclusions were reached on the lessons for Sri Lanka from the experience of East Asian countries. The stellar performance of East Asian countries can be ascribed to getting the fundamentals right and not to industrial policy per se. The issue of whether the East Asian model is duplicable in Sri Lanka, given that the contribution from industrial policy has been modest, should be contrasted with the risk of capture and rent-seeking. The recovery in East Asian countries has been largely due to the policy reversal in the direction of more neutral policies towards industry.

Once it is realised that industrial policy is not the proper response to market distortions, it behoves one to suggest an alternative, which is to formulate specific interventions through appropriate institutional arrangements. (i) Domestic distortions that have been identified as warranting intervention should not be addressed through trade policies. The proper instrument is a domestic subsidy because it avoids the consumption loss associated with protection. (ii) The subsidy should be appropriately targeted and not be a blanket subsidy. (iii) It should be the exception (that is a departure from neutral incentives) rather than the rule. (iv) It is necessary to isolate the evaluation of the need for subsidy or policy measure from any line ministry or group that has a vested interest in the subsidy or policy change. The evaluation can be conducted by an independent body such as a public commission. (v) The work of such a body must be done in the public domain and must be subject to transparency. (vi) All assistance must have a sunset provision with no possibility of extension beyond the initial support. (vii) Special funds could be administered to support activities such as provision for small- and medium-scale enterprises with fixed resources based on the above-mentioned principles and one-time grants.

Opening the country to globalisation requires macroeconomic stability, which involves keeping inflation low and maintaining current account sustainability, in order to benefit from it. The next chapter examines the vital necessity of keeping inflation low.

Chapter 8

Avoiding Inflation in Sri Lanka in Order to Benefit from Globalisation

8.1 Introduction

Inflation has many aspects and connections to the overall economy. After clarifying key concepts and developments in inflation in Sri Lanka, this chapter traces the main consequences that inflation has on exchange rates, external balance and the rate of economic growth in Sri Lanka.

This chapter is divided into five sections. Following the introduction Section 8.1, Section 8.2 clarifies certain concepts that have come up in public discussion, Section 8.3 discusses in summary form the inflationary developments in the country in the last three decades to provide a context to the present discussion. Section 8.4 traces the consequences for four important macroeconomic prices: the general price level, exchange rate, interest rate and wages. Section 8.5 discusses the consequences of continued inflation.

This chapter finds that inflation poses a grave challenge to the country and that it could be the forerunner of a serious economic crisis. This does not seem to be appreciated by the officialdom. On the demand side, the Central Bank is more responsible for the increase in inflation than it has acknowledged even though the inflation originates from the fiscal side. On the supply side, external factors — increasing oil, agriculture prices and US dollar depreciation — have been contributory factors to inflation. The Central Bank has been using the exchange rate to stabilise prices. This is dangerous as it leads to greater external and domestic indebtedness, higher interest rates, the start of a wage–price spiral and a much-reduced growth path in the future compared to the last 5 years. All these factors contribute to the increasing probability of a future external crisis with reduced competitiveness of the country's exports and import substitutes, leading to reduced economic growth. Controlling inflation is more of a challenge as inflation expectations have begun to increase, and, in the short run, this involves the side effect of a reduced rate of GDP growth, which will impact the GDP growth in the future. Meanwhile, the international financial and economic environment has begun to deteriorate with the sub-prime mortgage crisis in the United States and its impact on other developed countries' financial markets. This makes it more difficult to navigate through rough weather with growth slowing down in developed countries and the access to short-term finance, in particular, becoming more difficult. It would be very difficult to raise external finance to meet the widening current account deficit.

The consequences of inflation specific to Sri Lanka can be summarised in the following way: Its proximate effects operate via four crucial macroeconomic prices of the general price level, the exchange rate, the interest rate and wages. It has the following substantial real effects: (a) Inflation hurts the weakest in society — the poor, the unemployed and those who eke out a hand-to-mouth existence — who face the gravest conditions when their meagre real incomes erode further. Some 15 per cent of the population remains below the poverty headcount ratio. (b) Inflation distributes income in favour of those who are able to pass on the high prices to others by the nature of their activities, and thus it is the unkindest tax of all. (c) Inflation particularly favours the government over the private sector, as the real value of the present high debt of the government to the public is reduced and those who hold cash balances find their real value reduced by the inflation tax. (d) Inflation makes exports less competitive and imports artificially cheaper and induces the government to depend on short-term high-cost foreign (sovereign) borrowings. (e) Inflation reduces growth in the medium-term and diminishes long-term growth prospects. (f) Inflation could exacerbate the economic and political uncertainty existing in the country, in particular with the accelerated war effort. The challenge is to bring down the rate of inflation or restore internal equilibrium, which will contribute directly to having a sustainable external equilibrium. During 2005–2015 there is only a limited effort to control inflation in the country and the danger of higher and more unstable inflation looms large on the horizon despite the drop in the inflation rate. High inflation rates are unstable given their impact on expectations and the price distortions they create. The control of inflation should become the highest priority of the government and the Central Bank. It cannot be done without the political will and courage of the leadership; the government will also have to mend its ways as it has become profligate. Controlling inflation cannot be seen in isolation without reducing government spending, switching expenditures appropriately and making the Central Bank more responsible and credible than it is at the moment.

The challenge is to address the three sources of inflation in the country. These are the fiscal deficits and money creation by the Central Bank, which are demand-side phenomena, and imported inflation, which arises mostly due to the inordinate rise in prices of food and fuel and is a supply-side phenomenon, also sometimes called "cost-push" inflation. However, cost-push inflation cannot proceed without the monetary authority accommodating the increases in costs by increasing the money supply. It is also true that reductions in the rate of growth of money can slow down income growth and reduce employment in the future. The extent of the slowdown will depend upon the nature of the economy: if the economy is flexible enough to accommodate short-run price changes without overshooting; if the monetary authority still has credibility such that the economic agents believe the Central Bank's pronouncements. Compared to the situation before 1977, the Sri Lankan economy is more flexible today given that import and foreign exchange controls have been reduced substantially. However, the Central Bank has not grown in stature since the mid-1990s. Its pronouncements are taken less seriously than before, which reduces its ability to use moral suasion and necessary economic leadership to address the inflation problem. It has to restore its reputational capital by taking a clear and transparent stance with respect to inflation and it should not appear as another public relations effort of the government in predicting higher growth, lower inflation and improved external balance when these three goals have become elusive given the current fiscal and monetary framework. But, the Central Bank's task is made all the more difficult by a government that has expanded expenditures rapidly in areas and activities that have questionable economic validity. Meanwhile, war expenditures are also increasing rapidly, adding to aggregate demand with no counterbalancing reduction in expenditures on other activities.

8.2 Inflation and its Related Concepts

It is important to understand what inflation is in order to address its challenges. Inflation is a continuing increase in the rate of price change. It is not just a one-time increase in the general price level. It is also not the increase in prices of some goods; rather, it is a continued rise in the general price level, reflecting pressure on all goods and services. If the price of one or two goods rises due to say a supply shock, as was in the case of fuel and food import prices, other things remaining the same, it would lead to a reduction in the demand for these as well as other goods and services are given that each individual or enterprise has a budget constraint. The fact is that the rise in fuel prices will lead to other prices also to rise (given that energy is an important input). But, this is not inflation itself if it is a one-time shift in costs. This is because consumers and enterprises will react to the price increase by consuming or using less of the goods that have increased in price, substituting more of those that have not gone up in price, and working within the budget constraints. Famously, Milton Friedman declared in his 1968 address to the American Economic Association that "inflation is at all times and everywhere a monetary phenomenon."[1] Some have characterised this as only a monetarist's view of inflation. But, it is not so. Empirically, it has been shown that no sustained increase in the price level has been possible without an increase in the rate of change in the money supply. To be sure, there could be a phenomenon of cost-push inflation in the short run, arising from a supply shock, but it cannot be sustained without an increase in the money supply. All transactions need money, whether they be currency or demand deposits held by the public. It is in this sense that inflation is a monetary phenomenon. There could be little or no inflation in a specie or commodity money world because the supply of commodity money cannot be increased quickly without putting additional resources into increasing these types of money. This is the reason why the introduction of paper money saw increased inflation in the world. So, when some dismiss this interpretation of inflation as a monetarist view, they deny the close and empirically found association between the rate of increase in money supply and a sustained increase in prices.[2]

---

[1] Friedman, M (1968).

[2] For those who are mathematically inclined, inflation is the rise in the rate of price change with respect to time, or the time derivative (dp/dt) and not just "dp." If the rate of price

The circumstances in Sri Lanka, as in most developing countries, are that the fiscal authorities dominate the fiscal–monetary policy framework. In the case of Sri Lanka, this is readily seen, not only in the recent past but also in earlier periods. Nothing is more dangerous than allowing monetary policy to be dominated by fiscal policy and to be politicised to a large degree.[3]

8.3 Inflation Episodes and Consequences

Sri Lanka has experienced four inflation episodes over 35 years with continuing inflation episodes: the 1973–1975 episode, the 1980–1981 episode, the 1988–1989 episode, and the most recent and continuing 2006–2008 episode.

The 1973–1975 inflation episode was related to the first oil shock when the OPEC cartel raised the price of oil more than fourfold within a couple of years. Crude oil that was a mere $2.72 in 1970 rose to above $10.70 a barrel in 1973. At that time, Sri Lanka had a closed economy. National output and employment were less exposed to international prices, particularly with respect to imports, including oil imports. Even so, there was a large shock to the economy that led to a rise in the inflation rate to 11.0 per cent — the first time such a threshold was reached since the CCPI was introduced in 1952. The government at the time took strong measures to contain inflation by increasing taxes (lowering the fiscal deficit) and increasing price controls.[4] The impact of the 1973 budget was contractionary after some 10 years.[5] The adjustment to the imbalance was

---

change increases at one time and continues at the same rate after the price change, that is not inflation in itself unless it begins to trigger changes in the rate of change in the general price level. In other words, inflation is not associated with changes in the level of prices but its rate of change.

[3]Fry (1998). He found that fiscal dominance is associated less with the Central Bank's neutralisation of increased government borrowing from the banking system.

[4]Little *et al.* (1993). Of course, increasing price controls does nothing to reduce excess demand. It leads to a case of repressed inflation, where queues for goods get longer, instead of the prices rising higher. There is one side effect that may be helpful: if people's inflationary expectations are dampened by reigning in the rate of liquidity growth, then the inflation rate will be reduced. However, there is no empirical evidence to support the view that price controls reduce inflation expectations.

[5]Karunatilleke (1986).

mainly through reducing expenditures. There was no adjustment of the exchange rate even though the real exchange rate had to depreciate with the negative terms of trade shock to restore equilibrium. The reduction of overall expenditure would also have led to a fall in the demand for non-tradable goods, which would have led to a fall in their prices, leading to a fall in the real exchange rate.[6] Thus, it was not through a deliberate change in the nominal exchange rate or a devaluation. In effect, this approach amounts to putting the burden of adjustment mostly on quantities rather than on price (the exchange rate).[7] The imbalance was reduced, but the economy suffered an unnecessarily large reduction in output.[8] In addition, future growth was affected by the use of price controls, higher taxes and the general uncertainty created by public policy due to a coalition government that included Marxist parties.[9]

In the second inflation episode in 1980–1981, two factors combined to raise the inflation rate (average) to 22.1 per cent, the highest rate recorded since the CCPI was compiled. The expansionary impact of the fiscal operations was the highest recorded in absolute amount since gaining independence in 1948.[10] The overall fiscal deficit was 23.1 per cent of GDP. The factor that led to the expansion was the tremendous increase in the public expenditure that the government initiated at the time with large investments such as the Mahaweli project (a large river diversion scheme) and the new parliament complex. The negative contractionary impact of the second oil shock in 1979–1980 (which led to a decline in net foreign assets) was more than offset by increased public expenditures. This time, the government used the exchange rate to switch expenditures away from the tradable sector to the non-tradable sector and production away from the non-tradable to the tradable sector to help with

---

[6]Tradable goods are those that have their prices determined in the world market such as exportables (i.e. exports and their substitutes) and importables (i.e. imports and their substitutes).

[7]Of course, the real exchange rate was adjusted insufficiently due to the "switching effect" of reduced expenditures.

[8]Athukorala and Jayasuriya (1994).

[9]The Minister for Finance was Dr. N. M. Perera, the head of the *Sama Samaja Party* that wanted to herald in a socialist economy and change the capitalistic structure of the economy. See Rajapatirana (2008).

[10]*Ibid.*

the adjustment. Nevertheless, the 1980–1981 episode was qualitatively different from the earlier episode since the economy was more open and prices were allowed to allocate resources following the liberalisation of the economy in 1977. The reduction in quantitative import restrictions contributed to the increased flexibility of the economy and a part of the adjustment would reduce the price of tradables (note that tradable prices are given to small countries like Sri Lanka) to non-tradables, a measure of the real exchange rate. Consequently, the handling of inflation at that time did not compromise future growth as it did in the 1973–1974 episode.

The third inflation episode (1988–1989) was more associated with another large expansion of public expenditures (refer to Figure 8.3A). The two oil shocks had abated and the 12.8 per cent inflation that prevailed in 1988–1989 was mostly generated domestically. Whereas the earlier inflation was associated with terms of trade shocks, the third episode was largely the manifestation of a "Dutch disease" created by large aid inflows when the Mahaweli scheme's implementation was reaching a peak.[11] This was the result of the monetisation of net capital inflows.[12] The amounts involved were so large that even an attempt to sterilise the inflows through the sale of government securities would not have been successful. Besides, this would have led to high interest rates and posed a considerable problem to the private sector.

The fourth episode of inflation began in 2006 and continued past the mid-year mark for 2008, reaching a high point in April and declining in July and August, associated with increased reserve targets and seasonality factors (Table 8.1A). Again, supply shocks associated with the rise in energy and food prices combined with domestic expansionary policies led to a 29.9 per cent inflation rate measured by the CCPI and a 28.2 per cent rate measure by the CCPI index in April 2008. The fiscal deficit rose to

---

[11] A Dutch disease is the manifestation of an appreciation of the real exchange rate due to a booming export which is temporary in nature, as was the case with the discovery and export of natural gas in Holland that increased export revenues, which led to a fall in the relative profitability of other exports and their decline, leading to a worsening of the trade balance over the longer term.

[12] Deepak and Rajapatirana (1989). The authors warned that liberalisation would not succeed much given that the macroeconomic policy was unsupportive and unnecessarily expansionary. While the government was liberalising the economy, it was creating large macroeconomic imbalances that worked against liberalisation.

7.0 per cent of GDP in 2006 and declined slightly to 6.9 per cent of GDP in 2007. Two features stand in marked contrast to the earlier episodes in the approach to inflation. To date, there has been limited success in combating inflation as evidenced by the continuing trend of money supply growth in excess of output growth and recourse to short-term sovereign debt to meet the external current account deficit. The CCPI rose to 13.7 per cent in 2006 and further to 17.5 per cent in 2007. There was also the associated attempt to sterilise a part of the inflows from sovereign borrowing that led to high domestic interest rates and contributed to increasing the size of the public sector.[13] Finally, there was a large increase in war and security-related expenditures compared to expenditures of the 1988–1989 episode during which time the JVP uprising took place. The Central Bank responded to the rising inflation by formulating tight monetary targets but inflation accelerated until April and has come down slowly during the three months (May, June and July). As mentioned, a part of the decline in inflation was be associated with seasonality factors and not due to tight monetary targets alone, which implies that there was still the prospect of rising inflation in the economy as large fiscal deficits persisted and the Central Bank's routine financing of these deficits created a continuing inflation bias in the economy.

Of the last three of the four inflation episodes, the one that resembled the last episode in terms of the inflation rate at that time was the 1980–1981 episode. But, the comparison ends there since the reason for the inflation during the 1980–1981 episode was the large capital inflows. The extent of inflation, on the other hand, has more of domestic origin. Moreover, there were important qualitative differences between the two episodes. The increases in public expenditure and capital inflows that occurred during the 1980–1981 episode were largely associated with investments that were undertaken after some evaluation, while the public expenditure expansion during the 2006–2008 episode was more related to public consumption. The public investments envisaged at that time are not the result of careful feasibility studies, such projects as the Mattala International airport in the South, and the New Airline (Mihin), both

---

[13] It is noted that if one regresses Net Foreign Assets on Net Domestic Assets (as the dependent variable), there is a very high correlation coefficient giving strong evidence of sterilisation. This leads to the inevitable rise in interest rates with consequences for private sector borrowing.

these politically motivated projects made large losses. Moreover, the terms of the foreign funds borrowed in the recent episode were much more unfavourable to Sri Lanka given that they were borrowed at commercial terms (8.5 per cent) for 5 years. Finally, the initial conditions that were obtained in the fourth inflation episode had greater imbalances compared to 1980 with respect to the level of total debt, high levels of employment that made the economy more susceptible to inflation and the lack of a strong commitment to control inflation since none of the leading international financial institutions were involved in the economy in a significant way at the time, either with respect to financial flows or support programmes. In fact, the largest capital provider to Sri Lanka at that time, was the Islamic Republic of Iran (with some $450 million). Iran was not known to support high-return projects but those that support its narrow political objectives, given that the US, EU, and other major nations were contemplating tightening sanctions against it. In contrast, during the 1980–1981 episode, some six to seven countries were major donors of external assistance to Sri Lanka within a well-defined macroeconomic framework that was monitored as well. The Central Bank had to restrain fiscal expansion in order to be able to keep prices stable and support a more viable current account deficit in the balance of payments. It could have used the Fiscal Management (Responsibility) Act (FMRA) targets to begin to restrain public expenditures. There is little evidence that the target of a fiscal deficit of 5 per cent of GDP could be achieved in 2010. On the contrary, since it was a Presidential election in 2010, it led to a growing deficit, hence the need to begin expenditure reduction immediately rather than later. The government argued that such fiscal restraint would be difficult with the ongoing war. However, this implies that the government had to act with greater restraint in other areas of expenditure precisely because it was incurring large war-related expenditures.

8.4 Inflation and Macroeconomic Imbalance in Sri Lanka

The inflation in Sri Lanka is the manifestation of a macroeconomic imbalance. Inflation data for Sri Lanka ranged from 26.6 per cent in July 2008 to 24.9 per cent in August 2008. While inflation measured by the CCPI (N) has come down, Sri Lanka has the highest inflation rate for the South Asian Region, with inflation rates in the 11 per cent to 12 per cent range in Bangladesh, India, Nepal and Pakistan. Since all these countries face the same external environment, the reasons for higher inflation in Sri Lanka are mainly domestic in origin and are related to the large fiscal deficits that have become endemic in the country since the early 1980s. Hence, the resolution of the inflation problem has to be necessarily related to the fiscal situation and the creation of money. In other words, the rate of money growth in the country which causes inflation has its origin in the fiscal deficit and its financing through banking sources. The macroeconomic imbalance is related to the goods market, the factor market (capital and credit markets and the labour markets) and the external sector (which manifests as an unsustainable balance-of-payment outcome in the medium term). The policy response to inflation must be considered in relation to these markets, which involves the four macroeconomic prices they determine, namely, the general price level, the exchange rate, interest rate and the wage rate.

(a) The Goods Market and the General Price Level

The sustained increase in the general price level has to be confronted and brought under control to restore equilibrium. The macroeconomic imbalance which has manifested as inflation indicates that the rate of growth of money supply has exceeded the rate of growth of output. Both consumers and producers have a notion of their equilibrium amount of cash balances for different purposes. Inflation takes place when the money supply exceeds the cash balances desired by individuals and enterprises. When this happens, these economic agents try to reduce the cash balances by spending it on goods and services, which then leads to a general and sustained increase in the price level as long as the disequilibrium persists. Inflation is a dynamic phenomenon and not a once-and-for-all change in the general price level. Also, inflation cannot be sustained at a steady rate. It tends to accelerate and is unstable as the rate increases.

Moreover, inflation does not affect all commodities and services factor markets uniformly. Some prices move faster than others, while some experience larger increases than others. Thus, inflation interferes with the efficient working of markets by distorting relative prices and providing wrong information to economic agents. It also creates expectations that cannot be satisfied easily and sets in motion dynamic forces that are difficult to anticipate or control. For these reasons, it is vital that inflation is not allowed to get out of hand. It has implications that go way beyond economics, to politics and even social relations. Inflation is the unkindest tax of all. It leads to a greater impact on the poor and the economically weak who cannot defend themselves against it particularly consumers.

Inflation rewards debtors and taxes creditors. In the Sri Lanka case, the largest debtor being the government, inflation is a convenient device for it to reduce the real burden of debt. Twenty-five per cent inflation (average for six months) translates into a significant reduction in the real value of domestic debt service and the principal. Private debtors are also rewarded in a similar way. Persistent inflation destroys long-term credit markets. That is why, in Latin America, long-term credit was so spare. Long periods of price and interest rate stability are necessary to create long-term credit markets as seen in North America and other parts of the developed world, where 30-year mortgages are commonplace.[14] In countries where there is no history of monetary and price stability, lenders' horizons are narrow. Mortgages can be as short having only a thirty-day maturity, which will raise transaction costs and make a long-term asset market an impossible goal.

(b) Inflation and the Exchange Rate

Sri Lanka has a managed float or what is called a "dirty float," where the Central Bank adjusts the nominal rate without following any formal rule for the path of the exchange rate. It provides great discretion to the Central Bank to adjust the exchange rate in such a way so as to keep inflation low. The exchange rate can be used as an additional instrument to manipulate the inflation rate, but with a clear danger of losing reserves. The Central Bank has kept the exchange rate, as it claims, on a stable path but has allowed it to appreciate since 2007. This is more tempting for the Central Bank since it can use the exchange rate to keep prices from rising further. However, this is damaging to the economy since an appreciated exchange rate acts as a tax on exports and a subsidy on imports. It will harm both export- and import-substituting activities.

There are three points of evidence that the Central Bank has been using the exchange rate as a stabilisation device. First, the exchange rate

---

[14] The sub-prime mortgage crisis in the United States may restrict easy access to the mortgage market for some, but it is unlikely that there would be a dearth of long-term mortgages for eligible borrowers even at the height of the crisis.

has not been moved to reflect the divergent exchange rates between Sri Lanka and its trading partners. By keeping the exchange rate from moving when domestic inflation is in the neighbourhood of 25 per cent while the average inflation among Sri Lanka's competitors and trading partners is less than 10 per cent during the 2006–2008 period, Sri Lanka has become less competitive since its costs are higher. This has led to a decline in Sri Lanka's share in world exports. Second, in order to keep the exchange rate in a narrow and actually narrowing band, the Central Bank had to borrow foreign exchange from commercial banks and by floating sovereign bonds. The first of Sovereign bond for US$500 million in 2007 and the second for US$373 million was issued. The total borrowings for the year amounted to over US$1000 million. In March 2008, the government raised another $150 million and the Treasury bill market opened to foreigners up to 10 per cent of outstanding stock.[15] Some of these transactions have implied interest rates as high as 8.5 per cent for 5-year periods. The Central Bank has thus, in effect, borrowed abroad to keep the exchange rate appreciated. As is well known in the "Dutch disease" literature, inflows of capital lead to an appreciation of the exchange rate.[16] The Central Bank has been trading off high inflation for a loss of reserves and accumulating sovereign debt. This approach has also allowed it to keep domestic interest rates relatively low since it did not have to offer high interest rates to sell government paper locally. But, with its attendant exchange risk and maturity mismatch (borrowing short to invest long term), overall risks to the economy increased. Third, there is an attempt to restrict imports in a non-transparent way with only customs announcements to restrict the allowance of so-called white goods (cookers, refrigerators, TVs, and the like).[17] Similar *ad hoc* announcements have been made to restrict the import of motor cars.[18]

---

[15] Dias Bandaranaike (2008).

[16] Corden and Neary (1982).

[17] It is not unusual for foreign-employed Sri Lankans to buy duty free goods to sell some of these goods in the domestic market since the conversion of the foreign exchange through this means is more favourable (more Rs. per US $) given that the exchange rate has appreciated. The returning workers will get less money in a straight conversion of foreign exchange into Sri Lankan rupees.

[18] It may be pointed out that banning the import of cars while permitting the import of parts to assemble them in Sri Lanka is counterproductive. There is an old study which showed that such assembly has negative value added. That is, when inputs and outputs are valued

Inflation has a specific effect on external balance. Inflation affects the goods market in a particular way, and movements in the goods market have an immediate impact on external balance and the competitiveness of the economy. The main effect in this respect operates via the real exchange rate. First, one version of the real exchange rate known as the Purchasing Power Parity (PPP) exchange rate is determined by the relative price levels between the country in question and its trading partners. For instance, the August 2008 Sri Lanka exchange rate of the Rupees per US dollar (Rs. 107.5) stands in contrast to the exchange rate that was obtained 4 years earlier of around Rs. 101.19. If there was a free market for foreign exchange (or a floating rate) in Sri Lanka (there is none, since it is a managed or dirty float), then the exchange rate should reflect, say, 25 per cent inflation in Sri Lanka over this period, and around 8 per cent inflation over the same period, among Sri Lanka's competitors. A PPP exchange rate calculation indicates the appreciation of the exchange rate by nearly 9 per cent in 2008. This degree of appreciation is not insignificant given the depreciation of the US$ in world markets. This has led to the complaint from private sector exporters and from those who produce import substitutes that the exchange rate is not favourable for them to maintain the present level of activity. Some foreign firms located in Sri Lanka are planning to move out given the cost squeeze implied by the appreciation of the rupee.

Another definition of the real exchange rate is the ratio of tradable to non-tradable goods. This definition is important for allocating domestic resources in the goods and services market and maintaining macroeconomic equilibrium.[19] The series of the real exchange rate estimated on this basis also indicates an appreciation (see Table 8.2A on Real Exchange Rate). Tradable goods are those that have their prices determined in the world market such as exportables (i.e. exports and their substitutes) and importables (i.e. imports and their substitutes). Since Sri Lanka is a small country, having no monopoly power, it has to take world prices as given. Non-tradable prices are those that are determined in the domestic market

---

at international prices, the former exceeds the latter, which implies that every time a car is assembled, national income falls equal to the extent of the negative value added (see Little *et al.* (1970)). One has to worry that the assemblage of cars in Sri Lanka is also subject to negative value added.

[19] This concept and model is the so-called Australian macroeconomic model originally developed by Salter (1959).

for which there is no trade with the rest of the world (or goods and services that cannot be resold). It is these non-tradable goods' prices that are related to monetary policy since the supply of money determines domestic prices.[20] Thus, the higher the inflation, the higher the domestic price of non-tradables and the more appreciated the exchange rate. This measure of inflation shows an appreciation of nearly 12.8 per cent.

The third definition of the exchange rate, one that is favoured by the IMF, is the Real Effective Exchange Rate (REER), which is a variant of a PPP definition, and also indicates an appreciation of the Sri Lanka rupee by double digits beyond 2007.

With the exchange rate kept within a very narrow band, partly by borrowing abroad, there is the danger that rising interest rates (with inflation) and a nearly fixed exchange rate would provide a one-way option for the exchange rate to attract speculation and induce quick movement in and out of the rupee, leading to a crisis reminiscent of the East Asian financial crisis of the late 1990s. Allowing foreign nationals to hold deposits in Sri Lanka and subscribing to up to 10 per cent of Treasury Bills increased Sri Lanka's foreign exchange risk exposure significantly. In addition, the near fixed rate character of exchange rate management by the Central Bank hinders its ability to control the money supply. This is the so-called "Unholy Trinity" where a fixed exchange rate, capital mobility and independent monetary policy are not compatible.

Even if the nominal exchange rate is kept unchanged or is changed less frequently, real exchange rate movements take place. This is through changes that affect the supply and demand for non-tradable goods due to money growth and fiscal imbalances. Also, under a managed float as in Sri Lanka, if the Central Bank is reluctant to change the nominal exchange rate, the real exchange rate appreciates or depreciates and moves in and out of equilibrium in relation to the given position of (comparative static) equilibrium. In other words, an adjustment takes place either through proper management or through its neglect; the latter will lead to less desirable outcomes. A more flexible exchange rate policy will not only keep

---

[20]The domestic price level can be regarded as the weighted average of two prices: $PD = aPT + bPN$; PN and PT are price of non-tradables and price of tradables, respectively, and "a" and "b" are the weights in GDP. For a small economy like Sri Lanka (relative to the rest of the world), tradable sectors tend to be large and therefore the weight "a" is substantially higher compared to "b," the weight of non-tradable goods. If world prices were assumed to be unchanged, then $dPD = dPN$, given that $da = 0$ in the short run.

the economy more competitive but will also provide more potency to the monetary policy. With a nearly fixed exchange rate and foreign borrowing, the money supply has become endogenous to some extent, rendering the monetary policy less effective.

An appreciation of the exchange rate, as has been the case since 2007, induces two effects that move the economy further away from (comparative static) equilibrium. First, the relative price of tradables falls in relation to non-tradables, encouraging the consumption of tradables and discouraging their production. Second, the relative price of the non-tradables rises, and the opposite effect takes place, namely, a discouraging the consumption of non-tradables and encouraging the production of non-tradables. These two effects combine to increase the trade deficit (exports less imports), moving the economy further away from equilibrium and leading to a larger balance-of-payment deficits. If the moment away from equilibrium is transitory, then it makes sense for the government to finance the deficit. If, on the other hand, the change in relative prices is permanent, then the economy has to adjust.[21] There is no other alternative.

In terms of the standard definition of the real exchange rate, the Central Bank has to devalue the rupee by increasing the amount of rupees per US dollar. This counters the effect of inflation, which has raised the relative price of non-tradables to tradables in the first place (Appendix A: Table 8.2A & Figures 8.1A & 8.2A). However, it is imperative that the Central Bank controls the money supply to prevent the devaluation from being nullified by a rise in the price of non-tradables. If that happens, then it would begin continuous bouts of inflation and devaluations and could lead to a wage–price spiral as workers fight to keep their real wages from falling.

The case of Sri Lanka in terms of this framework is as follows: There was a substantial macroeconomic imbalance as evidenced by the increasing current account deficit (combined trade and services deficits) with a small surplus in the balance of payment in August 2008. This has been achieved mainly through foreign borrowing that was to be repaid with large repayments falling due in 2009. The exchange rate has appreciated in 2008 and the prospects were for further increases in the fiscal deficit.

---

[21] There is a basis to believe that the change in relative prices is permanent given that cost increases are not easily reversible since an important element of variable costs is the wage and money wages are not easily reversed. Of course, inflation will reduce real wages, but workers will clamour for wage increases.

This meant that the government would have had to take recourse to a larger inflation tax.[22] A very simple and indicative exercise shows that if the fiscal deficit cannot be brought under control, the inflation tax has to be raised to nearly double that of the past 3 years. In such a situation, the first best remedy is to reduce the fiscal deficit through a reduction in expenditures rather than an increase in revenues. An attempt to increase revenues will interfere with incentives and would be counterproductive. Hence, a combination of policies needs to be considered to avoid a crisis. First, reduce the deficit by getting rid of non-essential low-priority public expenditures, and aim to reduce the domestic financing of the deficit to say 2 per cent or half of the present extent of domestic financing. This would reduce the inflation tax to 28 per cent or half of the required inflation tax when the fiscal deficit is 4 per cent of GDP. Of course, the government can avoid raising the inflation rate altogether by only financing with non-bank sources, which will raise interest rates to very high levels.

(c) Money market and interest rates

When a country has experienced significant and long bouts of inflation, interest rates tend to be very high. This is because lenders have to assume greater risks and because the return to lending corrected for inflation declines. One can talk about a nominal rate of interest and a real rate of interest. A nominal rate of interest is merely the rate at which interest rates are expressed in percentages uncorrected for price level changes, such as "x" rupees per loan or the "fee" for using the loan. A real rate on the other hand takes into account the rate of inflation.[23]

---

[22] Inflation tax can be estimated in the following way: $\tau = \partial/\mu$, where "τ" is the inflation rate, "∂" is the fiscal deficit as a ratio of GDP and "μ" is the ratio of high-powered money to GDP. When numbers are plugged in for mid-2008, the following emerges for "τ": the estimated domestic financing of the 2008 deficit of 4 per cent of GDP (the original estimate of 3.7 per cent of domestic financing of deficit may not be feasible). Similarly, high-powered money of Rs. 290 million (estimated for mid-2008) and a GDP figure of Rs. 4,191 trillion yields 7 per cent of GDP. Thus, the inflation tax will turn out to be raised to 44 per cent (compared to 28 per cent) for a 3-year period. Clearly, this is not feasible without the risk of runaway inflation and a devastating loss of competitiveness (See Edwards (1989) for the conceptual basis of this estimate).

[23] In most cases, the standard formula to compute the real rate is as follows: The real interest rate is defined as $r = (1 + i)/(1 + dp/dt)$, where "r" is the real rate of interest, "i" is the nominal rate and "dp/dt" is the rate of inflation.

A rise in the rate of inflation lowers the real rate of interest. When this happens, lenders will not extend credit unless they are compensated for the loss of income by inflation. Hence, to induce them to lend, the nominal rate must rise in a competitive economy and it must be raised where there are interest rate controls. The upshot of the adjustment to inflation is that the supply of loanable funds becomes limited, overall. However, some loans may be demanded in order to take advantage of the inflation rate by speculation. For instance, during times of inflation, economic agents want to hold assets that go up in value faster than the inflation rate. Thus, holding real estate and price-increasing stocks become attractive and the spectrum of investment becomes skewed towards such investments rather than those that will increase long-term productivity.

Inflation in the last few months of 2008 has been 25 per cent per year (CCPI) and lending rates for short-term loans by the state banks (for good customers, around 22–28 per cents) have remained below this inflation rate. This has led to negative real lending rates. Such negative rates increase demand for loans overall, and provide a subsidy to prime borrowers with respect to the loans they have to repay (now at negative rates — unless the loans were made in variable rates, which is hardly the practice in Sri Lanka). This skews loans towards the well-to-do among all customers.[24] It should not be a surprise to see that private sector credit would increase under the circumstances. When the Central Bank restricts credit by reducing high-powered money (raising monetary targets), this raises interest rates on repurchases and, consequently, nominal rates of interest would rise. This would reduce the subsidy and the demand for credit.

When overall credit is restricted, it is likely that the private sector would have to adjust more than the public sector. This is due to two reasons. First, the state-owned banks are less able to restrict credit to their large state-owned corporation clients than private-owned banks whose clientele is mainly in the private sector. Second, less financial discipline is found in state-owned corporations (the so-called soft budget constraint). State-owned corporations can and do emphasise the "essential" nature of their enterprises to ensure themselves steady access to credit even when money markets become tight. Equally, state-owned corporations provide "finance" in the form of unpaid debts to each other when efforts are made

---

[24] This is the so-called "Iron Law of Interest Rates" which says that wherever there is a subsidy, the loan portfolio of banks becomes skewed in favour of larger and more well-to-do borrowers (see Gonzalez Vega (1976)).

to contain aggregate demand to reduce inflation. Thus, for example, the Ceylon Electricity Board has to accommodate large unpaid bills of other state corporations. This is a form of credit expansion that is hardly accounted for in standard monetary programmes designed to reduce aggregate demand. Thus, both the price (interest rates) and the quantity of credit are affected by inflation. In the final analysis, inflation is more damaging to the private sector's than to the public sector. Empirical studies done on inflation found a negative association between inflation and economic growth.[25]

(d) Inflation and Domestic and External Debt

At the end of April 2008, Sri Lanka's total government debt amounted to Rs. 3,238 million or Rs.162, 000 per person.[26] As a ratio of GDP, it stood at 85.1 per cent in 2007. Debt service (both domestic and external debt) has amounted to 85 per cent of government revenue, leaving little room for financing capital projects. As indicated, inflation helps to reduce the real value of the debt and the real transfer to the public from the debt service. The government borrowed from captive sources such as the Employees Provident Fund, National Savings, banks and from other sources such as the Central Bank. Recently, however, the government has reduced its borrowing from the Central Bank and other banking sources. Borrowing from bank sources increases the amount of high-powered money, which leads to higher inflation.

The situation is very different with respect to the foreign debt since it has to be repaid in foreign exchange with an export surplus. Foreign debt stood at Rs. 1,355 million, or 44 per cent of total debt, in 2007. In the past, most of the foreign debt was at concessional terms (at low interest, longer-term and with grace periods). Funds from the IDA carry a 70 per cent subsidy to the borrower. Such loans are now not available to Sri Lanka given that Sri Lanka's per capita income has exceeded the IDA cut off; now, the country is considered a "blend country" for IDA and World Bank funds. Foreign debt poses a large risk, given that it has to be repaid in foreign currency and is subject to exchange risk (say between the US$ and the Euro or Japanese yen). Inflation, by leading to the appreciation of the real exchange rate, makes it more difficult to

---

[25] Fischer (1981).
[26] Dias Bandaranaike (2008).

generate export surpluses. Already, the rate of export growth has fallen compared to the 2006–2008 period, while the import bills have increased due to the high prices of fuel and agriculture imports. This has led to an increase in the trade deficit which, in turn, has led to greater external borrowing, making future debt repayment problematic. In other words, without strong efforts to control expenditure, the government has been forced to borrow externally. But, those borrowings are now being constrained as evidenced by the downgrading of the country's credit rating by the Fitch Ratings Agency and others. Attempts to float a foreign bond have been under-subscribed even at high junk bond rates.

Meanwhile, domestic borrowing is become limited as funds from captive sources had become scarce. Private institutions and individuals are reluctant to buy government paper at going rates because of inflationary expectations, negative returns and vulnerability to inflation. It is more profitable to hold assets such as land as a hedge against inflation rather than fixed income assets.

(e) Inflation and the Labour Market

There has been a spate of wage demands in 2008. The 25 per cent average inflation over the 2006–2008 period led to a substantial decline in real wages. Some of the wage demands were met purely on welfare grounds, particularly in the case of public sector employees who have typically low wages (and also typically low productivity). A further demand of Rs. 5000 per month per employee was supported by the JVP and led to a one-day token strike. In addition, there were demands by government circles that the private sector also grant wage increases to at least partially offset the increase in the cost of living.

Increases in wages and salaries were the largest items in 2008 in public expenditures that contributed to the increase in the fiscal deficit. Given that there is increasing demand for wage increases with every bout of inflation, there is the danger that a wage–price spiral could be building up. Such an eventuality would prove to be very risky. The Treasury and the Central Bank could lose control of inflation at enormous peril to the country, with the civil war continuing in 2008, the threat of restricted access to funds from Western countries, based on the alleged human rights violations. The increasing demand for wages suggests that inflation expectations have been building up from 2006–2008.

The labour market plays a vital role in the inflationary process. Since the country continues to have high employment, labour can be bid away only with offers of higher wages. With a tight labour market and critical skill shortages, (partly due to emigration), employers are more willing to yield to high wage demands. Meeting some of these demands becomes inevitable, but a widespread clamour for wage increases could worsen the already unstable macroeconomic situation and lead to even higher inflation, given that labour costs are a large component of the total costs of firms. Yielding to wage increases would be self-defeating since cumulative rounds of wage and price increases will make inflation rise and real income decline further.

Unskilled labour is non-tradable.[27] Their wages are highly susceptible to the domestic monetary policy. Since the price of non-tradables is a function of money growth, a rise in these wages has a strong impact on the real exchange rate.[28] In a more stable environment, wages would reflect worker productivity as the competition among enterprises can lead to wages that are commensurate with the productivity being offered. However, at times of inflation, wage increases are not necessarily related to productivity.[29] Rather, especially in the Sri Lankan context, wage increases are more closely associated with trade unions that have their own political agendas. Their power would be high given their large membership, the importance of the particular sector and the connection to a strong political party.

Finally, inflation has a crucial influence on wages and labour markets, particularly when controlling inflation requires stringent monetary and fiscal policies. High inflation necessitates strong measures which favour the public over the private sector. The latter will be squeezed when

---

[27] Workers who go abroad for jobs are relatively more skilled compared to those who are domestically employed at low real wages. In this sense, the convention that unskilled labour is a non-tradable is not unreasonable.

[28] One could easily write the Real Exchange Rate (RER) in functional form as many economists do; it the ratio of Price of Tradables divided by the Price of Non tradables. Where the price of non-tradables is usually taken to be equal to the wages of unskilled labour.

[29] The exhortation by the governor of the Central Bank, Cabraal, that the private sector should raise productivity to become more competitive is very puzzling given that inflation leads to an appreciation of the exchange rate and is counterproductive to increasing productivity. Using the PPP example, it is unlikely that the private sector, particularly in the tradable sector, would have been able to raise productivity when inflation has compromised their ability to compete. In fact, the rates of productivity growth that would be required to offset the appreciation of the rupee were not achieved even during the miracle growth period of the East Asian economies.

measures to control inflation are put in place. Consequently, the private sector will undertake fewer investments and have less ability to borrow from banks or the stock market, with the result that the adaption and incorporation of technology will be restricted and delayed. This will have a negative impact on growth.

8.5 Consequences of Continued Inflation

If inflation were not being brought under control, it is highly probable that Sri Lanka will face a crisis. Evidence for such an eventuality is mounting in different ways. Utilising this discussion, a crisis can arise from the following sources.

First and foremost, there is a worrisome lack of concern regarding the high rate of inflation that the country was facing as such inflation is necessarily destabilising. The reaction of the Central Bank, the Treasury, and its coterie of advisers is to associate high inflation with high growth. But there is a significant qualitative difference between the high inflation of 1980–1981 and the inflation of 2006–2008. The 2006–2008, inflation is part of a Keynesian boom and bust phenomenon in which public expenditure and credit expansion create increases in nominal income and output in the short run only to decline in the future due to instability. Macroeconomic stability is a requirement for medium-term growth. It is clear that domestic policy is implicated by the high inflation in Sri Lanka, contrary to the assertions by the Central Bank.

Second, attempts to bring inflation under control have succeeded. However, the Central Bank has begun to tighten monetary targets more, achieving a slowing down of inflation. But, as mentioned, part of the decline is expected due to seasonality factors. Given the relatively underdeveloped nature of the money market, once aggregate demand begins to increase due to increased public expenditures, the Central Bank will not have many instruments left to reign in the rate of growth of liquidity. Liquidity is already high given the large domestic debt overhang, and a small increase in liquidity leads to large changes in the rate of inflation. It is getting increasingly difficult to convince the domestic financial markets to buy government and Central Bank securities despite the higher nominal rates that are being offered. In addition, the credibility of the Central Bank has been damaged because of its overly muscular and over-sensitive reactions to criticisms and every prediction about the rate of inflation by the Central Bank during 2008. Analysts have begun even to question the motives of the Central Bank's management as it announces different indexes of inflation even though there is little to criticise about the use of different indexes for different purposes.

Third, total domestic debt has increased so much that a large part of the current revenue is utilised to service this debt — an alarming 85 per cent of government revenue is dedicated to service debt. The amount remaining to undertake other expenditures was therefore limited with the result that there is continued recourse to ever rising fiscal deficits which have not seen a stable path of consolidation. Thus, the deficit which declined to 6.9 per cent of GDP in 2007 was expected to rise once again further in 2008 and 2009. It was shown that to the extent that the deficit is financed by bank sources, the government can use inflation tax and the Central Bank to take recourse to money printing and collecting seigniorage. It was shown that for a given magnitude of a fiscal deficit as a proportion of GDP and reserve money as a proportion of GDP, the inflation tax has to increase as the deficit increases. Also, given the current level of domestic debt, there will be an increasing tendency to increase the inflation tax.

Fourth, with increasing debt, and rising inflation, the government has the chance to inflate away debt, as some Latin American countries did in the 1980s with grave consequences. The temptation and the incentive to do so are there. Given the government's aversion to borrowing from multinational financial institutions that would insist on greater macroeconomic stability, there is no such guard at the moment.

Fifth, external debt had to be paid with foreign exchange through an export surplus either through goods and services or through a transfer of assets. However, the appreciated rupee does not augur well to increase exports. The trade deficit reached US$3,800 million in 2007. As mentioned earlier, attempts to borrow more sovereign debt have run into problems as only half of the $300 million was subscribed even at "junk bond" interest rates. And, higher rates are required by foreign lenders. Of course, some may ask why foreign lenders advance funds when there is already a downgrade of the country's creditworthiness. Lenders to sovereign governments tend to take bets that there will be rescue operations mounted by international financial institutions if there is the possibility of a debt default. The financial crises of the 1980s in Latin America and the crises of the 1990s in East Asia took place as lenders bet that there would be rescue operations, as there were. To be sure, they will get less than the full value of their debt in a crisis ("take a haircut" in common parlance), but the risk presents a one-way option since fees and penalty rates are collected from these governments up front. Thus, the larger lenders benefit while smaller lenders get a few cents per dollar in such a crisis. Moreover, a nearly fixed exchange rate combined with high interest rates and some capital mobility attracts "hot money" that can fly out as easily as it flies in, creating enormous problems for the management of the balance of payments in the short run.

Finally, given increased domestic imbalance and the looming external payments problems, the government would be forced to impose trade and exchange restrictions, taking the country back to the pre-1977 era. In fact, some of the advisers to the government, who have been uncomfortable with a liberalised economy given their leftist political ideologies, would favour "selective control" of imports and exchange allocations. Bureaucrats would not be uncomfortable with it, given that they get to administer these controls, providing them with increased administrative power and, at times, even pecuniary rewards. Of course, tightening a liberalised regime is fraught with great danger since a lot is at stake as labour and capital are entrenched in liberalised economic activities. One is bound to lose and face retrenchment. The economic future of the country is thus in a delicate state. It has a greater bias towards a real major crisis rather than towards the muddling through that it has done in the last 5 years.

With inflation, as prices go up, the cost of production goes up, making exports less competitive. One way to deal with it in the short run is to allowed the exchange rate to reflect the change in relative price. In the next chapter, we discuss increase in export, which has become an important priority as Sri Lanka has a large debt to repay. That being the case, we cannot afford to have high inflation in order to service our debt.

It is important for Sri Lanka to have low inflation to have competitive exports and help service debt.

Appendix A

Table 8.1A. Basic Indicators of the General Price Level, 1987–2008

Year	CCPI (1952=100)	% Change	CCPI (2002=100)	% Change	GCCPI (1989=100)	% Change	WPI (1974=100)	% Change	GDPD (1996=100)	% Change
1987	652.8	7.7	—	—	—	—	414.9	13.4	38.4	7.0
1988	744.1	14.0	—	—	—	—	488.7	17.8	42.8	11.5
1989	830.2	11.6	—	—	103.8	—	532.9	9.0	46.9	9.6
1990	1008.6	21.5	—	—	124.6	20.0	651.1	22.2	56.3	20.0
1991	1131.5	12.2	—	—	138.9	11.5	710.8	9.2	62.5	11.0
1992	1260.4	11.4	—	—	152.0	9.4	773.0	8.8	68.7	10.0
1993	1408.4	11.7	—	—	164.8	8.4	831.8	7.6	75.2	9.5
1994	1527.4	8.4	—	—	172.6	4.7	873.4	5.0	82.3	9.3
1995	1644.4	7.7	—	—	179.3	3.9	950.7	8.9	89.2	8.4
1996	1906.7	15.9	—	—	202.5	12.9	1145.1	20.4	100.0	12.1
1997	2089.1	9.6	—	—	220.1	8.7	1224.3	6.9	108.6	8.6
1998	2284.9	9.4	—	—	235.2	6.9	1298.7	6.1	117.8	8.4
1999	2392.1	4.7	—	—	244.1	3.8	1295.3	−0.3	123.1	4.4
2000	2539.8	6.2	—	—	252.0	3.2	1317.2	1.7	131.3	6.7
2001	2899.4	14.2	—	—	279.6	11.0	1471.2	11.7	147.6	12.3
2002	3176.4	9.6	—	—	309.3	10.6	1629.0	10.7	159.9	8.4
2003	3377.0	6.3	—	—	319.0	3.1	1679.1	3.1	168.2	5.1
2004	3632.8	7.6	115.3	9.0	—	—	1889.0	12.5	183.0	8.8
2005	4055.5	11.6	128.0	11.0	—	—	2105.9	11.5	202.1	10.4
2006	4610.8[a]	13.7	140.8	10.0	—	—	2351.6[a]	11.7	224.9	11.3
2007	5416.1	17.5	163.1	15.8	—	—	2924.4		256.4	14.0
2008	—	—	199.9	22.6	—	—	3653.6	24.9	298.3	16.3

Notes: CCPI: Colombo Consumers' Price Index; GCCPI: Greater Colombo Consumers' Price Index; WPI: Wholesale Price Index; GDPD: GDP deflator; [a]Provisional; [b]Data for June 2008.
Source: Department of Census and Statistics. Central Bank of Sri Lanka, Annual Report (various issues).

Table 8.2A. Indices of Tradable Price (PT), Non-tradable Price (PN) and Real Exchange Rate (RER), 1990–2007 (2002=100)

Year	PT	PNT	RER
1990	41.1	30.3	135.7
1991	44.3	33.2	133.4
1992	48.5	36.5	132.8
1993	50.9	41.1	124
1994	54.6	45.5	120
1995	58.4	49.9	117.1
1996	65.7	55.1	119.4
1997	70.5	59.7	118
1998	71	65.2	108.9
1999	77.4	69	112.1
2000	83.4	83.5	100
2001	91.4	94.1	97.1
2002	100	100	100
2003	105.3	105.4	100
2004	113.5	115.1	98.6
2005	120.5	126.8	95
2006	127.5	141	90.4
2007	140.3	160.5	87.4

Notes: PT = Implicit deflator for manufacturing value added; PN = Implicit deflators for value added in construction, utilities and other non-government services; RER = (PT/PN)*100. A decrease in the index indicates real exchange rate appreciation (decrease in profitability of tradable production relative to non-taxable production).
Source: Compiled from national accounts data of the Central bank of Sri Lanka, *Annual Report* (various issues).

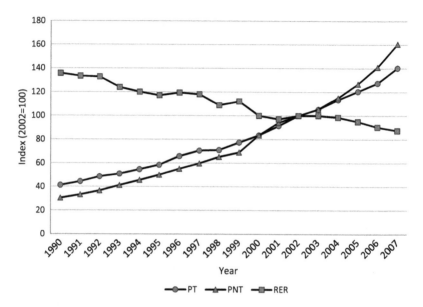

Figure 8.1A. Indices of Tradable Price (PT), Non-tradable Price (PN) and Real Exchange Rate (RER), 1990–2007

Source: Compiled from national accounts data of the Central Bank of Sri Lanka, *Annual Report* (various issues).

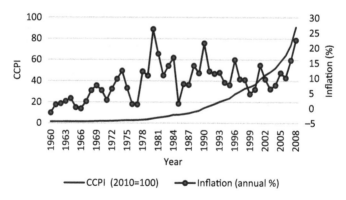

Figure 8.2A. Colombo Consumer Price Index Base (2010=100) and Year on Year Inflation in Sri Lanka (1960–2008)

Source: The World Bank, *World Development Indicators and Department of Census & Statistics Reports*.

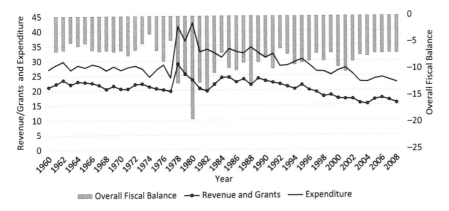

Figure 8.3A. Revenue/Grants, Expenditure and Overall Fiscal Balance (as a percentage of GDP) in Sri Lanka (1960–2008)

Source: *Central Bank Annual Report*, 2022.

Chapter 9

Export Growth and Appropriate Macroeconomic Policy: A Necessary Nexus

9.1 Introduction

Since 2005, Sri Lanka's trend export growth rate has fallen as has the share of export value added in GDP and the share in world trade. While trend import growth has also fallen, it remains higher than the export growth rate, leading to a trade deficit that has to be financed through running down reserves, borrowing from abroad, or curtailing imports (see Figures 9.1–9.3). Each method that lies at the centre of the macroeconomic and export nexus has different consequences for the economy. How we handle these choices will determine whether we can sustain growth beyond the post-war boom. We are looking here for sustained growth and not just one-time growth spurts. Sustained export growth will depend on a macroeconomic framework that needs to underpin necessary and far-reaching incentive reforms.

This chapter traces the links between macroeconomic policies and export growth to identify what appropriate macroeconomic policies would help to achieve a sustainable rate of export growth, given the current state of the world economy, domestic resources and policy constraints. We note that the falling export growth trend cannot be looked at in isolation. It is the result of international demand and domestic macroeconomic, trade and related policies. Sri Lanka cannot influence world demand and supply. The implication is that we take terms of trade as given

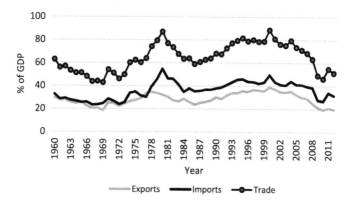

Figure 9.1. Sri Lanka Trade Trends, 1960–2012: Exports, Imports and Trade (as a percentage of GDP)

Source: The World Bank, *World Development Indicators*.

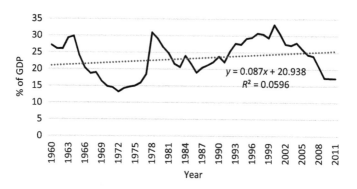

Figure 9.2. Merchandise Exports as a Share of GDP (1960–2011)

Source: The Central Bank of Sri Lanka, *Annual Report*.

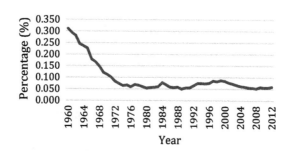

Figure 9.3. Sri Lanka's Share of World Exports, 1960–2012 (Per cent)

Source: The Central Bank of Sri Lanka, *Annual Reports*.

and have to address the issue through domestic policies going beyond the export sector. World experience suggests that macroeconomic policies are often implicated in falling export growth, slow GDP growth and indeed growth collapses. Microeconomic or incentive policies are vital for strong export growth, but they are not discussed in this chapter, given the wide dimensions of the topic at hand. Thus, the chapter does not discuss individual exports or activities related to them. Nevertheless, each export activity will face its microeconomic constraints ranging from access to resources, markets and responses to overall macroeconomic policies. We do believe these are important, but are not discussed in this chapter. We also do not discuss services or labour exports.

This chapter is organised as follows. After the introduction in Section 9.1, Section 9.2 discusses the analytical framework to examine the macroeconomic and export growth nexus. Section 9.3 takes a historical perspective. Section 9.4 discusses macroeconomic policies and their evolution. Section 9.5 examines export performance measures and their evolution. Section 9.6 notes other sectors and policy considerations including the incentives they operate under. Section 9.7 gives the main derivations and implications for the nexus and examines policies that have an overall impact on the economy including the export sector, which comprises fiscal and monetary policies and external borrowing. Section 9.8 examines the role of Foreign Direct Investment (FDI), trade facilitation and institutions that impinge on export growth. Section 9.9 provides the conclusions on appropriate macroeconomic policies to bring about export growth.

9.2 The Analytical Framework

Sri Lanka follows a Small Open Economy framework with an open current account and some degree of capital account openness as appropriate for Sri Lanka. This approximates our current situation best, save for some short-term and unpredictable departures from it (e.g. the 2006 to July 2009 period when the Central Bank used a virtually fixed exchange rate). Since February 2012, Sri Lanka has had a fixed but adjustable exchange rate, upwardly flexible real wages and real interest rates, which lie at the core of the macroeconomic framework.

The origin of the framework we are using in this chapter is the Australian model of a Small Open Economy (ASOE)[1] that traces the

---

[1] This Australian Open Economy macroeconomic model was developed by Salter (1959) and refined by Cordon (1977).

movement of these "macroeconomic prices" (namely, the real exchange rate, real wages and real interest rates) that influence trade and export growth outcomes. ASOE with its division between tradable goods (exportable namely, exports and their substitutes) and importables (imports and their substitutes) and non-tradable goods (mostly services, utilities and construction) provide the mechanics of the relationship of exports to macroeconomics and also enables the interpretation of historical export outcomes. A greater supply of exportables matched by a reduction in importables will improve the trade balance. The prices of exportables and importables are determined in the world market. Non-tradable prices are determined in the domestic market by domestic supply and demand and affected by domestic fiscal and monetary policies.

In this framework, the real exchange rate is the ratio of the price of non-tradable to tradable. This definition of the real exchange rate is relevant and useful to analyse domestic resource allocation. An appreciation of the exchange rate is a rise in the relative price of non-tradable to tradable. And, conversely, a fall in the relative price of non-tradable (or a rise in the price of tradable) is a depreciation. An appreciation that raises the relative price of non-tradable induces an increase in the supply of non-tradable and a reduction in the demand for non-tradable (i.e. through production and consumption effects). Depreciation, on the other hand, raises the relative price of tradable and has the opposite effect of increasing the supply of tradable and reducing domestic demand for tradable. Thus, a depreciation can improve the trade balance, while an appreciation will worsen the trade balance. In other words, the real exchange rate defined in this way is an important macroeconomic price influencing the domestic allocation of resources and affecting internal and external macroeconomic balance (See Figure 9.4).

There is also the standard definition of the real exchange rate in Purchasing Power Parity (PPP) terms, a variant of which is used by the IMF and the Central Bank of Sri Lanka. It serves as an important indicator of competitiveness. In that framework, other things remain the same: An appreciation reduces competitiveness, while a devaluation helps to either maintain or increase competitiveness. We note that the competitiveness of Sri Lankan exports was reduced during the appreciation of the Sri Lankan rupee in the 2006–2010 period. This real exchange rate, termed the Real Effective Exchange rate (REER), appreciated during this period. A fall in competitiveness leads to a reduction in the growth of

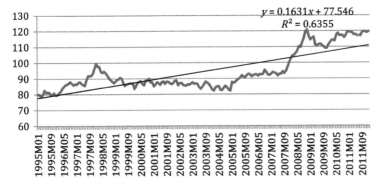

Figure 9.4. Monthly Movements of the Real Effective Exchange Rate (REER), 1995 (M01)–2011 (09)

Source: Darvas (2012). Based on 67 trade partners, covers 90 per cent of world trade and uses fixed average weights based on the 1998–2003 period.

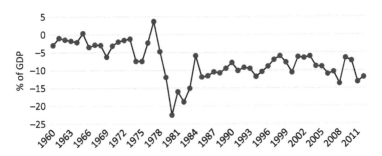

Figure 9.5. Trade Balance as a Percentage of GDP in Sri Lanka (1960–2012)

Source: The World Bank, World Development Indicators.

exports. The fall in turn could lead to a decline in imported goods needed for exports (Figure 9.5).

In the AOE framework, the three macro prices are related in well-defined ways. First, the real exchange rate is influenced by interest rates. In an open economy, interest rates determine capital flows which in turn influence the nominal exchange rate and hence the real exchange rate (see footnote 3), noting that the real interest rates determine capital flows. Similarly, an important component of non-tradable prices P_N is influenced by real wages of non-skilled workers when expressed as first differences, namely, $dP_N/dP_T = f(dW_N/(dP/dt))$.[2] Thus, attaining medium-term external and internal balance depends on these macroeconomic prices and the time paths to reach such equilibriums. In other words, the four principal markets — goods, capital, foreign exchange and labour — are integrated. In very simple frameworks, attainment of equilibriums in three markets ensures that the four markets are in equilibrium according to Walras's Law. A disturbance like an external shock causes macro prices to adjust, leading to a new configuration of these prices. Government policies can either support or hinder this adjustment. Most of the time, governments do not allow the adjustment process to take place on its own. It may lead to undesirable slowness or greater sacrifices than a government is prepared to make in terms of foregone employment or longer periods of slow growth.

In either definition of the exchange rate, an appreciation worsens the trade balance, while a depreciation ceteris paribus improves it when there is appropriate macroeconomic management, which avoids inflation and does not allow real wages to run ahead of a nominal devaluation (Figure 9.4, shows two episodes of appreciation peaks in 1997 and 2008–2009). And, the real effective exchange rate helps maintains a current account balance over the trade cycle. In fact, GDP or aggregate output can be divided into tradable goods and non-tradable goods that constitute the supply side of the economy. In the absence of readily available indices of tradable and non-tradable prices, the real exchange rate we use is a proxy, namely, the ratio of world prices (or major trading partners) to domestic price indices and nominal exchange rates. This is a variant of the PPP definition used by the IMF and the Central Bank of Sri Lanka.[3]

---

[2] Wages of skilled workers are technically determined by tradables since their prices are determined in the world market. The time derivative, $dW/dPN/dt$, represents marginal wages in the non-tradable goods-producing sector, hence the relationship between non-tradable prices and wages, and the relationship between the real exchange rate and economy-wide wages.

[3] The most commonly used measures compute the ratio, where Nominal Exchange Rate (NER) denotes the nominal exchange rate (measured as domestic currency per unit foreign currency), PW is an index of foreign prices and PD is an index of domestic prices (most often used are the Consumer Price Indexes (CPIs)). NER and PW are weighted averages computed across trading partner countries. The country weights are based on export shares. An increase (a decrease) in the index denotes depreciation (appreciation). The data used in the graph are from Darvas (2012). The data are based on fixed 1998–2003 weights

9.3 A Historical Perspective on Macroeconomics and Trade

Dividing the perspective into three periods, 1960 to 1977, 1978 to 2003 and 2004 to 2011, and identifying important regime changes for macroeconomics and export growth outcomes, allows us to provide a good historical perspective on the nexus between export growth and macroeconomic policy. The periods were chosen to represent each policy regime irrespective of the political makeup of the period. Thus, for instance, the first period was characterised by a policy regime of increased trade controls despite the half-hearted effort by the UNP to liberalise the economy during 1965–1970. That period was sandwiched by the restrictive regimes of the SLFP from 1960–1965 and 1970–1977. The second period (the longest covering 26 years) included the 1994–2003 government of President Chandrika Kumaratunga who, while politically on the left of centre, followed mostly right-of-centre economic policies. The last period was dominated by President Mahinda Rajapaksa's left-of-centre administration, which in some senses harks back to the leftist policies of the 1970–1977 period. The outcome of the slowing down of export growth and the decline in the export-to-GDP ratio were the result of external conditions and the domestic policy situation.

9.3.1 *The 1960–1977 Period*

The first period, 1960–1977, is distinguished by its relative macroeconomic stability, given low inflation and manageable current account deficits in the balance of payments. However, that early decade (1960–1977) saw the introduction and progressive tightening of exchange controls and increased trade protection. The macroeconomic implications of these two factors were that, first, Sri Lanka lost its character of an open economy with the imposition of import and exchange controls. Earlier, excess demand for tradable goods would spill into the current account so that the current account would worsen and lead to a fall in reserves. But, this could not happen with the introduction of exchange controls. Second, with the

---

and cover 67 trade partners, more comprehensive than the Central Bank's weights which are based on 24 trading partners. Besides, in the Darvas's estimates, the domestic price bases have not been changed often as is the case for the Central Bank of Sri Lanka's new price series.

increase in protection, the bias against exports had to increase and it did. And, the growth of exports slowed due to external conditions arising from the fall in world demand due to the first oil shock and the bias against exports arising from the introduction of import and exchange controls (see Appendix A: Table 9.2A). The ratio of exports to GDP was the lowest for the three periods. One outcome of it was that prices were no longer as important as before in determining the trade outcome. The question that then arises is why non-tradable prices did not rise.[4] One simple explanation is that there was excess capacity, but there was no increase in employment to speak of. Perhaps there was a reallocation of labour from exportable goods production to the production of non-tradable and import substitutes. The other possibility is that the tradable sector contracted. At that time, the labour market was flexible and real wages could adjust.

The 1965–1970 sub-period led to a partial attempt to restore the role of prices by adopting the Foreign Exchange Entitlement Certificate Scheme (FEEC) in 1968. With this scheme (copied from Pakistan), a multiple exchange rate system was put in place. All external transactions were divided into an A category and a B category. Transactions under the A category, which included essential imports (rice, flour, sugar and fertiliser) as well as traditional exports (tea, rubber and coconut), were to be conducted at the official exchange rate. B category transactions, which included non-traditional exports and non-essential imports, were conducted at an exchange rate with a premium (depreciated rate) and the rate was determined by the prices for FEECs. Thus, traditional exports (tea, rubber and coconuts) were converted at a fixed rate of exchange, while the non-traditional exports got a higher rate originally determined in the market for these certificates and carried a premium. Initially, the premium went as high as 65 per cent when the exchange rate for non-traditional exports rose to this level, but it was later fixed at 45 per cent. These certificates could be used to import goods from a permissible list (included in A category). The government at the time made an effort to cut down agricultural imports through a package of measures to increase import

---

[4] Of course, measured domestic prices reported in the CCPI included many subsidised items on the one hand and controlled prices on the other. Another part of the evidence is that reported prices were below the import and exchange rate premium in the open market. The GDP deflator was not particularly high and fitted the trend in price increases witnessed since 1960. In point of fact, inflation had remained dormant until 1978 and rose to 12.1 per cent. Real wages fell from 1971 until 1978.

substitution in agriculture, particularly rice. While some function of prices was restored with the FEEC scheme, its protagonists did not mind that the system taxed traditional exports, our main foreign exchange earner, and subsidised unproven non-traditional exports. Two main macroeconomic effects arose from the FEEC scheme. It helped to raise the price of tradables by a small percentage (due to a small percentage increase in non-traditional exports from a very low base) due to an increase in the production of importables with import substitution policies, particularly for agriculture. However, the bias against exports continued given the high import protection that became necessary to contain excess demand without spilling into the trade balance.[5] It is not clear if import substitution in agriculture at the time encouraged by the UNP led to greater efficiency in that the domestic resources costs of producing $1.00 of rice in Sri Lankan Rupees were lower than the accounting or shadow exchange rate that prevailed at the time. It is instructive to note what happened to the macroeconomic prices at the time. The REER index (1980 = 100) for total exports hardly moved between 1965 and 1970. It rose from 50 in 1965 to 51 in 1970. This did not help exports.[6] In addition, the nominal rate also indicates the fact that exports were taxed through an exchange rate premium between the official (FEEC) rate and the curb market rate for the US dollar in Sri Lanka. Thus, the premium for the US dollar rose from 56 per cent in 1968 to 65 per cent. The other price that is relevant is what happened to real wages. There was a slight increase in real wages between 1965 and 1970. They rose by 2.2 per cent for workers in wage board trades. But, in relation to 1968, real wages of these workers declined by nearly 11 per cent. But, it is noteworthy that there was hardly any change in the trend in wage rates. The general price level rose by nearly 8 per cent following the partial liberalisation of the foreign exchange rate and the trade regime. Real interest rates declined with the increase in inflation combined with an easy money policy and aid inflows. Between 1965 and 1970, the commercial banks' real deposit rate was −2.4 per cent while the

---

[5] It is surprising that the IMF went along with the Foreign Exchange Entitlement Certificate (FEEC system — a classic multiple currency arrangement) as it extended a Stand-by Arrangement at the time which was later abandoned as Sri Lanka could not meet some of the agreed targets for net domestic asset expansion. The World Bank helped create an Aid Group for Sri Lanka at that time, not as much for efficiency as to meet some of its own and other donors' resource transfer goals.

[6] See Table SA-17 in Athukorala and Jayasuriya (1994).

lending rate was −2.9 per cent. Real interest rates hardly moved up during this period.

The 1970–1977 sub-period is a remarkable one for the economic history of this country, with particular relevance for the nexus between macroeconomics and trade policies. The period saw the full flowering of the trade control regime that came into existence in the early 1960s, following a short respite from controls during 1965–1970. Trade controls became most stringent during this 1970–1977 sub-period. Some compared Sri Lanka's controls to the type of controls that were found in the former Soviet Union with one hundred per cent quantitative restrictions on imports. It introduced a huge bias against exports and a wide variance in the rates of protection among activities. At the same time, more price and quantity controls were put in place with the worsening of foreign demand due to the first oil shock. The left-of-centre coalition that included the *Lanka Samasamaja Party* (LSSP) and the Communist Party was very committed to increasing control of the economy. There was a definite and strong ideological shift towards greater control of the economy. The Marxist parties campaigned on the premise that Sri Lanka would be transformed into a socialist economy. Following the victory of the left parties, the leading SLFP coalition partner accepted their policies. And later, the SLFP's enthusiasm for greater control of the economy and takeover of private property seemed even more than that of the Marxist parties.[7] The SLFP–Marxists parties' coalition took over private property and nationalised the largest bank in Sri Lanka at the time — the Bank of Ceylon; they also ended up nationalising plantations and passing the Business Undertaking Acquisition Act of April 1971 and the Termination of Employment of Workers Act 33 of 1971. The first act dampened private enterprise, while the second entrenched labour union power at the expense of the unemployed. During this period, the first oil shock struck, raising the price of oil and creating difficulties in managing the economy, due to the increased import bill with the sharp increase in the price of oil.

To sum up, the whole period of 1960–1977 had a mixed outcome for the trade and macroeconomic nexus. First, the move from price-based policies to quantity-based policies made adjustment to external shocks more difficult (complicated by the first oil shock of 1973–1975) and

---

[7] One explanation is that Prime Minister Bandaranaike was convinced that the *Janatha Vimukthi Perumuna* (JVP) rebellion of 1971 was caused by the youth who could be appeased by a hard turn to the left.

changed the character of the nexus between macroeconomic policies and trade outcomes. Domestic prices were controlled as were interest rates while the nominal exchange rate remained fixed. The fall in world demand for Sri Lanka's exports and steady rise in import prices particularly for oil and grains imposed a heavy burden on the economy. But, the macroeconomic policy remained non-expansive. The Trotskyite Finance Minister, Dr. N. M. Perera, was inordinately fiscally conservative. Yet, the economy could not benefit from this quantity-based stability. This was because the bias against exports increased as import restrictions increased. The supply side of tradable sectors was constrained by nationalisations and the threat of business takeovers which made the reallocation of labour in line with changing incentives difficult. Since there were stringent exchange controls, the exchange rate did not ration resource use, nor did the balance of payments lead to huge losses in reserves since everything was controlled. Domestic prices particularly of non-tradables were highly controlled (a state of repressed inflation existed), and consumer and fertiliser subsidies and selective credit controls remained in place.[8] The fiscal deficit was kept under strict control and reserves were kept low, but this did not threaten macroeconomic stability. It led to price stability at the expense of efficiency that could have been achieved by using relative prices to allocate resources, rather than depend upon quantitative restrictions. The fiscal deficit was kept low with an average of 6 per cent of GDP for the period with a low standard deviation of 1.13. The current account deficit in the balance of payments averaged 2.5 per cent of GDP (Appendix A: Figure 9.2A) with a low standard deviation of 1.56. Meanwhile, as expected, the ratio of exports to GDP was only 19 per cent, the lowest for the three periods. GDP growth was also the lowest for the three periods. The nexus between macroeconomic policy and exports was least strong during 1970–1977.[9] Low growth of export was the price that

---

[8] Surjit Bhalla had reworked the CCPI, replacing subsidised items with market prices, and found a consistent understatement of market prices. Thus, the CCPI understated the price level by 44 per cent in 1971, by 56 per cent in 1974 and by 57 per cent in 1976. See Bhalla and Glewwe (1986).

[9] The real exchange rate (both the Australian Open Economic Model (AOEM) and the PPP rates) did not indicate the likely appreciation given that domestic prices did not reflect actual prices due to price control of principal consumption goods as well as other tradables. Non-tradable prices (those of utilities, construction and retail and wholesale trade) were similarly controlled.

was paid for an over-cautious approach to macroeconomic management and protectionist trade policies at the time.[10] Sri Lanka's shares of exports in GDP declined from 25.5 per cent in 1970 to 15.2 per cent in 1977 and its share in world trade declined at the same time. Macro prices behaved as expected when they are corrected for repressed inflation; exchange rate premiums rose and real wages declined. Some noted that the left-of-centre coalition was not very friendly to workers despite the rhetoric to the contrary. Athukorala and Jayasuriya (1994) showed that the economy was unnecessarily squeezed with tight macroeconomic policies when it was already experiencing a negative external shock from the first worldwide increase in oil prices. However, the squeezing of domestic demand did not lead to a diversion of resources to the tradable sector, particularly exports, given the stringent import control regime in place and expectations that the economy would be controlled even further if the coalition were to remain in power. In the event, the coalition was weakened when the Marxist parties left it in 1975.

9.3.2 The 1978–2003 Period

In contrast to the 1960–1977 period, the 1978–2003 period was one of more openness in the macroeconomic framework and movement towards a liberalised economy. The openness of the economy arose from the replacement of quantitative restrictions (QRs) with tariffs, and the adoption of a unified and devalued (by 45.1 per cent) market-based exchange rate (in contrast to the earlier FEEC scheme and the later Convertible Rupee Account (CRA) scheme). Import tariff rates were reduced which led to a reduction in the bias against exports combined with a more competitive market-based exchange rate. The replacement of quantitative restrictions with tariffs increased the flexibility of the economy and, in combination with the flexible exchange rate that was adopted, the economy could withstand external shocks better than before, with prices adjusting instead of quantities.

In addition to the trade liberalisation and the exchange rate reforms, interest rates were allowed to be market-determined which also helped to increase the ability to withstand external shocks. In effect, real wages

---

[10]This point was made succinctly by Athukorala and Jayasuriya (1994) in their elegant analysis of macroeconomic policies and their outcomes at that time.

were also allowed to adjust within limits with the movements of the real exchange rate (after all, real wages in the non-tradable sector are a part of the numerator of the real exchange rate) defined as the ratio of the price of non-tradable goods to tradable goods. The real exchange rate depreciated by about 40 per cent. Meanwhile, real wages also rose, initially by 25 per cent, but fell to the pre-liberalisation level in 5 years. As expected, tradable prices rose while non-tradable prices also adjusted over time. The initial boost to the production of tradable goods softened when inflation caught up with the huge public expenditures. It seems that the government's policy of liberalising the economy was throttled by the massive public expenditure boom. With prices allowed to find their equilibrium levels, the economy became more inflation-prone than before. Admittedly, though, instead of the repressed inflation of the earlier period, the new period saw open inflation. This meant that there had to be greater vigilance to guard against open inflation than before.[11]

Exports would fare better with the reduction of the bias against them than in the earlier regimes. However, this was not to be, given the competing public expenditure programmes that the government launched in early 1981. In hindsight, we can see the liberalisation of 1977–1978 was mostly undone by a massive public expenditure programme that included the Accelerated Mahaweli Development Project, the ambitious urban housing programme to build some 100,000 houses and the construction of one million rural dwellings. No doubt, the initially created greater headroom for the private sector with the new policies came to be limited, by the very ambitious public investment (Mahaweli project) and expenditure programmes, was not seen before in the Sri Lankan economy. This rivals even the ambitious public expenditure programme of today.

What did these developments imply from the macroeconomic policy and export nexus? A number of outcomes can be identified. First, the trade and exchange regime liberalisations helped to give an initial boost to exports and the ratio of exports to GDP rose to 26 per cent during the period (see Appendix A: Table 9.2A). However, that impact was later muted by an appreciation of the exchange rate due to the large public investments that raised the price of non-tradable goods significantly. It is to be noted that public expenditures are relatively more intensive in the

---

[11]At the same time, an open economy imposes macroeconomic discipline as very expansionary policies will lead to current account deficits that have to be financed by running down reserves or increasing foreign borrowing.

use of non-tradable goods (compared to private expenditures) so that a given amount of expenditure by the public sector produces a higher rate of appreciation for the same amount of expenditure by the private sector. Second, it leads to the now well-known and better-appreciated phenomenon of the Dutch disease.[12] The large inflows of capital associated with the public expenditure programmes appreciated the exchange rate to such an extent that the private sector, especially the export sector, could not cope with the competition for factors of production that the public sector virtually commandeered through the foreign assistance funds that it received. Third, because imports were restricted almost for a period of 17 years (1960–1977, with a short respite in 1968–1970) which had resulted in a huge pent-up demand for imports. Also, imports had become cheaper because of the appreciation of the rupee. The highest recorded imports, for the three periods during this time. Fourth, the current account deficit rose to high levels (to 5.6 per cent of GDP) not only because of private sector imports but also to accommodate the large capital inflows arising from foreign aid programmes at concessional interest rates, with long grace and maturity periods. Fifth, GDP growth rose to 4.8 per cent for the 1978–2003 period, the highest rate seen up to 2003. Finally, the threshold level for inflation was breached during this period. Inflation reached the highest level in the post-war period up to this time of 10.8 per cent (see Appendix A: Table 9.2A). It would be instructive to see how this precedent compares with the later periods and how it impinges on exports.

9.3.3 The 2004–2011 Period

The macroeconomic policy during this period was dominated by the escalation of the civil war following the end of the uncertain truce signed

---

[12] Given the AOEM we are using, the Dutch disease phenomenon is the increase in non-tradable prices associated with the increase in expenditures that leads to an appreciation of the exchange rate and creates a burden on exporters whether it arises from a natural resource shock from natural gas discoveries in Holland (as was the case of the Dutch guilder) or an increase in expenditure arising from foreign aid as was the case for Sri Lanka in the 1982–1985 period. Two elements of Dutch disease are the inflow of capital and the increase in the price of non-tradables. Connecting the Dutch disease phenomenon with the relation between the real exchange rate and growth, a recent view suggested that Dutch disease lowers economic growth. Thus, economic policy should contain any Dutch disease effects (Magud and Sosa (2010)).

under the Cease Fire Agreement (CFA) in 2002 and the coming into power of President Rajapaksa with the United People's Freedom Alliance (UPFA) coalition that was placed ideologically to the left of centre (Mahinda Chintana policies define the parties' political agenda). Meanwhile, well into this period, the financial market problems in the USA spilled into Western Europe and Japan in 2008 and reduced the demand for Sri Lanka's main exports — particularly garments. Following the end of the civil war in May 2009, the special access of Sri Lanka's garments to the European Union under GSP Plus was lost, on the alleged neglect of human rights during the last stages of the war with the LTTE. The civil war pervaded the early part of this period and led to large fiscal deficits, high inflation and a loss of reserves on a substantial scale. The current account deficits were financed from sovereign borrowing. Also, until late 2007, the pain was not felt as much because there was access to funds, as expensive as they had become when Sri Lanka was accumulating large foreign debt by historical standards. After refusing to get accommodation from the IMF, the government relented and sought a Stand-by Arrangement (SBA) from the IMF. After some delay, a $2.6 billion SBA was extended by the IMF in July 2009 following the end of the civil war in May 2009 when LTTE forces were defeated convincingly on the battlefield.[13] The SBA led to a build-up of foreign exchange reserves with the relieving of pressure on the balance of payments. It was concluded in late 2012, the only successful SBA programme extended to Sri Lanka.

Many features of this period are summarised in Appendix A in Table 9.2A. The fiscal deficit was brought under control with the implementation of the SBA. The period to 2011 had a fiscal deficit to the GDP ratio of 7.5 per cent, higher than the 1960–1977 period but lower than the 1978–2003 period. A similar pattern emerged with respect to the current account deficit of the balance of payments with 4.4 per cent of GDP in the

---

[13] The delay was presumably due to the US Secretary of State, Hilary Clinton, instructing the US Executive Director to communicate to the IMF Board that the US Government would vote against an SBA for Sri Lanka. This was the first known case in the history of the IMF when the US Government objected to a specific operation. Traditionally, the US Director, as do others, only comments on IMF policies and refrains from voting against individual loans. Even after the open disagreement with the Iranian government in the early 1980s, the US did not vote against an IMF Standby for Iran, but abstained from voting on it. But, the objection to the Sri Lankan SBA was withdrawn by the US. The Indian government, it is reported, helped to end this impasse.

last period, higher than the first period but lower than the second. However, the export-to-GDP ratio declined to 21.7 per cent of GDP while it had risen to 26.1 per cent in the second period, which witnessed a strong liberalisation of the trade regime at the beginning. GDP growth rose to 6.5 per cent for the whole period. Inflation rose to 10.2 per cent, higher than the first period but lower than the second period by a small margin.

During the early part of this period (2004–2006), the economy was moving along with a 4.5 per cent GDP growth rate with large debt-financed fiscal deficits, an exchange rate that was virtually fixed and a rising recourse to foreign borrowing. The incompatibility of a virtually fixed exchange rate, a partially open capital account (at least for inflows) and an independent monetary policy was either not realised by the Central Bank at the time or having realised it the Central Bank did not act on it.[14] The real exchange rate appreciated significantly between 2005 and 2009 (see Appendix A: Table 9.1A). Inflation, as measured by the GDP deflator, picked up and reached the highest appreciation in 2008. Reserves fell to a low level, rating agencies downgraded Sri Lanka's creditworthiness and funds to fight the war were partially raised by raising traditional tariffs as well as by introducing new para tariffs during the 2005–2010 period. In mid-2010, the government reduced protection by a modest amount by reducing surcharges and eliminating some taxes on imports such as the Port and Airport Levy and the Social Responsibility Levy.

With this modest relaxation, surcharges were reduced to 15 per cent across the board. Earlier, there existed the VAT, Social Responsibility Levy, Nation Building Tax and Excise duties. There was also a special commodity levy on 22 essential imports. They were all para tariffs leading to similar protective and revenue effects and created a bias against exports. Para tariffs were reduced from 39.9 per cent on all tariff lines (a total of 6,520 tariff lines) to 27 per cent. We note that the total protection rate had increased compared to the pre-2001 period, many types of tariff-like devices came to be used and the trade regime became increasingly unpredictable with several changes, especially in agricultural imports. Even the case of motor cars is revealing. After reducing tariffs from 300 per cent in June 2010, many rates were re-instituted.[15] This type

---

[14] The so-called unholy trinity was not realised by the authorities or if realised was ignored. A fourth aspect must be added, to the unholy trinity, namely, not going to the IMF!

[15] Motor cars deserve special mention. They are imported Complete Knocked Down (CKD) and are new, but older models are subject to a tax of 300 per cent, so domestic

of policy uncertainty could not be conducive for all investments, whether FDI or domestic investment.

The economy made a good recovery after 2009 due to (a) restoration of peace and upbeat expectations, (b) the SBA signed in July of that year which helped to restore macroeconomic stability aided by improved commodity prices, (c) better harvests in 2007 and 2008, and (d) somewhat improved external conditions in 2009; while both exports and imports declined in 2009, the decline in imports was less than that of exports. After some reticence, the Central Bank allowed the rupee to depreciate from Rs. 108 to the US dollar to Rs. 132 and above in February 2012. After the Treasury's announcement in the budget speech in November 2011 that it was devaluing the rupee by 3.0 per cent, the Central Bank hesitated until February 2012 when it allowed the exchange rate to float. The Treasury's announcement that the rupee was to be devalued was unusual. Traditionally, it is the Central Bank that is charged with the responsibility of maintaining the par value of the rupee under the Monetary Law Act of 1949 as amended in subsequent years. However, it was the Treasury that signalled the departure from a hard peg.[16]

Macroeconomic management improved in terms of reducing the deficit following the SBA. However, post-SBA stability could have turned out to be a transitory phenomenon. We already saw some signs that fiscal discipline could be hard to maintain. Fiscal deficits could have gone above 6.5 per cent of GDP in 2012 while inflation had begun to edge up. Meanwhile, the Central Bank of Sri Lanka (CBSL) was again using reserves to keep the rupee from depreciating and borrowing to maintain the exchange rate. In other words, we saw a repeat of the pre-SBA situation with respect to the fiscal deficit, holding the peg and allowing public expenditure to grow faster beyond the SBA (2009–2012) corset.

---

prices of cars reflect this QR premium. More recently, car parts came to be taxed at low rates compared to the past, leading to an increase in effective rate of protection (ERP). To make matters worse, the government reduced the excise tax on motor cars to induce greater domestic value addition, thus compounding the inefficiency of producing for such a narrow market.

[16] It is also likely that the IMF signalled its concerns that an appreciating rupee would produce the same conditions that had brought the economy close to a macroeconomic crisis in 2007–2008. A couple of instalments of the SBA were pending despite the claim made by the CBSL that IMF money was more expensive than commercial funds, which was clearly not the case.

What did these developments imply for the macroeconomic policy and export nexus? Growing fiscal deficits contributed to higher rates of inflation (e.g. inflation rose to 22.6 per cent in 2008). High inflation contributed to an appreciation of the exchange rate. When combined with the introduction of many para tariffs, the bias against exports increased. The SBA helped introduce a measure of fiscal discipline and limited further external borrowing at commercial rates. The $2.6 billion SBA helped meet current external debt obligations that were falling due. Despite the depreciation of the rupee, the exchange rate remained unstable. It appreciated and depreciated with CBSL interventions (through state-owned banks), which seemed to continue to keep the exchange rate in a very narrow range. Consequently, the former problem of using reserves to keep the exchange rate from depreciating continued. When this was the case, both exporters and importers had difficulty in undertaking forward transactions given that hedging against the exchange rate (that would help stabilise the Rupee) became difficult. The rate as well as the exchange rate regime itself becomes unpredictable in these circumstances. This poses difficulties for exporters and those interested in investing in the export sector given that the rates of return to investment in the exportable sector also become unpredictable.

The government used the tariff regime to raise revenues to finance the war. Consequently, many tariffs and tariff-like measures were introduced during this period. Since 1995, there has not been an important trade reform. What was done in June 2010 was partial, incomplete and subject to continued uncertainty. Recent research found that Sri Lanka has one of the most complex trade regimes in the world (Pursell and Ahsan, 2011).[17]

The trade regime is particularly difficult for exports in the following ways, as noted in the International Trade Centre (ITC) survey (2010): Some 69.7 exporters complained about Non-Tariff Measures (NTMs) that were creating problems for exporters. There were many procedural obstacles, with clearances required from plantations, forestry ministries and other authorities. Bribery is rampant. Exporters found domestic barriers more severe compared to foreign barriers, due to issues of certification, government clearances and other procedural issues. The ITC survey found

---

[17]Pursell's and Ahsan's (2011) work stands in contrast to the World Trade Organization's (WTO) Trade Policy Review (TPR) that did not fully understand and analyse the effects of para tariffs, which makes the TPR an inadequate document for the understanding of the trade policy framework of Sri Lanka (see Athukorala, 2012a).

that trade barriers in Sri Lanka were one of the most onerous out of the eight countries surveyed up to 2011.[18]

In this narrative, within the three periods, four crucial trade regime changes can be identified. These are 1960–1962 when the trade regime began to be tightened; 1970–1977 when the trade regime was tightened even further; 1978–2003 when it was liberalised; and 2005–2010 when the trade regime was somewhat tightened again. In each of these regimes, the macroeconomic and export nexus underwent changes with significant movements in the macroeconomic prices and export outcomes. In the 1960–1962 episode, when import and exchange controls were introduced, domestic prices were partly disconnected from foreign prices. Consequently, excess demand in the economy was more prone to being reflected in rising prices than falling reserves. Yet, prices did not rise significantly during this period due perhaps to excess capacity, a more flexible labour market and conservative demand management by the treasury and the CBSL. In the 1970–1977 episode, with greater import and exchange controls, there was a tendency for prices to rise but inflation was repressed. Excess demand manifested in long queues and rationing and was controlled by a rather conservative Minister of Finance. In the final episode, 2005–2010, the civil war escalated, and war spending expanded aggregate demand; prices rose high in the 1982–1985 period, but were brought under control with better demand management supported by the IMF Stand-by. This last period also saw the attempt to use the exchange rate as a nominal anchor in which monetary policy became subservient to an overvalued exchange rate target, supported by foreign borrowing at commercial rates.

9.4 Macroeconomic Policy and Their Evolution

Macroeconomic policy is meant a mix of fiscal and monetary policies. They are considered together because, for all practical purposes, their impacts on export growth are inseparable in Sri Lanka. On the fiscal side, fiscal deficits, revenue and expenditure policies, and the methods of financing are relevant as are the levels of government debt, both domestic and external. For monetary policy, money supply, credit policies, reserve levels, and nominal exchange and interest rates are relevant.

---

[18] International Trade Centre (2011).

Monetary policy influences exchange rates through its impact on prices, wages and interest rates. Recent inflation paralleled the 1980–1985 inflation due to huge public expenditures with effects on macro prices. Macroeconomic policy influences levels and rates of change of exports and imports. And, to keep the nexus stable, governments must try to avoid two adverse macroeconomic outcomes, namely, inflation and balance-of-payment crises as they impinge on tradable goods strongly with implications, particularly for exports.

Inflation: Sri Lanka has experienced four inflation episodes in the period covered between 1960 to 2011. It is instructive to examine the macroeconomic and export growth nexus. There was the 1973–1975 episode, the 1980–1981 episode, the 1988–1989 episode and 2006–2009 episode. Two inflation episodes are relevant to the export outcome: the second inflation episode of 1980–1981 and the 2006–2008 episode.

It is the 1980–1981 episode that is the most relevant for recent inflation. Then, inflation rate rose to 26.1 per cent (CCPI: 2002 = 100), the highest rate recorded at the time since the CCPI was compiled. The overall fiscal deficit rose to19.2 per cent of GDP in 1980. The factor that led to the expansion was the tremendous increase in public expenditure that the government initiated at the time with large investments in the Mahaweli multi-purpose project, the new parliament complex and similar public expenditures.

The inflation episode that began in 2006 and continued until 2008, reaching a high point in June and declining in July and August. The episode was associated with increased money supply, public expenditure and seasonality factors. Again, supply shocks associated with the rise in energy and food prices combined with domestic expansionary policies led to a 22.6 per cent inflation rate in 2008 as measured by the CCPI (2002 base). The fiscal deficit rose to 7.0 per cent of GDP in 2008 and rose to 9.9 per cent of GDP in 2009. This is in contrast to the earlier spike in inflation which was associated with a similar deficit. This underscores the link between inflation and the method of financing the fiscal deficit. A single-digit inflation has been broadly maintained. With respect to handling the current account deficit in the balance of payments, there was no attempt to switch expenditure using the exchange rate until February 2012. Instead, the government accumulated a large sovereign debt even after the SBA was effective and continued to use the exchange rate as a nominal anchor using sovereign borrowings (some 300–400 basis points above

LIBOR) for five-year sovereign loans. Unlike in the earlier episode, Sri Lanka had gained access to the international bond market and borrowed nearly $3.0 billion US dollars, exceeding the funding from the SBA. The contrast between the two episodes (1980–1981 and 2006–2008) is clear. The earlier episode did not entail large external debt given that the country had access to substantial concessional funds. Also, there was no civil war to fund during the earlier episode. In addition, in the earlier episode, the nominal exchange rate was allowed to depreciate, while in the latter episode, the nominal exchange rate was virtually fixed and this led to the rapid decline in reserves.

But, what does the contrast of macroeconomic imbalances entail for export growth? First, it is not a helpful environment when the inflation rates rise since it distorts relative prices.[19] Export firms, especially those who invest in the exportable sector, find it difficult to predict their future income and expenditure streams and therefore rates of return to investment. Second, inflation and high current account deficits increase uncertainty with respect to expanding the output of exportables at a given capacity in the normal course of a day-to-day business. These decisions become more difficult when the behaviour of the exchange rate is erratic, at least even when the direction of change could not be predicted. If not, the extent of the change gives a steady direction within some past variance norms. Of course, exporters can hedge but hedges tend to be short term, expensive and add to the costs of exporting goods.

9.5 Export Performance Measures and their Evolution

Trade, as a percentage of GDP (the so-called trade ratio which is the sum of exports and imports divided by GDP), has declined from 87 per cent in 1980 to 54 per cent in 2011 (See Appendix A: Figure 9.2A). There was an expansion of the non-tradable sector in contrast to the tradable sector,

---

[19] It is to be noted in macroeconomic literature that high variance in inflation is associated with high inflation rates. Even average values for inflation in Sri Lanka are associated with higher standard deviations. Similarly, larger current account deficits in the balance of payments are associated with greater appreciations of the exchange rate, in each of the periods used earlier. It is also clear that the greater the appreciation of the rupee, the greater its variance (indicated by higher standard deviations).

arising mainly from the expansion of public administration. Given that the size of the government sector increased, which was typically of low productivity, a greater share of the country's resources, both financial and human, was switched from the high-productivity private sector activities to low-productivity activities in the public sector. The tradable sector was subject to greater competition, and it was highly productive, particularly the export component of the tradable sector. In addition, when fiscal and monetary policies are expansive, the economy overheats as it did and leads to increasing external imbalances. The size of the domestic market is such that export growth is essential for achieving a higher GDP growth (Appendix A: Figure 9.1A). As already noted, the total share of exports in GDP declined as did the share of Sri Lankan exports in world exports. Taken together, these trends indicate that the Sri Lankan economy been lost competitiveness. This may be attributed, inter alia, to an overvalued exchange rate (before the introduction of a more flexible exchange rate policy in February 2012) and an inadequate liberalisation of the economy despite the mid-2010 trade reforms.

World trade is mostly in value-added products and their importance increases over time, allowing an even greater division of labour in the world. The ratio of value addition of manufactures in Sri Lanka's GDP rose from 10.4 per cent in 1980 to 12.3 per cent in 1983 and rose to 16.0 per cent in 2000. But it fell sharply to 13 per cent in 2010 raising some questions as to why it occurred. First, as noted earlier, non-tradable sectors expanded faster than tradable sectors (they have higher value addition ratios). Second, Sri Lanka's export competitiveness has fallen as evidenced by the fall in the share of Sri Lanka's exports in world exports. Third, even within the tradable sector, exports face greater competition from importable, more specifically import substitutes and non-tradable domestic resources. Finally, the appreciation of the real exchange rate imposes an onerous burden on exports. One reason for it is the Dutch disease phenomenon associated with capital inflows related to the large public expenditure programmes. Thus, as in the earlier episode when Mahaweli-related expenditures created a Dutch disease problem by raising non-tradable prices, a similar occurrence seems to be taking place as in the past.

Other measures of export performance are needed to tell the export growth story: These are (a) a bias against exports, (b) effective protection rates between exports and imports, (c) variance in protection, (d) non-tariff and para tariff barriers including Commodity Export Subsidy Scheme (CESS),

(e) effective exchange rates for exports and imports, (f) the role of FDI, (g) trade facilitation and (h) institutional support.

A bias against exports arises when the Effective Exchange Rate for imports (EERm) in domestic currency, saved from imports, exceeds the domestic currency equivalent of a dollar (EERx) earned in an export, due to tariffs, subsidies and taxes, and other barriers that raise the domestic currency prices of exports.[20] While no precise estimates exist for Sri Lanka, one can see that the protection accorded to importable must exceed those provided for exports in domestic currency given that export subsidies do not exist, while there are positive taxes on exports in terms of the cesses. It makes little sense to tax exports while at the same time trying to raise export growth.

With respect to effective rates of protection (ERP) of primary commodities, among importables, maize is the most protected agricultural commodity in the small sample of 9 agricultural commodities (Table 9.1), with an ERP of 232.58 per cent, followed by potatoes with an ERP of 149.09 and the third rank among the nine commodities being for fresh milk which has an ERP of 101.18 per cent. Out of exportables, the most unprotected commodity is fresh coconuts which have a negative ERP of 46.65 per cent, while tea is taxed (or dis-protected) at negative −3.97 per cent and latex rubber is unprotected at 1.08 per cent. Similarly, for other trade measures, import substitutes are protected with tariffs and other trade measures while exports are not protected unless there are subsidies to offset the bias against exports. But, export subsidies are not allowed under WTO rules.

As there have not been economy-wide estimates of ERP since the year 2000, this small sample of nine commodities confined to the agricultural sector provides a few examples of the protective structure. Some specific comments can be made confined to the agricultural sector in the narrow range of nine commodities. First, there is a tendency for resources to be drawn into the most protected sectors as they are the most profitable. Second, the negative sign for ERP in Table 9.1 indicates a tax or opposite of protection, what trade economists call "dis-protected or un-protected" in the case of exportables. Thus, the protection of importables implies a

---

[20] A bias is defined as follows:

$B = (EERm)/(EERx) - 1$.

In other words, when the (EERm) > (EERx), then $B > 0$.

tax on exports, as small as it could be, given that exports are subject to international competition. Third, it is important to realise that these ERP estimates apply to primary commodities, which means that the protection at this level makes it less profitable as activity moves up the value-added chain. Finally, there is a wide variance in protection, from −46.65 to 232.58, implying a wide variance in incentives. And therefore, investment in the tradable sector, in general, and in the exportable sector, in particular, has lower profitability compared to both import substitution and non-tradable sectors. In other words, the higher profitability of some primary commodities over others, particularly importables, leaves fewer incentives to expand production and to invest in the exportable sector. Thus, it is not surprising that agricultural exports are less attractive for investment compared to the industrial sector. We can only hazard a guess about the relative attractiveness of agricultural inputs production used in industrial production in this small sample. Goods such as latex rubber, coconut and milk powder are inputs into manufacturing rubber gloves, sandals, biscuits and confectionery. They raise costs of production on a range of exports. Overall, while nominal protection influences the level and composition of consumption in the economy, ERPs show the incentive structure that relates to different economic activities on a value-added basis.[21]

In the small sample presented in Table 9.1, there are large differences between NRP and ERP rates for the same product in the same year, which arises from incorporating inputs into the analysis. Thus, not only are the domestic prices of primary agricultural products affected by agricultural protection but also the domestic prices of tradable inputs, which influence the cost structures of the various agricultural activities and also the non-agricultural activities that use these inputs. This effect on the intermediate inputs is not captured by the NRPs. The very high and positive ERPs for import-competing activities stand in contrast to the negative ERPs for exportables. These indicate a strong anti-trade and anti-export bias in the trade regime. A third finding is a wide dispersion in NRPs and ERPs across the various agricultural activities, as though policymakers intended to guide resource allocation in the sector in a highly selective way, departing from the principle of neutrality that allows markets to determine

---

[21] ERP is equal to the value added estimated by taking into account trade protection divided by the value added at free trade prices. $(Vj - Vj^*)/Vj^*$), where Vj^* represents value added per unit of output at border prices for the output and tradable inputs, given the exchange rate.

Table 9.1. Nominal and Effective Rate of Protection: Nine Agricultural Commodities for 2009/2010

	Primary Commodity	Tradable Commodity	NRP (%) of Tradable Commodity	ERP (%) of Primary Commodity
Import-competing	Paddy	Rice	6.75	36.49
	Potatoes	Potato	54.24	149.09
	Maize	Maize	102.18	232.58
	Red onions	Red onion	3.00	0.70
	Green gram	Green gram	17.27	18.71
	Fresh Milk	Milk powder	74.93	101.18
Exportables	Made tea	Made tea	−2.12	−3.97
	Rubber latex	Rubber Latex	−1.42	−1.08
	Coconuts: Fresh nuts	Desiccated coconut	−30	−46.65

Source: Alberto Valdes *et al.*: What is the Cost of a Bowl of Rice? *World Bank Policy Note*, May 2012 (unpublished).

resource allocation rather than using public policy on a selective basis. The upshot of this approach is that unless there is a compelling infant industry argument, productive efficiency is compromised, including for those in the export sector in a fundamental way.

9.6 Other Sectors and Policy Considerations

As noted, one cannot look at export growth in isolation. For example, export growth depends on incentives for exports as well as other factors. Imports are important for export growth for several reasons. For imported inputs, for relative incentives (if importables have a high return), resources will be drawn to that sector, reducing the profitability of exports. A tariff on imports is a tax on exports (Lerner Symmetry theorem).[22] An import

---

[22] The theorem holds that a tariff on imports is a tax on exports. P_1, an import with a tariff of t_x, leads domestic relative price of imports to exports to rise to $P_1(1 + t_x)$, then the relative price will become $P_2/P_1 (1 + t_x)$ where P_2 is the export good. But, foreign prices remain the same in foreign currency at say $(P_2/P_1)^*$ — the new domestic relative price $P_2 / P_1 (1 + t_x) > P_2/P_1)^*$. Domestic relative price upon foreign price is $P_2/P_1 (1 + t_x)/(P_2/P_1)^* = (1 + t_x)$. Thus, a 10 per cent tariff on importables is equal to a tax on all exportables. In the

tariff can also lead to an appreciation of the exchange rate and hurts exports.

Likewise, incentives for a particular group of exports can either help or hinder total export growth. Sri Lanka has tried to do this on several occasions and failed at it, each time, e.g. FEEC scheme (1968–1970) and CRA (1971–1977). Both schemes taxed traditional exports and subsidised new or non-traditional exports. The outcomes in both cases were disappointing, to say the least. Sri Lanka's overall exports suffered at that time. There was no way that around 5 per cent of non-traditional exports could grow so strongly and rapidly to overcome the disadvantage or implicit tax created by the multiple exchange rate.

In a similar vein, taxing raw materials and intermediate exports to increase domestic value added does not serve efficiency or maximise GDP or total value added. It has become quite fashionable to go back to the old idea that increasing domestic value added per se would be more beneficial to the country than taxing raw materials and final goods at similar rates. Consequently, one sees today that many raw material and intermediate goods exports are either banned or face high export taxes. With such a measure, the domestic price of these goods must fall, giving an advantage to the exporter of the final good in that value chain. Two consequences follow from this policy. The production of raw materials and intermediate goods is discouraged as their profits fall due to the imposition of an export tax. The country would not have an improvement in performance as these goods are taxed. Also, since world trade is fast becoming a trade in value added, it puts this country at a disadvantage compared to others in the same line of business.[23]

Exchange Rate: The appreciation of the Sri Lanka rupee, *vis-à-vis* a basket of currencies representing its trading partners in the 1990s and since 2005, has acted as a tax on exporters and a tariff on those importing goods, raising the profitability of the importers and producers of importables. The

---

presence of non-tradable goods, this symmetry is broken. But, for small economies like Sri Lanka, non-tradable sectors are small, so a qualified Lerner theorem applies.

[23] Prema-Chandra Athukorala showed that value added in China, the world's largest exporter of the iPhone, only adds 3.2 per cent of value added to that product even though it earns billions of dollars by processing the final stage of the iPhone. If China had incentives to increase domestic value added, it would not be the world's most successful exporter today (Gamani Corea Foundation Lecture, 2012).

nominal exchange rate in October 2012 was Rs. 126.75 to the US dollar. When we compare it with the exchange rate that prevailed in 2005, which was Rs. 100.50 to the US dollar, we can determine the time path of the nominal exchange rate implied between 2005 and 2012. It suggests that the exchange rate should have depreciated at 3.37 per cent a year. This implies an average exchange rate of Rs. 122.62 in 2011 in comparison with the actual rate at that time Rs.110.56, which gives a 9.83 per cent overvaluation in 2011, i.e. $100*(110.56-122.62)/122.62 = 9.83$ per cent. This is likely to be more of an underestimate than an overestimate given that the exchange rate rose to Rs. 138 to the US dollar a couple of months before October 2012 and fell to a lower level due to CBSL intervention by selling US dollars. A part of is an overshooting of the exchange rate, which is a well-known phenomenon, and the rate would settle to a lower rate depending on macroeconomic conditions at the time. Of course, no one can predict what the rate is going to be. For that, we have a market. This implies a tax of 9.83 per cent on exports (since foreign prices are fixed). We use the nominal rate here since it is the rate that market agents use to make their day-to-day decisions. Also, the nominal rate becomes a crucial variable to estimate the REER.

Meanwhile, Sri Lanka's competitors had devalued their currencies to take into account the difference between their domestic inflation rates and those of their competitors. Thus, Sri Lankan exporters were in a quandary; their narrow profit margins were squeezed as they had to pay similar wages, salaries and rents compared to those countries producing import substitutes. By delaying the devaluation, the exporters paid a substantial price in terms of forgone exports as did the country as a whole.

A comparison of average real exchange rate indexes provides a long-term perspective of the three periods (see Appendix A, Table 9.1A on an implied overvaluation during this period). The average value for the real exchange rate was 63.2 for the 1960–1977 period. It appreciated and took the value of 94.2 during 1978–2003 given the Dutch disease phenomenon and it fell to 88.8 during the last period of 2004–2011. Of course, averages hide spikes in the real exchange rate, both up and down. As noted, there was an appreciation that spiked in 2008. It could have gone even higher were it not for the Central Bank selling dollars to the market and losing reserves in the process. Similar to inflation, high rates of appreciation are associated with large variance as indicated by the high standard deviations for each period. Two spikes are observable in 1997 and 2008. However, there were high spikes in early 1980 as a result of appreciations associated with the Dutch disease.

There are other effects of the appreciation in addition to the Dutch Disease effect. Because imports grew much faster than exports, the trade balance widened and the government borrowed at commercial rates without seeking IMF support initially. This led to paying higher interest to commercial lenders compared to the lower interest paid under the SBA programme. It also has to be factored in that it raised the cost and delayed the necessary depreciation of the rupee. Meanwhile, downgrading Sri Lanka's creditworthiness by the rating agencies due to the accumulating liabilities would have discouraged FDI. This additional cost had to be factored in too.

FDI: A good environment for FDI also helps exports, for FDI provides resources, management and know-how for exports as well as access to foreign markets. Empirical work supports the close link between export growth and FDI (Athukorala and Rajapatirana, 2000). Sri Lanka required an investment of 35 per cent of GDP to achieve 8 per cent growth. National savings amounted to 25 per cent of GDP, which meant that the savings/investment gap amounted to 10 per cent of GDP. That is currently equivalent to $6 billion. This amount needed to be raised through a mix of debt and non-debt, creating inward flows. As a lower-middle-income country, Sri Lanka no longer had access to grants and concessional financing. The headroom for commercial borrowing was also being reduced. Hence, a major share of the financing of the gap of $6 billion needed to take the form of non-debt, creating inflows, particularly FDI, which could boost export performance. It is noteworthy that Sri Lanka's total stock of FDI amounted to about $6 billion and a flow of FDI $752 million. Malaysia had an FDI stock of $73 billion and attracted $8 billion in 2008. The corresponding figures for Vietnam, which initiated market-oriented reforms much later than Sri Lanka, were $43 billion and $8 billion.

Trade facilitation: Supporting infrastructure helps exports by reducing the cost of exporting at the border and even behind the border. Similarly, delays at the border due to unhelpful procedures, customs clearances, costs of certification and corruption act as barriers to exports (ITC Survey: Sri Lanka 2010). Reform of the customs and certification procedures would help improve Sri Lanka's export competitiveness since the higher costs associated with these procedures act as a tax on exports.

Infrastructure: Good and supportive infrastructure, such as roads, ports and loading facilities, helps keep costs down and raises returns to export. Infrastructure also helps provide competitive production and good trade facilitation of exports. Since 2005, the government has been spending large amounts of resources on creating and improving infrastructure. This would help in the long run by reducing the cost of transport and providing more competitive prices for use of power and water among other cost-reducing measures. But, like all investments, to be efficient, the government must follow proper evaluations to see the rate of return to these activities corrected for all-round or external effects or externalities. Otherwise, there is no guarantee that this money will be properly spent so as to lead to greater efficiency and increased competitiveness.

Institutional support: Fiscal and monetary authorities, as well as institutions such as Export Development Board and other government entities such as Customs and certification agencies, can help or hinder export growth. Their record has not been encouraging. Using export cesses to tax exports and attempting to promote exports through bureaucracies have not been successful in most countries, while some East Asian countries are the few exceptions. Even there, the investment has been with the private sector. Government agencies support what private agents have identified as feasible and profitable avenues for investment and export. Most importantly, when government initiatives have not borne fruit, they have closed down such projects. This type of planned exit is essential to prevent public resources from being wasted but governments refuse to close down bad projects and use the institutions created to provide sinecures for political supporters. This has been the case in Sri Lanka with all political parties that have been in power.

9.7 Main Derivations and Implications for the Nexus

Narrow Profit margins: Exporters operate with narrow margins given the intense international competition they face compared to those who produce for the home market (import substitutes). They face export taxes and para tariffs (such as CESSES and other trade constraints.) While export subsidies are not allowed under WTO rules, export taxes are allowed.

Cesses: It does not make sense to tax exports and hand over the tariff revenue to bureaucrats to disperse the revenue according to their will. Their activities may not be pernicious, but are worthless and wasteful. The bureaucratic processes of the Export Development Board have to be noted.

Real wages and productivity: Real wages and productivity are important determinants of export growth because they in turn determine export competitiveness. When fiscal and monetary policies are expansive and raise the price level, labour demands higher money wages and if they succeed, then the country's competitiveness declines, if there is no matching increase in productivity. For example, wages in Bangladesh for textile and garment workers are lower than in Sri Lanka, but Sri Lanka still retains its competitiveness in the activity because productivity is higher in Sri Lanka.

Real wages in terms of the AOEM are closely related to the real exchange rate defined as the ratio of non-tradable goods prices to tradable goods prices (P_N/P_T). Non-tradable prices are closely correlated with wages of unskilled workers (wages of skilled workers on the other hand are highly correlated with tradable goods). A rise in this ratio or the real exchange rate is an appreciation. Non-tradable prices are largely determined by monetary policy. So, when the monetary authority exhorts the exporters to increase productivity (rather than allow the exchange rate to depreciate), it is asking these firms to increase productivity over and above a rise in P_N (or an appreciation of the real exchange rate). So, with a 9.83 per cent appreciation, it would have been impossible to match it with productivity increases. In fact, during the height of the growth spurts in East Asia in the 1970s, none of the four Tigers could raise their total factor productivity above 7–8 per cent per year. In contrast, Sri Lanka's TFP for the last 30 years increased only 1.0 per cent per year.

Besides, with the incentive framework remaining largely unchanged since 2004, an increase in productivity could not take place. Consequently, the appreciation reduced Sri Lanka's competitiveness when at the same time Sri Lanka's competitors in South Asia devalued their currencies. Thus, the decline in Sri Lanka's competitiveness can be approximated in the following way, taking into account three elements involved in the loss of competitiveness[24]: a rise in the price of non-tradable, a fall in

---

[24] In broad terms, the loss in competitiveness is equal to the rate of appreciation of the real exchange rate less the growth in productivity.

productivity and the relative depreciation of currencies by Sri Lanka's competitors.

9.8 Fiscal and Monetary Policies to Support Export Growth

Fiscal Policies: Overall fiscal deficits were high since the late 1990s (See Appendix A: Table 9.2A). They were 8.4 per cent of GDP in 1998, 9.5 per cent in 2000, 8.5 per cent in 2002, 7.0 per cent in 2005 and 8.0 per cent in 2010. These reflected increases in public expenditure, bidding away of resources from the private sector (crowding out), involuntary open market operations caused by attempting to keep the exchange rate from depreciating and of course the high inflation. The cost of living as shown by the CCPI with 2002 is 9.6, 9.8 per cent in 1998, 6.2 per cent in 2000, 11.6 per cent in 2005, 22.6 per cent in 2008 and 6.2 per cent in 2010 (Department of Census & Statistics of Sri Lanka).[25] World interest rates were at an all-time low with the LIBOR at 3.0 per cent. Sri Lanka was able to have its bond sales over-subscribed due to the relatively high coupon rate paid by its bonds and the "Good Housekeeping Seal" provided by the IMF's SBA.

The relationship of fiscal policies to export growth comes about in three ways. (i) A large fiscal deficit financed from monetary sources creates inflation and leads to an appreciation of the exchange rate. (ii) Borrowing from domestic sources through Treasury Bills (TBs) and securities raises the interest rate, encouraging inflows of portfolio capital given that the capital account in Sri Lanka is partially open at least for inflows, which also leads to an appreciation of the exchange rate. (iii) Domestic inflation leads to demand for higher wages, raising real wages of the whole labour market. While import-competing activities can pass on the cost increase to the protected domestic market, exporters facing world competition cannot raise the price as their profits are squeezed, leading them to adjust production downward. This triggers a decline in the export growth rate. These developments occurred in 1981–1985 and 2006–2010.

---

[25] Base changed from 2002 = 100 to 2007 = 100 as reported by the Central Bank database.

Monetary Policies: The relationship of monetary policy to exports comes directly from the management of the exchange rate, which is the responsibility of the Central Bank. Allowing inflation to rise either through fiscal deficit financing or through loose monetary policy overall leads to the undue expansion of private sector credit and leads to an appreciation of the exchange rate. And, when the Central Bank sells foreign exchange to the market to support the exchange rate, it leads to an involuntary open market operation since dollars are exchanged for rupees, leading to a reduction in liquidity in the domestic money market and a rise in interest rates. When the exchange rate adjustment is delayed, its cost rises cumulatively and the adjustment has to be larger, leading to both adverse expectations about the economy on the part of market agents as well as making the policy adjustment more drastic and disruptive, setting off the further expectation of exchange rate actions and tight monetary policies to battle the inflation.

Monetary policy misjudgements can cause foreign borrowing and lead to higher interest rates when the economy is on an unstable path, discouraging FDI but encouraging short-term capital flows or the "carry trade." These have adverse repercussions on the rate of export growth arising from the appreciation, on hasty and unpredictable outflows that can raise short-term interest rates and increase uncertainty in the short-term capital market, and in the foreign exchange market raising the cost of hedging.

Finally, a loose monetary policy could lead to higher inflation and increased wage demands that run ahead of productivity growth. But, worse, inflation hides real prices and distorts decisions with respect to the purchase of inputs, carrying inventories and trade finance.

Sri Lanka's 2005–2011 period shows the manifectation of this relationships and the situation was partially saved by the government's decision to go to the IMF in July 2009, reluctantly, after decrying such an effort for a couple of years and thereby accumulating higher amounts of debt compared to an early adjustment of the exchange rate.

The situation was also greatly helped by the end of the war that had made enormous demand for resources, leading to a high level of tariffs (that had an indirect but real impact on exports), creating fiscal deficits and raising interest rates to command resources for the war effort.

The future challenge was how to manage the macroeconomic policy to limit export growth.

9.9 Conclusions: Appropriate Macroeconomic Policies to bring about Export Growth

Fiscal consolidation is imperative to create conditions for strong export growth and better resource allocation overall. External pre-commitment such as the SBA helped avoid some of the problems associated with deficits during the 2009–2012 period. But SBA arrangements must be designed particularly to lead to near-term action to cut expenditures and raise the return to public expenditure, allowing headroom for private investment. The 2003 budget balance legislation should be resurrected to implement the fiscal consolidation. But, equally important are measures to improve the incentive structure overall by reforms in the trade, regulatory and non-bank financial sector areas. It would require greater collaboration among the international financial institutions including the World Bank, Asian Development Bank and bilateral lenders. Finance without policy change would not help exports or overall productivity increases in general. It could make things worse. The ideological commitment not to privatise also led to an appreciable cost. Perhaps we could learn from China, Vietnam and India. Just changing leadership in the state-owned enterprises without changing incentives and ownership will not help.

A flexible exchange rate policy would be helpful to raise competitiveness and export growth. One cannot say what level of the nominal exchange rate will prevail. It would depend on a host of factors including future supply, demand for foreign exchange, rate of domestic versus foreign rates of interests, net capital inflows and net access to Sri Lanka's bond market. It would be necessary to make the exchange regime (note that it is not the rate but the regime) predictable and not try to fix the exchange rate again to around Rs. 125 US dollar by using reserves. Also, to say, as some officials have done, that the exchange rate needs to remain overvalued to keep the rupee value of foreign debt low is clearly wrong and would damage the economy. Keeping the exchange rate overvalued would tax exports, reduce competitiveness and be self-defeating because, after all, repayment of debt has to be made in foreign currency. It would amount to what Keynes described as "a widow's cruise," an unending journey to nowhere!

More open trade policies should be adopted by reducing overall import protection, reducing the bias against exports, and reducing the variance in protection and the barriers to the production of both exportables and importables. *Ad hoc* trade measures as done recently, by raising and lowering tariffs and para tariffs at will should be avoided. One must make the trade regime predictable and resist the pressures to give benefits to one group of exporters and those producing for the domestic market. There is much scope to reduce trade barriers because they are inordinately high when para tariffs make up total protection. Selective controls to deal with the trade deficit are equally self-defeating. Such policies distort relative prices and do little or nothing to reduce excess demand for importables created by expansive macroeconomic policies.

Barriers to FDI should be reduced by improving the investment climate by going beyond economic policies to issues of rule of law, protection of property rights and good governance. The government needs to get rid of the Termination of Employment of Workmen (special provision) Act No. 45 (1971) and the Revival of Underperforming Enterprises and Underutilised Assets Act (2011). It should help make the labour market more flexible and improve the regulatory environment to provide the proper atmosphere for private sector development. Since the year 2000 and even before, a new group of Asian development giants emerged. China, India, Vietnam and Thailand increased their GDP growth rates and their exposure to world trade, and have been providing outstanding support to private enterprises, investment and exports. They do not have ideological blinders to preclude winning approaches to development, such as stable macroeconomics, competitive markets and well-aligned incentives to promote exports.

The credibility of policymaking institutions should be restored by being consistent, not by putting out pie-in-the-sky forecasts but by increasing the confidence of the economic agents that the government is committed to reforms and would maintain effectiveness despite external shocks. This would involve going beyond macroeconomics and even economics to law, good governance and remaining business friendly. Of course, credibility cannot be earned by press statements but has to be earned by hard data and demonstrable results.

Export and imports are at the centre stage of globalisation. Therefore, factors that determine exports and imports have an important bearing on globalisation. Sri Lanka's past history, especially the 1970–1977 period, has shown that globalisation-unfriendly policies have not been able to increase growth and improve income distribution. The next chapter looks into the relationship between globalisation and income distribution. Paul Krugman's observation that globalisation leads to worsening of income distribution has not been the case in Sri Lanka.

Appendix A

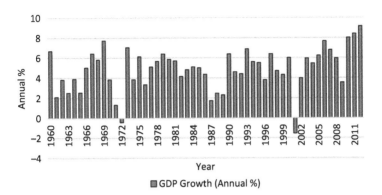

Figure 9.1A. GDP Growth (Annual Percentage) (1960–2012)

Source: The World Bank, *World Development Indicators*.

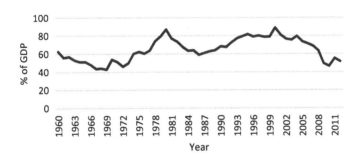

Figure 9.2A. Sri Lanka Trade as a Percentage of GDP (1960–2012)

Source: The World Bank, *World Development Indicators*.

Table 9.1A. Implied Overvaluation of the Rupee During 2005–2012 (Nominal Rates)

	2005	2006	2007	2008	2009	2010	2011	2012
Actual Average Annual LKR/USD Exchange Rate	100.50	103.91	110.62	108.33	114.94	113.06	110.57	126.75
Implied LKR/USD Exchange Rate	100.50	103.89	107.39	111.01	114.75	118.62	122.62	126.75
Implied Overvaluation (%)	0.00	0.03	3.01	−2.41	0.17	−4.68	−9.83	0.00

Source: Central Bank Reports (various issues): Assumes 2005 and 2012 exchange rates are broadly stable.

Table 9.2A. Macroeconomic Outcomes and Macro Prices (Annual Averages and Rates)

Macro Variables	Periods		
	1960–1977	1978–2003	2004–2011
Fiscal Deficit (% of GDP)	$\bar{X}$:5.96 δ:1.13	$\bar{X}$:9.67 δ:2.81	$\bar{X}$:7.52 δ:1.033
Current AC/ GDP	$\bar{X}$:2.53 δ:1.56	$\bar{X}$:5.58 δ:3.58	$\bar{X}$:4.42 δ:3.00
Exports/ GDP	$\bar{X}$:18.69 δ:4.67	$\bar{X}$:26.09 δ:3.99	$\bar{X}$:21.73 δ:4.26
GDP Growth (Annual %)	$\bar{X}$:3.97 δ:1.87	$\bar{X}$:4.76 δ:1.92	$\bar{X}$:6.49 δ:1.58
Inflation Rate	$\bar{X}$:6.56 δ:2.47	$\bar{X}$:10.77 δ:4.89	$\bar{X}$:10.22 δ:3.53
REER	$\bar{X}$:63.21 δ:12.06	$\bar{X}$:94.16 δ:32.64	$\bar{X}$:88.77 δ:13.69
Real Interest Rate	$\bar{X}$: 2.28 δ:1.08	$\bar{X}$:4.33 δ:4.70	$\bar{X}$:2.58 δ:2.84
Real Wage Rate	$\bar{X}$:81.06 δ:10.25	$\bar{X}$:95.5 δ:11.39	$\bar{X}$:80.96 δ:8.90

Note: $\bar{X}$ = Average, δ = Standard Deviation.
Source: Central Bank of Ceylon (various years), Athukorala and Jayasuriya (1993), Indraratna (2012), Athukorala and Rajapatirana (2000) and Institute of Policy Studies (2011).

All the figures in this appendix are based on data from the annual reports of the Central Bank of Sri Lanka from various years, World Development Indicators, the Institute of Policy Studies and cited works of a host of researchers on Sri Lanka over the years. The motivation to use the export/GDP ratio as a measure of export performance was dictated by the concern that had dealt with export growth per se. This would force us to use all other variables in a similar manner in terms of rates of change with exception of measuring inflation. One exception is of course is the inflation measure, given that it is always a dynamic phenomenon but it does influence levels of real wages, interest rates and exchange rates. The export-to-GDP ratio captures a part of the supply side of the export process. The analysis is comparatively static.

Chapter 10

Globalisation, Poverty and Income Distribution in Sri Lanka

10.1 Introduction

Sri Lanka had a good reputation in international development circles based on its poverty reduction strategy and improving income distribution. That reputation was built up in the 1960s and 1970s. For instance, in a famous debate between Amartya Sen and Surjit Bhalla, Paul Grewwe held that Sri Lanka was a good model that was able to achieve higher levels of welfare with better policies, leading to relatively low levels of poverty compared to other countries in the developing world. Income distribution was also relatively better than in many other developing countries.

10.2 Different Views on Globalisation and Income Distribution

Famous economist Paul Krugman in his Arndt-Corden Lecture at the University of Melbourne in 2018 remarked that he and other mainstream economists have underplayed the effect of globalisation on income distribution. Max Corden, who was present at the lecture, half humorously said that he did not think worsening income distribution was an inevitable result of globalisation. This chapter evaluates Krugman's claim of whether globalisation leads to a worsening of income distribution with respect to Sri Lanka. The worsening of income distribution was not inevitable as referred to by Paul Krugman.

However, when we consider a later period, 1978–1985, there was a worsening of income distribution, not arising out of globalisation but out of the Dutch disease problem which was associated with the inflow of capital for the Mahaweli project. The previous chapter and the paper by Cordon and Neary (1982) define what Dutch disease is. When we examine Sri Lanka's record with GF policies from 1978–1985, there was no improvement in income distribution as the theory would have predicted. On the other hand, when there were GU policies under the Sirimavo Bandaranaike-led coalition with Marxist parties, income distribution improved the Gini coefficient and its value fell to 0.41.

There were a number of reasons for this result: (i) The then Minister of Finance, Dr. N. M. Perera, who was also the leader of the Trotskyite party, imposed an income ceiling on business executives who earned more than Rs. 2,400 per month (a relatively low income in US dollar terms). (ii) A tax in the form of compulsory savings was imposed on middle-income families, or those who were earning a monthly income above Rs. 1200. (iii) There were very high import duties imposed by the Sirmavo Bandaranaike government under the tutelage of Finance Minister N.M. Perera, who introduced policies such as low ceilings on executive salaries, on the one hand, and created and expanded state ownership of leading enterprises under very stringent laws which allowed the government to take over private property at will, on the other hand. Such a strategy came to be challenged and the government lost the election in 1978, securing only eight seats in the parliament. Rising unemployment and restrictive policies on the mobility of persons within the country led to slow growth. The stringent and high trade barriers, including both tariffs and quantitative restrictions, made GU policies very unpopular. The Gini coefficient improved due to the draconian policies undertaken by the government to tax private enterprises or higher-income earners. As business-related income fell, incomes of those in the lower rungs of the income ladder were raised or prevented from falling with subsidies. The state takeover of private houses and tea and rubber plantations, to further the cause of making Sri Lanka a socialist heaven, failed. Following that time, the Trotskyites and the Communists would never win more than 10 seats in five decades. Sri Lanka may be a rare case where the income distribution improved with GU policies. But, such an approach could not be sustained because income kept falling and those restrictions led to reduced efficiency and increased costs.

Table 10.1. **GDP Growth Rates and Income Distribution Under Different Regimes (1956–2012)**

Time Period[c]	GDP Growth Rate[a] (%)	Income Share Lowest 20 Per cent	Gini Coefficient based on Monthly Income
1956–1964 (8)	(GU) 3.24 (1963)	3.9	0.49
1965–1969 (4)[d]	(GF) 4.84	—	—
1970–1977 (7)	(GU) 2.91 1973	5.0	0.41
(1977–1993) (16)	(GF) 4.90 (1978/1979– (1981/1982)	3.7	0.52
1978–2004 (26)[e]	(GF) — (1986–1987)	3.6	0.52
1994–2000 (6)	(GF/GU) 5.17		
2001–2004 (3)	(GF) 3.45 (1996–1997) (2003–2004)	4.1 (1996–1997) 3.8 (2003–2004)	0.48 (1996–1997) 0.50 (2003–2004)
2005–2014 (9)	(GU) 6.59 (2005–2012)[b]	4.5 (2012)	0.55 (2006) 0.55 (2009) 0.53 (2012)

Notes: [a]GF — Globalisation-Friendly, GU — Globalisation-Unfriendly.
[b]Years in parenthesis give the year of the income survey.
Since years for the period differ from the year of the survey, the data indicated are for the nearest year.
[c]Indicates the number of years in the period in which a government was in power.
[d]There was no consumer survey during 1965–1969.
[e]The 1978–2004 period includes the 1994–2000 period since the latter period under President Chandrika Kumaratunga followed the same policies towards globalisation as the earlier UNP period.
Source: GDP growth rates are from the Central Bank of Sri Lanka (CBSL) and the income shares of the lowest 20 per cent of income earners and the Gini Coefficient are from Consumer Finance Surveys of the CBSL based on monthly incomes.

Globalisation-friendly policies in large measure were similar to what Professors Bhagwati and Krueger defined as outward-oriented policies and GU policies were similar to inward-oriented policies. The concepts of GF and GU policies were broader, as they took into account trade, FDI and migration of labour. In this book, the factors taken into account are economics, ideology, politics and history.

The individual country volumes, written under the National Bureau of Economic Research, United States (NBER) project led by Professors Bhagwati and Krueger, use the concept of outward- and inward-oriented policies that have been widely adopted by the economist profession to analyse trade regimes.

The Gini coefficient improved to 0.41 due to ceilings on incomes (See Table 10.1). It was not a market-based process, but the result of large consumer subsidies to the lower 20 per cent of the population and high taxes on the upper 20 per cent of the population. What has to be realised is that this system could not have lasted long. And, it did not last. Large expenditure subsidies could not be sustained.

Finally, none of these aspects can be blamed on globalisation. In the case of Sri Lanka, results show that there has not been worsening of income distribution due to globalization. In the next chapter, we can see some of the challenges faced by Sri Lanka and the return to a globalisation path through better incentive policies and macroeconomic reforms.

10.3 Conclusions

Sri Lanka needs to return to fiscal discipline and create conditions to welcome FDI and other non-debt-creating inflows. More GF policies are the need of the day. They worked in the past in Sri Lanka and all over the developing world. In Asia, Bangladesh, China, India, Indonesia and Vietnam are good examples of countries that follow globalisation-friendly policies.

Chapter 11

The Future of Globalisation in Sri Lanka

As noted in earlier chapters, Sri Lanka has been open to globalisation with its GF policies through trade, FDI and migration of labour. The consensus in the world is that, following a short slowdown during COVID-19, globalisation resumed and many parts of the world followed globalisation-friendly policies.

However, this would not be true for Sri Lanka which went through a huge economic crisis and political crisis. There were country-wide demonstrations demanding the resignation of the president. In mid-May 2022, President Gotabaya Rajapaksa resigned. Meanwhile, Ranil Wickremesinghe was appointed as prime minister by the president on May 14, 2022. In line with the constitution, an election was conducted by the speaker among members of the parliament, which led to the appointment of Ranil Wickremesinghe as the new president of the country. He took on the enormous task of reviving the economy.

Reviving the economy would include raising GDP growth and repaying at least a part of the huge foreign debt, which is US$51 billion as of 2022. Meanwhile, the foreign exchange reserves have fallen. A formidable dollar shortage had developed. Sri Lanka lost access to the financial market following the pre-emptive declaration of bankruptcy by the CBSL. Even when supply ships had come to the port, there were no dollars to pay for the needed supplies. Countries such as China, India, Japan and the UK pledged their support to Sri Lanka in this economic crisis. Meanwhile, Japan offered to host a meeting of potential donors to pledge their support to the economic recovery of the country.

Long queues appeared for fuel, cooking gas, baby food and medicine in the country. Due to the introduction of new policies it was no longer necessary to stand in queues to get such essentials. Poor economic policies had created an equally difficult political situation and exacerbated the overall situation in the country.

Unlike in the past, support from the multilateral financial agencies, the IMF, World Bank and the Asian Development Bank was not able to provide bridging finance to supply crucial consumption items. These institutions had supported Sri Lanka in the past, as analysed in Chapter 6, with the IMF having provided 16 Stand-by Arrangements and extended fund facilities to help Sri Lanka over the last 50 years.

Because Sri Lanka was classified as a middle-income country, it did not have access to concessional finance from the IDA (the concessional window of the World Bank). In contrast to past situations of stress for the economy, at those times, the country did not have high debt obligations as it does now.

Behind the crisis were policies of past governments that mishandled the fiscal situation. Large amounts were spent on roads that were overbuilt with standards rivalling those in developed countries with 4- and 5-lane highways. The size of the traffic did not justify the roads. Large sums of money were spent on non-tradable goods that could not bring a return to pay the debt created by this type of infrastructure.

Economic management was poor, to say the least. The Central Bank did not bring about stability during this time. In addition to questionable expansionist monetary and fiscal policies, there was much misuse of public funds. SOEs were poorly managed. Large deficits were created by the Ceylon Electricity Board, the Sri Lankan Airlines and the Petroleum Corporation. The grandiose building of the tri force headquarters, remains a monument to rank waste of public expenditure, when there is no war. What all this means is that Sri Lanka was following GU policies and the results showed that they had negative impacts on access to foreign capital, with low GDP growth and fallen per capita income.

President Ranil Wickremesinghe is a committed GF leader who has demonstrated this commitment the previous six times he has held the post of prime minister. But, there were problems in the coalition government of 2015–2019 due to the ideological difference between President Sirisena and Prime Minister Wickremesinghe.

However, this time, it is likely to be more difficult due to a number of reasons. First, there is a political crisis with President Gotabaya who has admitted to genuine mistakes on his part. The Gotabaya government delayed going to the IMF, switched over to carbonic fertilisers and banned chemical fertilisers. Gotabaya lacked political acumen not being a politician but an army officer and the secretary of defence. He won the presidential elections by a large majority, particularly due to the Easter Sunday bombings by Muslim extremists.

Since Sri Lanka is a small country with an open economy, what happens in the rest of the developed world has a significant impact on its economy.

11.1 Sri Lanka's International Trade

For a small developing country in a strategic location, there are great opportunities for Sri Lanka to participate and benefit from international trade. Basically, whether these opportunities are exploited or not depends on the type of trade and economic policies pursued by Sri Lanka in response to the globalising world. In addition to domestic policy, the other variable is the opportunity set available to the country for exports and efficient import substitution available from the rest of the world. If the export basket of the country is favourable, referring to countries that import Sri Lankan products and services, then Sri Lanka can penetrate and expand those markets. The domestic policy design set can make a large difference to the trade outcome for exports and efficient import substitution.

Sri Lanka's comparative advantage lies in producing and exporting labour-intensive goods. It imports capital and technology-intensive products. The comparative advantage of a country can change over time and countries can produce and export goods which can have different factor intensities over time. For example, many countries in East Asia have changed the product intensity from labour to capital, both physical and human capital.

During the period from independence in 1948 to the 1970s, Sri Lanka produced labour-intensive goods, such as textiles, garments and basic goods (e.g. shoes, minor manufactured products and value-added products). The country has not transformed to more capital-intensive and technically advanced exports and import substitutes. A close look at Sri Lanka's trade regime reveals that there have been three broad transitions in the trade regime. Following independence, Sri Lanka produced the same goods that were produced since British investments in primary products such as tea, rubber and coconuts (mostly for the domestic market).

A transition in the trade regime took place with the left-of-centre politicians in the post-independence period from 1956–1976. They were very interested in reducing dependence on primary exports and establishing import-substituting industries such as steel, industrial products such as tires, and rubber products such as gloves and rubber for car vipers (and for other car parts such as bushes). Sri Lanka was unable to follow the reforms of the East Asian Economies which produced high and steady GDP growth. At that time, Sri Lanka could not join the group of countries that had managed to become successful trading nations. The ideological differences of the leadership between the 1978–2005 period of the two Presidents, J.R. Jayawardena and Mahinda Rajapakse, led to diametrically different approaches to the economic policy making. Tariffs were high and quantitative restrictions continued.

A number of factors can be identified as to why Sri Lanka failed to join the fast-growing East Asian economies. These included the ideological commitment to left-of-centre economic policies that had been practiced by India and the attempt to rely on import substitution as a way to initiate sustained growth. The 1970–1978 period was the high-water mark for left-of-centre economic policies that came to be known as inward-oriented policies with high protection, bias against exports, the use of quantitative restrictions over tariffs and implied wide variance in protection rates.

The final and dominant factor was the lack of fiscal and monetary discipline. These led to high inflation rates and investment in non-tradable goods that were not creating competitive production sources. Instead, large investments in infrastructure with low rates dominated by high levels of rent-seeking made exports and import substitutes non-competitive.

The future path of trade policies will be better, as the country has been chastened, having gone through the trauma of the inability to pay off its high debt acquired during the left-of-centre governments. The 2022–2024 IMF programme provides key policy targets to discipline fiscal and monetary policymaking and would also lead to the following of guidelines to improve structural policies.

Because of the War between Russia and Ukraine, demand for Sri Lankan exports and other goods, by Western European countries is expected to decline. The country needs to create a new policy environment, using globalisation-friendly policies, meeting the deadlines set under the IMF Extended Fund facility programme and setting domestic reforms including the privatisation of huge loss-making state-owned enterprises. Further, introducing a new competition policy law and implementing it well through a productivity commission established by the government (based on the Australian model) would help raise productivity growth and reduce the high costs and inefficiencies of state-owned enterprises. A strong reform programme will provide a base for high exports and competitive import substitution. Disciplined macroeconomic policies would be a *sine qua non* to have a better future and increase the benefits of globalisation policies for Sri Lanka.

11.2 Sri Lanka's FDI

Sri Lanka's future was looking good at the end of its 26-year civil fight in 2009. Its location at the centre of some of the world's most used shipping paths and proximity to India have given the nation an advantage when it comes to drawing FDI.

At the end of the War, it was expected that the economy would be growing, but this did not happen due to the constitutional crisis, under President Sirisena, followed by the Easter Sunday bombing and the COVID-19 pandemic. COVID-19 caused a major blow to tourism and caused numerous Sri Lankans working overseas to come back, as they lost their jobs. This followed a constitutional crisis in 2018 when the president at the time removed the prime minister, appointed a former prime minister and virtually suspended the constitution for 52 days. These developments discouraged FDI flows to Sri Lanka. In addition, the macroeconomic management of the country was poor with rising inflation and unsustainable current account deficit in the balance of payments.

As a result of these developments, Sri Lanka's foreign reserves fell to an all-time low. Consequently, Sri Lanka had to borrow large sums of dollars, which led to a huge debt repayment problem. The Central Bank declared a pre-emptive debt default. In such an environment, FDI fell to an all-time low. The economic problems that Sri Lanka was experiencing for over a decade led to large balance-of-payment deficits where the imports were 40 per cent higher than exports since 2014.

A large foreign trade gap emerged, with falling foreign exchange reserves and traditional sources of financing drying up. With the official declaration of an organised default, the associated problems arose with shortages of milk, food, fuel and medicines. Long queues were needed to meet large shortages.

With the election of Mr. Ranil Wickremesinghe as president by the parliament, there was an important change in the country. His experience as prime minister on six occasions and leader of the opposition opened a new chapter in the approach to the emerging economic situation. Sri Lanka went to the IMF for support, which led to a change in the economic situation with queues for essentials being shortened, leading to more countries willing to help Sri Lanka with access to foreign exchange resources. Sri Lanka further agreed to some measure of debt restructuring with the IMF and initiated the EFF programme to launch a reform to stabilise the economy and work towards economic recovery and GDP growth.

The future for FDI looks better than before because of the credible commitment to stability and recovery, and the willingness of some debtors to restructure debt in line with improved economic fundamentals.

While the domestic economic situation has definitely improved, there is still the challenge to sustain reforms. Some good signs are emerging, such as the increased rate of tourism, with the highest number recorded in March 2023, and some interest expressed by countries to invest in Sri Lanka in the coming years. Two major uncertainties remain: One, the reform programmes could be victim to irresponsible politics. Two, there is likely to be a decline in the growth rates of Sri Lanka's major export markets in Europe mainly due to the Russia's war with Ukraine and uncertain politics in the Unites States in the coming presidential election. A 50 per cent chance of success would be a fair assessment of the situation for the future of FDI and other non-debt-creating inflows.

11.3 Sri Lanka's Labour Migration

Since 1960, Sri Lanka has seen a momentous rise in labour migration as reflected in its net migration figures. The socialist policies in the 1950s and making Sinhala the official language led to outward movements of people from different ethnicities (Tamils and Burghers), especially people whose native language was not Sinhala. The restrictions on travel and essential food and the nationalisation of private organisations led to many professionals leaving Sri Lanka for Canada, Australia, the USA, Zambia and Papua New Guinea in search of employment and higher education. Further, the JVP insurrection in 1983 and the LTTE war led to migration of refugees, asylum seekers and skilled professionals from the northern and southern parts of the country. The outflow of migrants continued even after the war.

The determinants that have favoured outward migration have been pull factors such as the ease of migration policies, the demand for employment from specific sectors and occupations, and flexible education policies linked to migration. The 1970s showed a high demand for employment in oil-producing countries (Kuwait, Qatar, Saudi Arabia and Jordon) for unskilled workers, especially female domestic workers who have been an important source of foreign exchange earnings for Sri Lanka (8 per cent of GDP after merchandise exports in 2019). The GF policies, with the relaxation of foreign exchange controls and regulations, imposed on travel promoted migration from Sri Lanka.

From 2017 onwards, there has been continued political uncertainty (52-day constitution crisis), in particular following the Easter Sunday terrorist attacks that triggered greater outward migration. The COVID-19 pandemic initially led to an increase in the trend of inward migration, with less outward migration due to the closure of international airports. This position gradually changed with the opening of airports and the relaxation of strict quarantined procedures. The political uncertainty and bad policy decisions (import restrictions, tax reductions and banning of fertilisers) made in 2019 led to an economic crisis and shortages of gas and fuel, leading to long queues. The macroeconomic imbalances also led to an outward flow of skilled and unskilled workers.

Thus, we see that the globalisation-unfriendly policy decisions of making Sinhala the official language and placing restrictions on travel had a bearing on the patterns of migration. Chauvinistic Sinhala-oriented policies have led to events such as the JVP insurrection in 1971 and 1989, the civil war and the resultant outflow of migrants. GF policies, on the other hand, removed travel restrictions and allowed the inflow of skill and knowledge through the establishment of the export-processing zones, which created employment opportunities in Sri Lanka. However, there is still a constant increase in the number of unskilled workers moving to Middle Eastern countries for higher wages.

The future of migration will depend mainly on the favourable policy environment in Sri Lanka. Further, good educational policies through vocational training institutes and universities that can develop industry-focused curricula to allow on-the-job training in Sri Lanka will create the necessary human capital. Although one of the merits of outward skilled migration is the creation of an inflow of foreign exchange to the country, establishing GF policies will create employment opportunities leading to higher economic growth.

11.4 Conclusion

Whether Sri Lanka can take advantage of the opportunities offered by globalisation depends on the policy environment following the reforms that the new government intends to enact. The world economy will move towards greater openness from all the evidence that we can marshal. The issue is whether Sri Lanka will follow GF policies to help take advantage of the openness, join production networks, increase exports and FDI, and have what is called outward-oriented economic policies. The 1977–1983 period shows that those policies worked. However, there is emerging evidence that the world economy could experience a recession, in which case Sri Lanka would find itself in a difficult position of having to revive its economy.

The response of Sri Lanka to global economic development combined with its policy responses will determine the productivity, income distribution and GDP growth of the country. The response of the government in the period from 1970–1977 was a laboratory experiment, which revealed that high protection and domestic price controls (globalisation-unfriendly outlook) resulted in lower GDP growth, lower FDI and worsened income distribution. Armed with these experiences, new growth is expected in the future.

Chapter 12

Conclusions

The main aim of this book has been to examine the challenges of globalisation for a small economy like Sri Lanka. This book covers 60 years, a reasonable period to examine the main aspects of globalisation. Within these 60 years, the economy went through different phases of change and continuity that would be of value to other countries of similar size, endowments, policy orientation in terms of history and ideology, and adaptation to changing global economic conditions. Small countries have to adapt, while large countries influence the global economy.

The individual chapters take up different aspects of globalisation's impact on Sri Lanka. Given its size, Sri Lanka cannot influence global changes and events, but can only respond to them, seeking the best outcomes. However, it is worth a try to examine the main forces at work that produced the different outcomes of the exposure to the world. Earlier books on globalisation by eminent economists have examined globalisation from the perspective of larger countries and not at the ground level as this book is doing. This is a special feature of this book, compared to other books on globalisation over the last 20 years, which have become dated to some extent and missed important global changes such as the World Financial Crisis, lack of progress in international trading arrangements and a reduction in global capital flows to developing countries.

First, one of the strongest conclusions of this book is that globalisation cannot be analysed by economics alone, but economics has a lot to do with globalisation. This book has analysed combination of historical narrative, political dimension and ideological aspects of Sri Lanka's exposure to the world. While the analysis is mostly confined to the 1960–2020 period, it has a wider time span when the future of globalisation is discussed. It also deals with the situation before 1948 when Sri Lanka was under British colonial rule. Three significant drivers of globalisation, trade, foreign direct investment and labour migration were present in the British period from 1794–1948. This venture into history provides a good anchor for the later period analysed.

Second, the movements towards and away from globalisation were highly dependent on a few key factors. They were the ideological make-up of the government in power, and the performance of the economy in the earlier part of the election cycle. A failure of the previous government gave the new government the opportunity to undertake reforms that raised productivity growth. These reforms would include encouraging FDI, bringing about freer trade and open migration. The new government provided investment capital that led to greater investment, especially in the rural areas. Policies that were adopted to lead to freer trade, welcoming conditions for FDI and a liberal attitude towards outward migration were defined as "globalisation-friendly" (GF) policies. Policies that were in the opposite direction were named globalisation-unfriendly (GU) policies. We test the hypothesis that GF policies lead to lower levels of poverty and better income distribution, measured by the Gini coefficient. In other words, under GF policies, we expect a lower Gini coefficient and under GU policies a higher Gini coefficient.

Third, whether globalisation in Sri Lanka displayed any phenomena experienced by developed countries is an important question. Such alleged "de-globalisation," "slowbalisation" and "hyper globalisation" occurred in Sri Lanka. The general question of whether "globalisation has gone too far or not gone far enough" has also been raised. There is, however, no case of "de-globalisation" in the sense that the three indicators of globalisation used in this book — trade, FDI and emigration — have continued, and no reversals have taken place in these spheres. Similarly, there has not been any "hyper globalisation." If we look at the statistics at present, the trade-to-GDP ratio, the FDI-to-GDP ratio and migration rates have remained stable. There is a general agreement among mainstream economists that trade reforms, FDI and labour migration could play an important role in raising GDP growth, reducing poverty levels and improving income distribution. The slowing down of the economy was not due to globalisation but due to the lethargy of the public officials who delayed GF reforms. However, due to draconian policies by the government in power, there was a lower Gini coefficient even though there were globalisation-unfriendly policies in effect.

Fourth, there was greater political uncertainty in the SLFP–LSSP and Communist Party-inclusive coalition in 1970–1977. The differences in the ideologies of the two parties and among the party leaders caused uncertainty about the appropriate policy regime that was needed, which delayed GF reforms. During the second year of the coalition, from 2015–2019, the SLFP leadership proceeded to oppose proposals for trade and other reforms. Potential investors who had thoroughly investigated both economic and political conditions of the country would have noted the strong dissention between the coalition partners. Evidence of this situation was seen in President Maithripala Sirisena's dismissal of the UNP Prime Minister Ranil Wickremesinghe and appointment of a former defeated President Mahinda Rajapaksa who led the SLFP. Finally, these unconstitutional acts were reversed by the Supreme Court, but the dissension within the ruling government had become well recognised by potential investors, both foreign and domestic. The Easter Sunday bombing of high-end tourist hotels and churches confirmed beyond doubt the lack of cohesion within the government in the 2015–2019 period. The original intention to follow GF policies were thus faulted and then abandoned. In this case, the gains from globalisation could not be realised. The 2022 Supreme Court decision found fault with President Sirisena and his officials who were in charge of security for not acting to stop the Easter Sunday bombing by Muslim extremists. Large fines were imposed on the president and his team for dereliction of duty that led to a catastrophic reduction in revenues related to tourism and a consequent loss of creditworthiness of the country.

Fifth, globalisation as defined here — the process of integration with the world — with the benefits of specialisation, increased competition and raised productivity was not fully realised in the case of Sri Lanka, over the period covered by this book. Globalisation-unfriendly policies resulted in increased poverty levels and worsened income distribution. It is well established that during GU policies, poverty levels increased. During globalisation unfriendly policies, market adjustments were prevented from taking place because everything was controlled. There was a forced improvement in income distribution due to strong measures to produce that outcome which could not be sustained. This is established through a statistical analysis. The emergence of the COVID-19 pandemic led to increased incidence of poverty. For instance, the poverty rate increased from 4 per cent of the population to 12 per cent of the population as the government that came into power in November 2019 adapoted in GU policies. The cost of treating COVID-19 patients rose with the spread of the disease, which was less severe than among Sri Lanka's neighbouring countries. However, the initial success of controlling infections could not be maintained. While government policies played their role, Sri Lanka's population was less committed to prevention measures such as wearing masks, social distancing and minimising travel outside the home.

Sixth, Sri Lanka's economic policies are well known to change with the election cycle. Policy consistency was lacking over the entire period. Being a democracy, there were regular elections based on universal suffrage. However, due to the war with separatists LTTE, the northern and eastern parts of the country were not represented in parliament throughout the war years. Thus, that part of the country experienced difficulties with respect to integration with the rest of the world as well as to the rest of the country for nearly half of the 60-year period. Public administration was also truncated. This prevented a sizeable part of the population from living in the areas of conflict. The benefits of globalisation of greater specialisation and access to health, education and social services were not available to these parts. After the war, there was increased connectivity, but due to poor public polices with respect to extension services, subsidised fertilisers and seeds were not easily available in those areas. The reach of globalisation was limited by conflict. These parts have now become more integrated with the rest of the country than in the past, particularly due to the civil war, 1983 to 2009. That process continues but at a slower pace. Agriculture is now more protected than industries and services with subsided fertilisers, irrigation and extension services. There was little participation of agriculture in international trade due to its reduced presence in exports. Yet, an often-cited figure is that agriculture has low productivity compared to industries and services. Like in other low-income countries, more poor people live in rural areas than in urban areas. Globalisation has not touched agriculture in a significant way in Sri Lanka. In a sense, the protection of agriculture is a GU policy.

Seventh, this book attempts to answer some of the queries raised by leading economists like Paul Krugman who stated that income distribution had worsened due to countries' exposure to globalisation and GF policies. The evidence for Sri Lanka is less clear. For instance, during the height of the GU period, income distribution improved compared to the

GF period. The precise GU period was 1970–1977 during the coalition government of Mrs. Bandaranaike. With the communists and the Trotskyites, income distribution improved and the Gini coefficient was at 0.41 compared to the GF period of 1977–1985 when the Gini coefficient was 0.52. The Trotskyites Finance Minister Dr. N.M. Perera introduced policies such as low ceilings on executive salaries, on the one hand, and created and expanded state ownership of leading enterprises under very stringent laws which allowed the government to take over private property at will, on the other. Such a strategy came to be challenged and the government lost the election in 1978 after winning only eight seats in the parliament.

Policies relating to the slow growth rate, rising unemployment and mobility restriction of people within the country also was created. The stringent and high trade barriers, both tariffs and quantitative restrictions, made GU policies very unpopular. When the Gini coefficient improved, it was due to the draconian policies undertaken by the government to tax private enterprises. As business-related income fell, incomes of those on the lower rungs of the ladder were relatively increased or prevented from falling with subsidies. The state takeover of private houses and tea and rubber plantations to further the cause socialism failed. Following that, the Trotskyites and the communists did not win more than 10 seats in parliament for more than five decades. Sri Lanka maybe a unique case in which the observation by Paul Krugman would not hold. These draconian practices could not be sustained.

Eighth, as noted in Chapter 2, the classification of GF and GU policies influenced the outcomes of globalisation. Globalisation-friendly policies in large measure were similar to what Professors Bhagwati and Krueger defined as outward-oriented policies and GU policies were similar to inward-oriented policies. The concepts of GF and GU policies were somewhat broader, as they took into account trade, FDI and migration of labour. Where country studies were concerned, the concepts took into account economics, ideology, politics and history. Compared to individual country volumes written under the National Bureau of Economic Research, United States (NBER) project led by Professors Bhagwati and Krueger, this book takes into account the wider concepts such history, ideologies and politics.

Ninth, globalisation has been present in the world since the 1880s. What was missing then was the advanced technology relating to communications, transport and organisation of global production networks. There were greater economies of scale to be had in the modern manifestation of globalisation. Greater specialisation, "just-in-time" organisation and problem-solving at the assembly line with decentralised decision-making made enterprises more efficient. Access to parts and other inputs was better organised in the global production networks. Of course, the COVID-19 pandemic disrupted this smooth flow inputs and outputs.

Tenth, this book notes that scepticism about globalisation and its alleged ill effects is exaggerated as we see country after country returning to the global production networks that have been built in the last six decades. That process is not leading to de-globalisation. "Slowbalisation" was an epithet found in the editor's remarks in *The Economist* magazine at the height of the COVID-19 pandemic. The reduced GDP growth rate, mountains of debt, the pre-emptive declaration of the inability to repay borrowings and the very low reserves hardly sufficient for a week of imports are not related to globalisation per say. The IMF diagnosed that Sri Lanka's debt was not sustainable. It suggested that it was not a case of low liquidity but a solvency problem. Also, one needs to ask why, despite support by the IMF on 16 occasions, Sri Lanka's solvency problem persisted. Both the lender and borrower have to account for the lack of success. Some politicians pointed the finger at the IMF, but the fact is that out of the 16 accommodations, only six could be called successful cases, when IMF conditions were satisfied.

Eleventh, none of these above-mentioned issues can be blamed on globalisation. On the contrary, the way out is to reform the incentive system, led by trade reforms. Sri Lanka needs to return to fiscal discipline and create conditions to welcome FDI and other non-debt-creating inflows. More GF policies are the order of the day, which worked in the past in Sri Lanka and all over the developing world. In Asia, Bangladesh, China, India, Indonesia and Vietnam are good examples of countries that are following globalisation-friendly policies.

Finally, some have speculated on what would be the future of globalisation. The biggest clue is the rebuilding of the global production networks, leading to the success of a host of Asian countries. Further, the overcoming of the COVID-19 pandemic, the fourth industrial revolution and the 5G technologies that promise greater efficiency tilt the scale in favour of success in the future against the views of the pessimists.

Bibliography

Abeyratne, S. (1997). Trade strategy and industrialisation, In W. D. Lakshman (ed.). *Dilemmas in Development*, Colombo: Sri Lanka Economists Association.

Acemoglu, D. and Robinson, J. A. (2012). *Why Nations Fail: The Origins of Power. Prosperity and Poverty*. New York: Random House.

Adelman, I. and Sunding, D. (1989). Joan Robinson as a development economist. In G. R. Feiwel (ed.), *Joan Robinson and Modern Economic Theory*. (pp. 702–722). New York: New York University Press.

Adhikar, R. (1993). Policy reforms and export performance in Sri Lanka: Some observations. In R. Adhikari, C. Kirkpatrick, and J. Weiss (eds.), *Industrial and Trade Policy Reforms and Experience in Developing Countries* (pp. 186–197). Manchester: Manchester University Press.

Aldwinwin R. E. (1969 May/June). The case against infant industry tariff protection. *Journal of Political Economy*, 77, 295–305.

Aluwalia, M. S. (2002). Economic reforms of India since 1991: Has gradualism worked? *Journal of Economic Perspectives*, 16(3), 67–88.

Aluwalia, M. S. (2016). The 1991 reform: How home grown were they. *Economics and Political Weekly*, 51(29), 38–46.

Aluwalia, M. S. (2018). *India's Economic Reforms: Achievements and Next Steps, Asian Economic Policy Review*. Japan Center for Economic Research.

Amartya, S. (1987). *Hunger and Entitlements*. Helsinki: World Institute For Development Economic Research.

Athukorala, P. (1981). Import substitution, structural transformation and import dependence: A case study of Sri Lanka. *Developing Economies*, 19(2), 119–142.

Athukorala, P. (1993). Manufactured exports from developing countries and their terms of trade: A reexamination of Sarkar-Singer results. *World Development*, 21(10), 1607–1613.

Athukorala, P. (1995). Foreign direct investment and manufacturing for export in a new exporting country: The case of Sri Lanka. *World Economy*, 18(4), 543–564.

Athukorala, P. (2012a). China's rise in the world economy: Opportunities and challenges for developing countries. *Gamani Corea Foundation Lecture, Sri Lanka*. May 25 2012.

Athukorala, P. (2012b). Sri Lanka's trade policy: Reverting to dirigisme? *The World Economy*, 35(12), 1662–1686.

Athukorala, P. and Jayasuriya, S. (1994). Macroeconomic Policies, crises, and growth in Sri Lanka 1969–1990. *Asia Economic Papers*, 12(2), 1–28.

Athukorala, P. and Jayatilleke, S. B. (1989). Growth of manufactured exports, primary commodity dependence and net export earnings: Sri Lanka. *World Development*, 17(6), 897–903.

Athukorala, P. and Jayatilleke, S. B. (1996). *Macroeconomic Policies, Crises and Growth in Sri Lanka, 1969–90*. Washington, D.C.: World Bank.

Athukorala, P. and Rajapatirana, S. (2000). *Liberalisation and Industrial Transformation: Sri Lanka in International Perspective*. New Delhi and London: Oxford University Press.

Athukorala, P. and Rajapatirana, S. (2003). Capital inflows and the real exchange rate: A comparative study of Asia and Latin America. *The World Economy*, 26(4), 613–637.

Athukorala, P., Jayatilleke, S. B., and Kelegama, S. (2011). *Trade, Liberalisation & Poverty in South Asia: Reforms, Stylised Facts & Preview*. London: Routledge Studies in the Growth Economies of Asia.

Balassa, B. (1986). Towards renewed economic growth in Latin America. *The International Executive*, 28(3), 29–31.

Balassa, B. (1989). Outward orientation. In H. Chenery and T. N. Srinivasan (eds.), *Handbook of Development Economics* (Chapter 31, pp. 1646–1689). North Holland, Amsterdam.

Baldwin, R. E. (1969). The case against infant industry tariff protection. *Journal of Political Economy*, 77(3), 295–305.

Barro, R. J. (1972). Inflationary finance and the welfare cost of inflation. *Journal of Political Economy*, 80(5), 978–1001.

Bates, R. H. and Krueger, A. O. (1993). *Political and Economic Interactions in Economic Policy Reform: Evidence from Eight Countries*. Cambridge, MA: Blackwell Publishers.

Beason, R. and Weinstein, D. (1996). Growth, economies of scale, and targeting in Japan (1955–1990). *The Review of Economics and Statistics*, 78(2), 286–295.

Bertrand, T. (1985). *The Efficiency Costs of Taxation Issues and Tax Proposals in Sri Lanka*, Draft (mimeo).
Bhagwati, J. (2004). *In Defense of Globalisation*. New York, NY: Oxford University Press.
Bhagwati, J. and Panagariya, A. (2013). *Why Growth Matters: How Economic Growth in India Reduced Poverty and the Lessons for Other Developing Countries*. New York: Public Affairs.
Bhagwati, J. and Srinivasan, T. N. (1978). Trade policy and development. In R. Dornbusch and J. A. Frankel (eds.), *International Economic Policy* (pp. 1–38). Baltimore: John Hopkins University Press.
Bhagwati, J. and Ramaswami, V. K. (1963). Domestic distortions, tariffs, and the theory of optimum subsidy. *Journal of Political Economy*, 71(1), 44–50.
Bhagwati, J. N. (1978). *Foreign Trade Regimes and Economic Development: Anatomy and Consequences of Exchange Control Regimes*. Cambridge, MA: Ballinger Press.
Bhagwati, J. N. (1985). *Investing Abroad, Esmee Fairbairn Lecture 1985*. Lancaster: University of Lancaster.
Bhagwati, J. N. (1987). Outward orientation: Trade issues. In M. S. Khan, M. Goldstein, and V. Corbo, (eds.), *Growth-oriented Adjustment Programs* (pp. 257–290), Washington, D.C.: International Monertary Fund.
Bhalla, S. and Glewwe, P. (1986). Growth and equity in developing countries: A reinterpretation of the Sri Lankan experience. *World Bank Economic Review*, 1(1) 35–64.
Bird, G. (1996). The international monetary fund and developing countries: A review of evidence and policy options. *International Organisation Journal*, 50(3), 477–511.
Blinder, A. S. (1997). *Measuring Short-run Inflation for Central Bankers — Commentary. Review*. Federal Reserve Bank of St. Louis. pp. 157–160.
Bruton, H. T. (1970). The import-substitution strategy of economic development: A survey. *Pakistan Development Review*, 10(2), 123–146.
Buchanan, J. and Tullock, G. (1962). *The Calculus of Consent: Logical Foundations of Constitutional Democracy*. Ann Arbor: University of Michigan Press.
Buchanan, J. M. and Stubblebine, W. C. (1962). Externality. *Economica*, 29, 371–384.
Cabraal, A. N. (2008). Managing inflation, interest rates, and exchange rates: The balancing act. The Island, July 28.
Caves, R. E. (1996). *Multinational Enterprise and Economic Analysis* (2nd edn.). Cambridge: Cambridge University Press.
Central Bank of Sri Lanka (1980–2011). *Annual Reports*. Colombo.
Central Bank of Sri Lanka (1998). *Economic Progress of independent Sri Lanka 1948–1998*. Colombo.

Chai, S. (1998). Endogenous ideology formation and economic policy in former colonies. *Economic Development and Cultural Change*, 46(2), 263–290.

Chenery, H., Robinson, S., and Syrquin, M. (1986). *Industrialisation and Growth: A Comparative Study*. Oxford: Oxford University Press.

Cline, W. R. (1982). Can the East Asian model of development be generalised? *World Development*, 10(2), 81–90.

Coase, R. H. (1960). The problem of social cost. *Journal of Law and Economics*, 3, 1–44.

Corden, W. (1994). *Economic Policy, Exchange Rates and the International System*. Oxford: Oxford University Press.

Corden, W. M. (1966). The structure of a tariff system and the effective protection rate. *Journal of Political Economy*, 74(3), 221–237.

Corden, W. M. (1977). *Inflation, Exchange Rates, and the World Economy: Lectures on International Monetary Economics*. Oxford: Clarendon Press.

Corden, W. M. (1984). Booming sector and Dutch disease economics: Survey and consolidation. *Oxford Economic Papers*, 36(3), 359–380.

Corden, W. M. (1974). *Trade Policy and Economic Welfare*. Oxford: Clarendon Press.

Corden, W. M. (1997). *Trade Policy and Economic Welfare* (2nd edn.). Oxford: Clarendon Press.

Corden, W. M. and Neary, P. (1982). Booming sector and de-industrialisation in a small open economy. *Economic Journal*, 92(368), 825–848.

Corea, G. (1951). *The Instability in an Export Economy*. D.Phil. Thesis, Oxford University.

Corea, G. (1957). *Ceylon: The Instability in an Export Economy*. Colombo: Marga Institute.

Corea, G. (2008). *My Memoirs*. Ratmalana, Sri Lanka: Vishva Lekha Press.

Cuthbertson, A. G. and Khan, M. (1981). *Effective Protection to Manufacturing Industries in Sri Lanka*. Colombo, Sri Lanka: Ministry of Finance and Planning.

Darvas, Z. (2012). *Real Effective Exchange Rates for 178 Countries: A New Database. Working Papers 716*. Brussels: Bruegal.

Das Gupta, B. B. (1949). *A Short Economic Survey of Ceylon*. Colombo, Sri Lanka: Associate Newspapers of Ceylon.

Deepak, L. (1983). *Poverty of Development Economics*. Cambridge, MA: MIT Press.

Deepak, L. (1985). The Real Exchange Rate, Capital Inflows and Inflation: Sri Lanka 1970–1982. *Review of World Economics*, 121(4), 682–702.

Deepak, L. (2003). Free trade and Laissez faire: Has the wheel come full circle? *The World Economy*, 26(4), 471–482.

Deepak, L. and Rajapatirana, S. (1989). *Impediments to Trade Liberalisation in Sri Lanka*. Series: *Thames Essay* (51). Aldershot, Hampshire, U.K.; Brookfield, Vt., USA; London: Gower. Trade Policy Research Centre.

De Silva, H. (n.d.). Time for legistlating inflation targeting. *Financial Time, Sunday Times Newspaper, Sri Lanka, 16th March 2008*.

De Silva, K. (2005). *A History of Sri Lanka*. Sri Lanka: Penguin Books India.

De Silva, K. M. (1981). *A History of Sri Lanka*. Delhi: Oxford University Press.

Dias Bandaranaike, A. D. (2008). Rising government debt. *Financial Times*, July 98.

Diaz-Alejandro, C. (1965). On the import intensity of import substitution. *International Review for Social Sciences*, 8(3), 495–511.

Diaz, A. and Carlos, F. (1965). On the import intensity of import substitution. *Kyklos*, 18(2), 214–226.

Dollar, D. (1992). Outward-oriented developing economies really do grow more rapidly: Evidence from 95 LDCs. 1975–85. *Economic Development and Cultural Change*, 40(4), 523–544.

Dollar, D. and Edward, N. W. (1993). *Competitiveness, Convergence and International Specialisation*. Cambridge, MA: MIT Press.

Donges, J. (1976). A comparative study of industrialisation policies in fifteen semi-industrial countries. *Review of World Economics (Weltwirtschaftliches Archiv)*, 112(4), 626–659.

Dornbusch, R. (1980). *Open Economy Macroeconomics*. New York: Basic Books.

Dornbusch, R. (1992). The case for trade liberalisation in developing countries. *Journal of Economic Perspectives*, 6(1), 69–85.

Dutt, P. and Mitra, D. (2005). Political ideology and endogenous trade policy: An empirical investigation. *Review of Economic Statistics*, 87(1), 59–72.

Edwards, S. (1989). Exchange rate misalignment in developing countries. *The World Bank Research Observer*, 4(1), 3–21.

Edwards, S. (1992). Trade orientation, distortions and growth in developing countries. *Journal of Development Economics*, 39(1), 31–57.

Feenstra, R. C. (1998). Integration of trade and disintegration of production in a global economy. *Journal of Economic Perspectives*, 12(4), 31–50.

Fernandez, C. (1996). Development planning in Sri Lanka. In W. D. Lakshman (ed.). *Dilemmas of Development: Fifty Years of Economic Change in Sri Lanka*. Colombo, Sri Lanka: Sri Lanka Economists Association.

Fernandez, C. E. (1996). *Do Ideologies Have an Influence on Economic Policies in Latin America? The Cases of Argentina*. Brazil and Chile: Mimeo. AEI.

Fernando, L. (1997). Development planning in Sri Lanka. In W. D. Lakshman (ed.). *Dilemmas of Development: Fifty Years of Economic Change in Sri Lanka*. Colombo: Sri Lanka Economists Association.

Findlay, R. (1984). Trade and development, theory and Asian experience. *Asian Development Review*, 2(1), 23–42.

Fischer, S. (1981). Towards understanding the costs of inflation: II. *Carnegie-Rochester Conference Series on Public Policy*, 15(1), 5–41.

Fischer, S. (1991). Growth, macroeconomics and development. *NBER Macroeconomic Annual*, 6, 329–364.

Frankel, J. (2000). Globalisation of the economy. *NBER Working Papers 7858, National Bureau of Economic Research, Inc.*

Friedman, M. (1968). The role of monetary policy. *American Economic Review*, 58(1).

Friedman, M. (1994). *Money Mischief: Episodes in Monetary History.* New York: Harcourt Brace Jovanovich.

Fry, M. (1998). Assessing Central Bank Independence in developing countries: Do actions speak louder than words? *Oxford Economic Papers*, 50(3), 512–529.

Galbraith, K., Hicks, J. R., Hicks, U., Kaldor, N., Myrdal, G., Robinson, J., and Lang, O. (1959). *Papers by Visiting Economist: The Tasks of Economic Planning in Ceylon.* Sri Lanka.

George, A. L. (1979). The causal nexus between and decision making behavior: The "operational code" belief system. In L. S. Falkowski (e.d.), *Psychological Models in International Politics.* Boulder, Colorado: Westview Press.

Goldstein, J. (1993). *Ideas, Interest and American Trade Policy.* Ithaca, New York: Cornell University.

Goldstein, J. and Keohane, R. (1993). Ideas and foreign policy: An analytical framework. In J. Goldstein and R. O. Keohane (eds.), *Ideas and Foreign Policy: Beliefs, Institutions, and Political Change, Cornell Studies in Political Economy.* (pp. 3–30). Ithaca, NY: Cornell University Press.

Gonzalez-Vega, C. (1976). On the iron law of interest rate restrictions: Agriculture credit policies in Costa Rica and in other less developed countries. Ph.D. dissertation, Department of Economics, Stanford University.

Grubel, H. (1966). The anatomy of classical and modern infant industry arguments. *Weltwirtschaftliches Archiv*, 97, 325–344.

Guisinger, S. and Scully, G. (1990). "Pakistan." In D. Papageorgiou, M. Michaely and A. Choksi (eds.). *Liberalizing Foreign Trade.* Vol. 5. Washington, D.C.: World Bank.

Hall, P. A. (1989). *The Political Power of Economic Ideas: Keynesianism Across Nations.* New Jersey: Princeton University Press.

Harberger, A. C. (1996). Reflections on economic growth in Asia and the Pacific. *Journal of Asian Economics*, 7(1), 365–392.

Harrison, A. E. (1994). Productivity, imperfect competition and trade reforms: Theory and evidence. *Journal of Development Economics*, 36(1), 53–73.

Hayek, F. A. (1945). The use of knowledge in society. *American Economic Review*, 35(4), 519–530.
Hill, H. (1990). *Foreign investment and East — Asian development. Asian-Pacific Economic Literature*, 4(1), 21–58.
Hirschman, A. O. (1958). *The Strategy of Economic Development*. New Haven: Yale University Press.
Hirst, P. and Thompson, G. (2002). The future of globalisation. *Cooperation and Conflict*, 37(3), 247–265.
Hughes, H. and Krueger, A. O. (1984). Effects of protection in developing countries on developing Countries in exports of manufactures. In R. E. Baldwin and A. Krueger (eds.), *The Structure and Evolution of Recent US Trade Policy*, (pp. 388–416). Chicago: Chicago University of Chicago Press.
Indraratne, A. V. de. S. (1958). *Comments on the Ten Year Plan*. Colombo, Sri Lanka: Journal of National Chamber of Commerce.
Indraratne, A. D. V. de. S. (2013). The impact of the global recession on the Sri Lankan economy. In *GTU's Second International Conference on Globalised Market. The Theme: Meeting the Challenges of a Globalised Market. published in the Conference Papers*. A Revised and edited version is published in the *Sri Lanka Economic Journal*. Vol. 201.
Institute of Policy Studies. (1992–2003). *Sri Lanka — State of the Economy*. Colombo, Sri Lanka: Institute of Policy Studies.
International Trade Centre. (2011). *Sri Lanka: A Company Perspective — An ITC series on Non-tariff Measures*. Geneva: International Trade Centre.
Irwin, D. (1996). *Against the Tide: An Intellectual History of Free Trade*. Princeton, NJ: Princeton University Press.
Ito, T. (2001). Growth, crisis and the future of economic recovery in East Asia. In E. S. Joseph and S. Yusuf (eds.), *Rethinking the Asia Miracle*, (pp. 55–94). New York: World Bank and Oxford University Press.
Jayasuriya, S. (2004). *Exchange Rate*, In S. Kelegama (ed.), *Economic Policy in Sri Lanka: Issues and Debates*. Colombo: Vijitha Yapa, Sri Lanka.
Jeffrey, A. F. (2000). Globalization of the economy. NBER Working Paper No. w7858.
Jennings, I. (1950). *The Economy of Ceylon*. London: Oxford University Press.
Johnson, H. G. (1960). Cost of protection and the scientific tariff. *Journal of Political Economy*, LXVIII, 327–345.
Johnson, H. G. (1965). Optimal Intervention in the Presence of Domestic Distortions. In *Trade Growth and Balance of Payments. Essays in Honour of Gottfried Haberler*. Vol. 3. Chicago: Rand McNally.
Karunatilleke, H. N. S. (1971). *Economic Development in Ceylon*. New York: Praeger Publishers. pp. 181–182.
Karunatilleke, H. N. S. (1986). Fiscal policy and monetary policy in Sri Lanka with special reference to the period after 1977. *Sri Lanka Economic Journal*. Sri Lanka Economic Association.

Keesing, D. B. (1997). *Dilemmas of Development, Fifty Years of Economic Change in Sri Lanka*. Colombo: Sri Lanka Association of Economists.

Kelegama, S. (1989). The speed and stages of trade liberalisation strategy: The case of Sri Lanka. *Marga Quarterly Journal*, 10(1).

Kelegama, S. (1990). Open economic policy and its impact on domestic industrialisation in Sri Lanka. *Upanathi*, 5(1), 95–147.

Kelegama, S. (n.d.). The economic dimensions of the North-East Conflict in Sri Lanka. In R. Rotberg (ed.), *The Political Economic and Social Reconstruction of Sri Lanka*. Cambridge, MA: Harvard Institution of International Development.

Kelegama, S. (2006). *Development Under Stress: Sri Lankan Economy in Transition*. Colombo, Sri Lanka: Vijitha Yapa Publications.

Kelegama, S. and Wignaraja, S. (1991). Trade policy and industrial development in Sri Lanka. *Marga Quarterly Journal*, 2(4), 27–53.

Keynes, J. (1936). *The General Theory of Employment Interest and Money*. London: Macmillian Publishers.

Khatkhate, D. (1982). Anatomy of financial retardation in a less-developed country: The case of Sri Lanka 1951–1976. *World Development*, 10(9), 829–840.

Kim, J. and Lau, J. (1996). The sources of Asian Pacific economic growth. *Canadian Journal of Economics*, 29(1), 448–454.

Krishna, R. (1988). Ideology and economic policy. *Indian Economic Review*, 23(1), 1–26.

Krueger, A. O. (1974). The political economy of rent-seeking society. *American Economic Review*, 64(3), 291–303.

Krueger, A. O. (1978). *Liberalisation, Attempts and Consequences*. Cambridge, MA: Balinger Publication Company.

Krueger, A. O. (1980). Trade policy as an input to development. *American Economic Review: Papers and Proceedings*, 70(2), 288–292.

Krueger, A. O. (1984a). Trade policies in developing countries. In R. W. Jones and P. B. Kenen (eds.), *Chapter 11. Handbook of International Economics*, (Vol. 1, pp. 519–569). Elsevier.

Krueger, A. O. (1984b). *Problems of Liberalisation in the World Economic Growth*. A. C. Harberger (ed.). San Francisco, CA: ICS Press.

Krueger, A. O. (1995). The role of trade in growth and development: Theory and lessons from the East Asian experience. In R. Garnaut. E. Grilli and J. Riedel (eds.), *Sustaining Export Oriented Development: Ideas from East Asia* (pp. 1–30). Cambridge: Cambridge University Press.

Krueger, A. O. (1997). Trade policy and economic development: How we learn. *American Economic Review*, 87(1), 1–22.

Krueger. A. O. (1978). *Foreign Trade Regimes and Economic Development: Liberalisation Attempts and Consequences*. Cambridge, MA: Balinger Publishing Company.

Krueger, A. (1998). Whither the World Bank and the IMF? *Journal of Economic Literature*, 36(4), 1983–2020.
Krueger, A. & Rajapatirana, S. (1999). World Bank Policies Towards Trade and Trade Policy Reforms. *World Bank Economic Review*, 717–740.
Krueger, A. O. and Tuncer, B. (1982). An empirical test of the infant industry argument. *American Economic Review*, 72(5), 1142–1152.
Krugman, P. (1987). *Learning to Industrialise*. London: McMillan.
Krugman, P. (1995), Growing World Trade: Causes and Consequences. *Brookings Papers on Economic Activity*, 25th Anniversary Issue, 26(1), 327–377.
Krugman, P. (1997). What ever happened to the Asian miracle? *Fortune*, 136(4), 26–29.
Lakshman, W. D. (1997a). *Dilemmas of Development, Fifty Years of Economic Change in Sri Lanka*. Colombo: Sri Lanka Association of Economists.
Lakshman, W. D. (1997b). Income distribution and poverty. In W. D. Lakshman (ed.), *Dilemma of Development: Fifty years of Economic Change in Sri Lanka*. Colombo: Sri Lanka Association of Economists.
Lakshman, W. D. (2012). *Exchange Rate as a Policy Instrument — A Critical Evaluation of Sri Lankan Experience*. Peradeniya, Sri Lanka: Prof.H.A.D.S Gunasekera Memorial Oration, University of Peradeniya.
Lall, S. (1990). *Building Technological Capability*. Paris: OECD.
Lange, O. (1936). Economic theory of socialism: Part I. *Review of Economic Studies*, 4(1), 53–71.
Lawrence, R. Z. and Weinstein, D. E. (1999). Trade and growth: Import-led or export-led? Evidence from Japan and Korea. *NBER Working Papers 7264*. National Bureau of Economic Research, Inc.
Levy, B. (1989). Foreign Aid in the making of economic policy in Sri Lanka, 1977–1983. *Policy Sciences*, 22(3/4), 437–461.
Lewis, W. A. (1954). Economic development of unlimited supplies of labour. *The Manchester School*, 22(2), 139–191.
Little, I. M. D. (1981). The experience and causes of rapid labor-intensive development in Korea, Taiwan Province, Hong Kong, and Singapore, Biai and possibilities for emulation. In E. Lee (ed.), *Export-led Industrialisation and Development*. Geneva: ILO.
Little, I. M. D. (1982). *Economic Development, Theory, Policy and International Relations*, (pp. 425–439). New York: Basic Books.
Little, I. M. D. (1994). *Trade and industrialisation revisited. Pakistan Development Review*, 33(4 Part 1), 359–389.
Little, I. M. D. (1999). *Collection and Recollections: Economic Annexes and their Provenance*, (pp. 213–240). Oxford: Clarendon Press.
Little, I. M. D., Scitovsky, T., and Scott, M. (1970). *Industry and Trade in Some Developing Countries*. London: Oxford University Press. Published for the Organisation for Economic Development, Paris.

Little, I. M. D., Richard, N. C., Corden, M., and Rajapatirana, S. (1993). *Boom, Crisis and Adjustment: The Macroeconomic Experience of Developing Countries*. Oxford: Oxford University Press.

Lucas, R. (1988). On the mechanics of economic development. *Journal of Monetary Economics*, 22(1) 3–42.

Maddison, A. (2001). *The World Economy. A Millennium Perspective*, Vol. 1, Paris: OECD Development Studies.

Magud, N. and Sebastian, S. (2010). When and why worry about Real Exchange Rate Appreciation? The Missing Link between Dutch Disease and Growth. *International Monetary Fund Working Paper, WP/10/271*.

Michaely, M. (1984). The timing and sequencing of a trade liberalisation policy. *Country Policy Department Discussion Paper.* Washington, D.C.: World Bank Group.

Michaely, M., Papageorgiou, D., and Choksi, A. M. (1991). *Liberalising Foreign Trade: Lessons of Experience in the Developing World*. Oxford: Basil Blackwell.

Myint, H. (1961). *Equilibrium and Growth in the World Economy*. Cambridge, MA: Harvard University Press.

Myint, H. (1985). Growth policies and income distribution. *Development Policy Issues Series, No. 1*. Washington, D.C.: World Bank.

Myrdal, G., Arnold, R., and Sterner, R. (1944). *An American Dilemma: The Negro Problem and Modern Democracy*. New York: Harper Brothers.

Nishimizu, M. and Robinson, S. (1984). Trade Policies and productivity change in Semi-industrialised countries. *Journal of Economic Development Economics*, 16(1–2), 117–206.

North, D. C. (1990a). *Institutions, Institutional Change and Economic Performance (Political Economy of Institutions and Institutional Change)*. Cambridge: Cambridge University Press.

North, D. C. (1990b). A transactions cost theory of politics. *Journal of Theoretical Politics*, 2(4).

Nurske, R. (1962). *Problems of Capital Formation in Underdeveloped Countries, and Patterns of Trade and Development*. Oxford: Oxford University Press.

Oliver, H. M. (1956). Industrialisation of Ceylon: Opinions and policies 1916–1951. *Ceylon Economist*, 3(3), 175–225.

Pack, H. (1993). Industrial and trade policies in the high performing Asian economies. *Background Paper for the East Asian Miracle*. Policy Research Department. Washington, D.C.: World Bank.

Pack, H. (2000). Industrial policy: Growth Elixir or poison? *The World Bank Research Observer*, 15(1), 47–67.

Panagariya, A. (2000). Evaluating the case for export subsidies. *World Bank Policy Research Working Paper No. 2276*. Washington, D.C.: World Bank.

Panagariya, A. (2023a). Modi will win a third term in 2024. *Money Control India*, 1 March.
Panagariya, A. (2023b). India is on the cusp of returning to a high growth trajectory. *The Hindu*, 2 February.
Papageogiou, D. Michaely, M. and Choksi, A. (1991), *Liberalising Foreign Trade: Indonesia, Pakistan and Sri Lanka*, Vol. 5, Oxford: Basil Blackwell.
Perera, A. (n.d.). Money, Printing, Inflation and Inflation Targeting. *Sunday Times Newspaper*, April 6 2008.
Prebisch, R. (1950). *The Economic Development of Latin America and its Principal Problems*. New York: United Nations Development of Economic Affairs, Economic Commission for Latin America (ECLA).
Prebisch, R. (1959). Commercial policy in the underdeveloped countries. *American Economic Review*, 49(2), 251–273.
Prebisch, R. (1964). *Towards a New Trade Policy for Development: Report/by the Secretary General of the United Nations Conference on Trade and Development*. New York: United Nations Conference of Trade and Development, UN, 125.
Pursell, G. and Ahsan, F. M. Z. (2011). Sri Lanka's trade policies: Back to protectionism. *Australia South Asia Research Centre Working Papers*. Canberra: Australian National University, 41.
Rajapatirana, S. (1987). Main author and director of The World Bank, World Development Report 1987. Oxford University Press, New York.
Rajapatirana, S. (1988). Foreign trade and economic development: Sri Lanka's experience. *World Development*, 16(10), 1143–1157.
Rajapathirana, S. (1993). Policy recommendations for export promotion. *Estudios De Economía*, 20(19), 1–25.
Rajapatirana, S. (1996). Trade policies, macroeconomic adjustment and manufactured exports: The Latin American experience. *Weltwirschaftliches Archive*, 132, 558–585.
Rajapatirana, S. (1997). *Trade Policies in Latin America and the Caribbean: Priorities. Progress and Prospects*. San Francisco, CA: International Center for Economic Growth.
Rajapatirana, S. (2000). *Currency Boards Versus Central Banks: Lessons from Sri Lanka's Monetary Experiences*. Peradeniya, Sri Lanka: Prof. H.A.de.S Gunesekara Memorial Oration, University of Peradeniya.
Rajapatirana, S. (2008). Demonetisation of the Sri Lankan Rupee: The anatomy of a monetary experiment, Dr. J.B. Kelegama Festschrift.
Rajapatirana, S. (2009). *Ideology and Economic Policy-Making: A Framework and Exploration of Comparative Experience*. (Mimeograph). Washington, D.C.: American Enterprise Institute.
Rajapatirana, S., de Mora, L. M., and Yatawara, R. (1997). Political economy of trade reforms 1965–1994: Latin American Style. *The World Economy*, 20(3).

Ratnayake, R. (1988). Trade policy and the performance of the manufacturing sector: Sri Lanka. *The Developing Economies*, XXVI-1.

Reinhart, C. N. and Trebesch, C. (2016). The International Monetary Fund: 70 years of re-intervention. *Journal of Economic Perspective*, 30(1), 3–28.

Riedel, J. (1984). Trade as the engine of growth in developing countries. *The Economic Journal*, 94(373), 56–73.

Riedel, J. and Athukorala, P. (1995). Export growth and the terms of trade: The case of the curious elasticities. In E. D. D.Currie (ed.), *In North South Linkages and International Macroeconomic Policy*, (pp. 29–45). Cambridge: Cambridge University Press.

Robinson, J. (1965). *The Accumulation of Capital*. London: MacMillan Publishers.

Rodrigo, C. G. (2001). *Does Sri Lanka Need Industrial Activism?* Colombo: Sri Lanka Economic Association Journal, New Series.

Rodrik, D. (1992). The limits of trade policy reforms in developing countries. *Journal of Economic Perspectives*, 6(1), 87–106.

Rodrik, D. (1993). The positive economics of policy reform. *American Economic Review*, 83(2), 356–361.

Rodrik, D. (1995). Trade and industrial policy reform. In J. R. Behrman and T. N. Srinivasan (eds.), *Chapter 45. Handbook of Development Economics* (pp. Vol.3, Part 2 2925-2982). North-Holland: Elsevier.

Rodrik, D. (2011). *The Globalisation Paradox: Democracy and the Future of the World Economy*. New York and London: W. W. Norton & Company.

Romer, P. M. (1992). Two strategies for economic development: Using ideas and producing ideas. In *Proceedings of the World Bank Annual Conference on Development Economics*. Washington, D.C.: World Bank, pp. 63–101.

Sachs, J. and Warner, A. (1995). Economic reform and the process of global integration. *Brookings Papers on Economic Activity*, 26(1), 1–118.

Sachs, J. D. (1985). External debts and macroeconomic performance in Latin America and East Asia. *Brooking Papers on Economic Activity*, 16(2), 523–573.

Salter, W. E. G. (1959). Internal and external balance: The role of price and expenditure effects. *Economic Record*, 35(71), 226–238.

Salter, W. E. G. (2008). Foreign receipts and payments and the miraculous exchange rate. *Financial Times*.

Sanderatne, N. (1995). *The Economy in Sri Lanka Year 2000: Towards the 21st Century*. Colombo, Sri Lanka: Center for Regional Development Studies. Ceylon Printers Ltd.

Sanderatne, N. (2000). *Economic Growth and Social Transformation: Five lectures on Sri Lanka*. Colombo: Tamarind Publications.

Santhirasekaram, S. and Amirthalingam, K. (2010). Direct and indirect effects of conflicts, violence and war on economic growth in Sri Lanka. *Sri Lanka Economic Journal*, 11(1), 31–60.

Scitovsky, T. (1954). Two concepts of external economies. *Journal of Political Economy*, 62, 143.
Selvaratnam, S. (1956). *Population Projections for Ceylon 1956–1981*. Colombo: Planning Secretariat. The Government Press.
Sikkink, K. (1991). *Ideas and Institutions: Developmentalism in Brazil and Argentina*. Ithaca, New York: Cornell University Press.
Singer, H. W. (1950). The distribution of gains between investing and borrowing countries. *American Economic Review*, 40(2), 473–485.
Snape, R. H. (1991). East Asia: Trade reforms in Korea and Singapore. In G. Shepherd and C. G. Langoni (eds.), *Trade Reforms: Lessons from Eight Countries* (pp. 103–115). San Francisco, CA: International Center for Economic Growth.
Snodgrass, D. R. (1966). *Ceylon: An Export Economy in Transition*. Illinois: Richard D. Irvin, Homewood
Snodgrass, D. R. (1998). The economic development of Sri Lanka: A tale of missed opportunities. Discussion Paper 637, 33. Cambridge, MA: Harvard Institute for International Development.
Solow, R. M. (1962). Technical progress, capital formation and economic growth. *American Economic Review*, 52(2), 76–86.
Spraos, J. (1980). The statistical debate on the net barter terms of trade between primary commodities and manufactures. *Economic Journal*, 90(357), 107–128.
Stein, B. (1954). Problems of economic development in Ceylon. *The Ceylon Historical Journal*, 3 & 4, 286–330
Stein, H. (1995). *On the Other Hand: Essays on Economics, Economists, & Politics*. Washington, D.C.: The AEI Press.
Stiglitz, J. (1996). Some lessons from the East Asian Miracle. *World Bank Economic Observer*, 11(2), 151–177.
Stiglitz, J. A. (1995). *Whither Socialism?* Boston: MIT Press.
Stiglitz, J. E. (1989). *On the Economic Role of the State*. A. Heertje (ed.). Oxford: Blackwell.
Stiglitz, J. E. (2001). From miracle to crisis to recovery: Lessons from four decades of East Asian experience. In J. E. Stiglitz and S. Yusuf (eds.), *Rethinking the Asia Miracle*. New York: World Bank and Oxford University Press.
Stiglitz, J. E. (2002). *Globalisation and Its Discontents*. New York and London: W. W. Norton & Company.
Stiglitz, J. E. (2006). *Making Globalisation Work*. New York: W.W. Norton & Company.
Stiglitz, J. E. and Weiss, A. (1981). Credit rationing in markets with imperfect information. *American Economic Review*, 71(3), 393–410.
Stolper, W. (1966). *Planning Without Facts: Lessons of Resource Allocations from Nigeria's Development, with an Input-Output Analysis of the Nigerian Economy 1959–60*. Cambridge, MA: Harvard University Press.

The Government of Ceylon. (1922). *Report of the Industries Commission.* Colombo: Government Record Office.

The Government of Ceylon. (1958). *The Ten Year Development Plan.* Colombo: Planning Secretariat, Government Publications Bureau.

Tybout, J. (1992). Linking trade and productivity: New research directions. *World Bank Economic Review,* 6(2), 189–211.

UNCTAD. (2019). *Key Statistics and trends in Trade Policy 2022-UNCTAD.* UNCTAD secretariat calculations based on UNCTAD TRAINS database.

Valdes, A. (2013). *What is the cost of a bowl of rice? The impact of Sri Lanka's Current Trade and Price Policies on the Incentive Framework for Agriculture.* Washington, D.C.: World Bank.

Vidanapathirana, U. (1993). *A Review of Industrial Policy and Industrial Potential in Sri Lanka.* SLEA-USAID. Publication Series. No. 4. Colombo, Sri Lanka: Sri Lanka Economic Association.

Vittachi, T. (1958). *Emergency '58: The Story of Ceylon's Race Riots.* Colombo: Lake House.

Wade, R. (1990). *Governing the Market: Economic Theory and the Role of the Government in East Asian Industrialisation.* New Jersey: Princeton University Press.

Weerakoon, D. and White, H. (1995). *How Open has the Sri Lankan Economy Become? Trends in Trade and Trade Taxes: 1977–1993.* Colombo, Sri Lanka: Institute of Policy Studies.

Westphal, L. (1978). The republic of Korea's experience with export-led industrial development. *World Development,* 6(3), 347–382.

Wignaraja, G. (1994). Outward-oriented trade policy and industrial performance in Sri Lanka. 1977–92. *Contemporary South Asia,* 3(3), 203–215.

Wignaraja, G. (1995). Outward oriented trade policy and industrial performance in Sri Lanka. *Marga Quarterly Journal,* 13(4).

Williamson, J. (1998). Sri Lanka's search for the right economic policies, Keynote address delivered at the conferences on 'Independent Sri Lanka: Economic Development 1948–1998 and prospects' held at Kalutara, Sri Lanka on 23–24 March.

Wolf, M. (2004). *Why Globalisation Works.* New Haven, Connecticut: Yale University Press, p. 398.

World Bank (1952). *The Economic Development of Ceylon.* Baltimore: Johns Hopkins Press for the World Bank.

World Bank. (1984). *Sri Lanka Recent Economic Developments, Prospects and Policies.* Washington, D.C.: The World Bank Group.

World Bank. (1987). *The World Development Report.* New York: Oxford University Press.

World Bank. (1993). *The East Asian Miracle: Economic Growth and Public Policy.* New York: Oxford University Press.

World Bank (2000). *Sri Lanka: Recapturing Missed Opportunities.* Washington, D.C: The World Bank Group.

World Bank. (2014). *What is the Cost of a Bowl of Rice: The Impact of Sri Lanka's Current Trade and Price Policies on the Incentive Framework for Agriculture.* Washington, D.C.: The World Bank Group.

World Trade Organisation (2010). *Trade Policy Review: Sri Lanka.* Geneva, Switzerland: WTO Secretariat and by the Government of Sri Lanka.

Yee, A. S. (1996). The causal effects of ideas on policies. *International Organisation*, 50(1), 69–108.

Young, A. (1995). The Tyranny of numbers: Confronting the statistical realities of the East Asian growth experience. *The Quarterly Journal of Economics*, 110(3), 641–680.

Zinsmeister, K. (1993). *MITI Mouse: Japan's Industrial Policy Doesn't Work.* Policy Review. Spring. No. 64, pp. 28–35. Washington, D.C.: Heritage Foundation.

Index

A
anti-colonial, 21, 76
asymmetric information, 167–168

B
balance of payments, 28, 33, 37, 61, 102, 118, 134, 140–141, 148, 189, 203, 215, 219, 223, 228–229, 253
Bandaranaike–Shastri Pact, 26, 99
blanket subsidy, 177, 179
British Empire, 21–22, 25, 94
Business Undertaking Acquisition Act, 32, 218

C
capital substitution, 10
causal beliefs, 89, 91–92
Cease Fire Agreement, 103, 223
colonial economy, 50, 63
comparative advantage, 13, 26, 33, 74, 81, 132, 142, 155, 158, 160, 166, 172–175, 178, 251
Convertible Rupee Account, 37, 220

COVID-19, ix, 10, 13, 151, 249, 253, 255, 259–260, 262
currency board system, 21, 94

D
debt overhang, 19, 152, 201
decreasing returns, 53, 69
dirigiste economy, 50
disorganised default, 152
diversification of exports, 120
Doha Development Round, 5
Donoughmore Constitution, 96
double taxation, 42
Dutch disease, 39, 41–42, 92, 102, 104, 118, 127, 175, 187, 192, 222, 230, 235–236, 246

E
East Asian Crisis, 15, 162, 165, 170
East Asian Miracle, 162
economic shocks, 8
effective rates of protection, 33, 44, 65, 103, 129, 231
equity, 106, 129, 162

exchange controls, 27–29, 33, 35, 39, 60, 64–65, 78, 100–101, 131, 183, 215–216, 219, 227, 255
expenditure control, 126
export processing zones, 41, 108, 255
export-oriented manufacturing, 124

F
Factor Price Equalisation, 3
first oil shock, 32, 62, 98, 114, 185, 216, 218
fiscal deficit, 16, 91, 106, 148, 183, 185–190, 195–196, 199, 202, 219, 223–228, 239–240, 244
Fiscal Management (Responsibility) Act, 189
foreign direct investment (FDI) flows, 31, 41, 96, 99, 253
Foreign Exchange Entitlement Certificate Scheme, 29, 78, 216

G
GDP growth rates, 40, 117, 242, 247
Generalised System of Preferences, 45
Gini coefficient, 246–248, 258–259, 261
government revenue, 116, 122, 134, 198, 202
Greater Colombo Economic Commission, 41, 101
gross domestic product (GDP) growth, ix, 13, 16, 19, 23–24, 29, 36, 40–41, 78, 91–92, 100, 113, 115, 117, 131, 141, 151, 159, 161–163, 170, 175–176, 182, 211, 219, 222, 224, 230, 242–244, 247, 249–250, 252, 254, 256, 258, 262

H
Harrod-Domar model, 71
Heckscher–Ohlin model, 3, 90
Hickenlooper Amendment, 31, 99
high-cost foreign (sovereign) borrowings, 182
history, ix–x, 1, 11, 13, 15, 19–20, 31, 35, 81, 90, 115, 134, 142, 150, 191, 218, 223, 242, 248, 257–258, 261
hyper globalisation, 1, 258

I
ideology, 1, 11, 13, 15–17, 19, 21, 27, 35, 42, 51, 83, 85–102, 104, 151–153, 155, 161, 248, 257, 261
import and exchange controls, 28, 35, 60, 78, 215–216, 227
import substitution, 16, 27, 29–30, 35, 45, 56, 60–61, 64–65, 68, 70–72, 76–77, 79–80, 107, 114–115, 122–123, 138, 142, 174, 216–217, 232, 251–253
import-substituting, 167, 191, 252
incentive package, 41
income distribution, ix–x, 2, 9–10, 13, 242, 245–248, 256, 258–261
increasing returns, 53, 58, 77
industrialisation, xi, 13, 27, 29, 41, 53–54, 56, 58–61, 68, 72–73, 75–77, 79–80, 140, 142, 155, 166, 173
inflationary financed deficits, 132
international monetary fund (IMF), 151, 223
International Trade Center, 44
intra-industry trade, 7
investment protection, 42

K
Korean boom, 26
Korean War, 25

L
lending programmes, 149
Lerner Symmetry theorem, 65, 233
liberalised economy, 37, 203, 220
liquidity, 129, 185, 201, 240, 262

M
macroeconomic stability, 22, 25, 28–29, 31, 94, 106, 119, 124–125, 179, 201–202, 215, 219, 225
Mahaweli project, 39, 117–118, 124–125, 127, 132, 186, 221, 246
market-driven economy, 100
market-driven policies, 163
market fundamentalist, 155
market socialist, 72
Marxist parties, 21, 32–34, 56–57, 62–63, 98–99, 186, 218, 220, 246
mercantilist strategy, 167
Millennium Challenge Corporation, 151
Ministry of Industries, 34, 40
Ministry of Planning and Implementation, 40
Multinational Financial Institutions, 109, 202

N
nationalisation, 12, 27–28, 31, 33, 50, 62–64, 96, 98–99, 101, 105, 114, 123, 254
nationalistic ideology, 27
negative factor productivity, 80
neo-classical, 52–53, 155, 157, 166

non-debt creating, 236, 248, 254, 262
non-essential imports, 29, 121, 128, 216
non-tariff measures, 33, 226
non-traditional exports, 29–30, 121–122, 124, 133–134, 140, 216–217, 234

O
oil shock, 32, 34, 62, 92, 98, 100, 114, 126, 185–187, 216, 218
OPEC cartel, 185

P
para tariffs, 43–44, 47, 103, 224, 226, 237, 242
political milieu, 11, 95
principal–agent problem, 74, 81, 161, 178
private entrepreneurship, 32
private sector-led expansionary policies, 150
privatisation policies, 40
productivity, 19, 22, 44, 46, 54, 60–61, 63, 66, 68, 72, 80–81, 125, 139, 153, 164, 167–168, 177, 197, 199–200, 230, 238–241, 253, 256, 258–260
public choice theory, 79, 160, 168
public expenditure programmes, 38, 41, 118, 221–222, 230

Q
quantitative restrictions, 32, 37, 41, 43, 47, 64–65, 107, 114, 166, 218–220, 246, 252, 261

R

real effective exchange rate, 117, 194, 212–214
real exchange rate, 37, 39, 45, 118, 125–126, 130, 186–187, 193–195, 198, 200, 205–206, 212–214, 219, 221–222, 224, 230, 235, 238
reflectionalist, 89
reform programme, 50, 106, 149, 253–254
reforms, xi, 3, 8, 10, 20–21, 24–25, 36–40, 43, 45, 62, 94, 100, 102, 106–108, 128–129, 131, 135, 139, 141, 150–151, 163, 175, 209, 220, 230, 236, 241–242, 248, 252–254, 256, 258–259, 262
Rice-Rubber Agreement, 25

S

Second World War, 21–22, 25, 55, 113, 147
slowbalisation, x, 13, 258, 262
small open economy, 3, 9, 11, 13, 211
socialist economy, 32, 50, 99, 186, 218
Soulbury Commission, 97
sovereign borrowing, 188, 223, 228
state-owned corporation, 197
Stolper–Samuelson models, 3
sub-prime mortgage crisis, 182, 191
supply-side market failures, 157–178

T

tariff protection, 101
Ten Year Plan, 49–50, 54, 56, 59, 66, 69–70, 77–78
Tequila crisis, 6
Termination of Employment of Workers Act, 32, 218
tight monetary targets, 188
total factor productivity, 19, 60, 68, 72, 80, 164, 238
trade and exchange control, 98
trade and exchange rate controls, 113
trade controls, 25, 27–28, 31, 44, 100, 103, 215, 218
trade protection, 28, 40, 91, 158, 215, 232
trade regime, 15, 21–22, 29, 36, 39, 43–45, 101, 114–115, 117, 128–129, 154, 163, 166, 217, 224, 226–227, 232, 242, 251–252
trade to GDP, 4, 5, 7, 258

W

World Financial Crisis, 2, 257

www.ingramcontent.com/pod-product-compliance
Lightning Source LLC
Jackson TN
JSHW011949070125
76732JS00002B/23